ADVANCE PRAISE FOR

QUESTS FOR QUESTIONERS: APPROACHES TO QUALITATIVE INTERVIEWS

"*Quests for Questioners: Inventive Approaches to Qualitative Interviews* is an invigorating collection of contributions from diverse perspectives about innovative understandings of interview practices. Whether you're experienced or new to research, this accessible book will stimulate you to think 'outside the box' conceptually and culturally, and to experiment with moving beyond the standard question-answer talk. It's a valuable resource that should be on every qualitative research reading list."

Rosalind Edwards, Professor of Sociology,
University of Southampton, UK

"Kathryn Roulston's edited book is an important, timely, thoughtful, and accessible collection. As someone who designs, conducts, and teaches interview-based qualitative research, I appreciate how useful that the range of discussions here are for scholars across disciplines and experience levels, as the authors consider a range of methodologies, including culturally responsive focus groups, object-based interviews, photo and graphic elicitations, and place-based interviewing. The variety of engagements with interviewing offered here will be applicable across courses, contexts, research projects, and readers' needs and interests."

Stephanie A. Shelton, Associate Professor of Qualitative Research,
The University of Alabama, USA

"In Roulston's edited volume, *Quests for Questioners: Inventive Approaches to Qualitative Interviews*, readers are introduced to innovative approaches to qualitative interviewing, as well as foundational theoretical and practical considerations for this approach to data generation. The volume offers new insights about culturally responsive approaches to interviewing, as well as rich discussions on how to engage with theory when re-conceptualizing interviewing practices. From the use of graphics to mobile methods to photo elicitation, this volume maps out new possibilities for what remains the most common approach to generating qualitative data. Indeed, this volume is a *key* and *essential* resource for qualitative inquirers seeking to deepen and expand their qualitative interviewing practices."

Jessica Nina Lester, Professor of Qualitative Research,
Indiana University, Bloomington

QUESTS FOR QUESTIONERS

QUALITATIVE RESEARCH METHODOLOGIES: TRADITIONS, DESIGNS, AND PEDAGOGIES
EDITED BY KATHLEEN DEMARRAIS, MELISSA FREEMAN, JORI HALL, AND KATHRYN ROULSTON

The *Qualitative Research Methodologies: Traditions, Designs, and Pedagogies* series is designed to encourage qualitative researchers to look both backward and forward in the field of qualitative inquiry. We invite authors to submit proposals for both single-authored books and edited volumes focused on particular qualitative designs situated within their historical, theoretical, and disciplinary/cross-disciplinary contexts. Pieces might include a tradition's or design's historical roots and key scholars, ways the approach has changed over time, as well as ethical and methodological considerations in the use of that particular research approach. They may also provide an introduction to contemporary designs created at the intersection of multiple, theoretical, and often assumed incommensurable historical paths. In addition, we encourage authors to submit proposals for books focused on the pedagogy of qualitative research methodologies that interrogate how we prepare researchers new to qualitative research methodologies with the theoretical, methodological, and ethical understandings and skills for their work.

Those interested in being considered for inclusion in the series should send a prospectus (https://zfrmz.com/rmlvGq7xgL2RTgPkByk9), CV, and cover letter to: Kathleen deMarrais (kathleen@uga.edu).

Books in the Series:
Focus Groups: Culturally Responsive Approaches for Qualitative Inquiry and Program Evaluation
by Jori N. Hall (2020)
Exploring the Archives: A Beginner's Guide for Qualitative Researchers
by Kathryn Roulston and Kathleen deMarrais (2021)
Autoethnography for Practitioners: A Transformative Process for Individual, Group, and Corporate Development
by Kathy-Ann C. Hernandez, Wendy Bilgen, and Heewon Chang (2022)
Quests for Questioners: Inventive Approaches to Qualitative Interviews
edited by Kathryn Roulston (2023)
The Action Research Dissertation: Learning from Leading Change
by Karen E. Watkins, Erica Gilbertson, and Aliki Nicolaides (2023)
Qualitative Research Design and Methods: An Introduction
by Kathleen deMarrais, Kathryn Roulston, and Janie Copple (2023)

QUESTS FOR QUESTIONERS

ℭ Inventive Approaches to
Qualitative Interviews

EDITED BY KATHRYN ROULSTON

Myers
Education
Press

Gorham, Maine

Copyright © 2023 | Myers Education Press, LLC
Published by Myers Education Press, LLC
P.O. Box 424
Gorham, ME 04038

All rights reserved. No part of this book may be reprinted or reproduced in any form or by any electronic, mechanical, or other means, now known or hereafter invented, including photocopying, recording, and information storage and retrieval, without permission in writing from the publisher.

Myers Education Press is an academic publisher specializing in books, e-books and digital content in the field of education. All of our books are subjected to a rigorous peer review process and produced in compliance with the standards of the Council on Library and Information Resources.

Library of Congress Cataloging-in-Publication Data available from Library of Congress.

13-digit ISBN 978-1-9755-0524-0 (paperback)
13-digit ISBN 978-1-9755-0525-7 (library networkable e-edition)
13-digit ISBN 978-1-9755-0526-4 (consumer e-edition)

Printed in the United States of America.

All first editions printed on acid-free paper that meets the American National Standards Institute Z39-48 standard.

Books published by Myers Education Press may be purchased at special quantity discount rates for groups, workshops, training organizations and classroom usage. Please call our customer service department at 1-800-232-0223 for details.

Cover design by Teresa Lagrange Design Service from Portland, ME.

Visit us on the web at **www.myersedpress.com** to browse our complete list of titles.

Contents

List of Figures and Text Boxes ... ix

Introduction ... xi

PART I Being Culturally Responsive in Interview Research

ONE Culturally Responsive Interviews: The Negotiation of Cultures ... 3
Lorien S. Jordan

TWO Beyond Qualitative Interviews: Toward Synergistic Conversations as Relational and Nation Building ... 23
Emma Elliott and Timothy San Pedro

THREE Culturally Responsive Focus Groups ... 43
Jori N. Hall and Joseph-Emery Lyvan Kouaho

FOUR Recruiting For and Conducting Virtual Focus Groups and Interviews With Low-Income Populations During the COVID-19 Pandemic ... 65
Brigette A. Herron, Darci Bell, and Jung Sun Lee

PART II Being Inventive in Theorizing Interviews

FIVE Cartographic Accounts: Qualitatively Mapping With Braidotti ... 87
Maureen A. Flint and Morgan P. Tate

SIX Intra-Action is For Everybody! (Re)Thinking the Qualitative Interview ... 109
Travis M. Marn and Jennifer R. Wolgemuth

SEVEN   Past, Present, Futures of Assembling Object-Interviews   127
Susan Naomi Nordstrom

PART III   Being Inventive in Eliciting Interview Accounts

EIGHT   Object Lessons: Considering Object-Interviews and Narrative Representation in Qualitative Research   147
Janie Copple

NINE   Experience in the Abstract: Exploring the Potential of Graphic Elicitation   169
Alison Bravington

TEN   Mobile Methods, Go-Alongs, and Walking Interviews   195
Kathryn Roulston and Maureen A. Flint

ELEVEN   Photo Elicitation With Native STEM Students and Professionals   215
Nuria Jaumot-Pascual, Tiffany Smith, Maria Ong, and Kathy DeerInWater

About the Authors   *237*
Acknowledgments   *243*
Index   *245*

List of Figures and Text Boxes

Figure 5.1:	Steve's Marked Map of Campus	92
Figure 5.2:	Ryan's Collage of Campus	94
Figure 5.3:	Leo's Campus Map	96
Figure 5.4:	Map of the Gusu Historic District, which encompasses the old city of Suzhou	103
Figure 8.1:	Book Cover	159
Figure 8.2:	Tracing Connections	160
Figure 9.1:	Concentric Circles	174
Figure 9.2:	Hub-and-Spoke	175
Figure 9.3:	Free Circles	175
Figure 9.4:	Pictor (a and b)	176
Figure 9.5:	Process	177
Figure 9.6:	Hierarchy	178
Figure 9.7:	Tree	178
Figure 9.8:	The Dynamics of the Timeline (a and b)	179
Figure 9.9:	The "Wiggle in the Line" (Sheridan et al., 2011)	180
Figure 10.1:	(a) Designing a Study Using Go-Alongs and Walking Interviews (p. 1)	206
Figure 10.1:	(b) Designing a Study Using Go-Alongs and Walking Interviews (p. 2)	207
Figure 11.1:	A Collection of Art	220
Figure 11.2:	New Formation	222
Figure 11.3:	Connection	223

Figure 11.4: Isolation — 224

Figure 11.5: Make It Beautiful — 225

Figure 11.6: Saktce and Tribal Plates — 226

Text Boxes

Box 3.1: Guidelines for Participation — 49

Box 9.1: Image-Focused Questions — 183

Box 9.2: Assessing Rigor in Graphic Elicitation — 188

Introduction

Kathryn Roulston

In the medieval period, knights undertook *quests*: adventures or expeditions that involved journeys into the unknown. Nowadays, it is not just knights venturing forth. Researchers from all over the world undertake quests into the unknown to investigate research problems and understand the world. In these expeditions, researchers frequently ask questions of others to learn about research topics. Whereas the noun "question" has Anglo-French derivations that originally conveyed the ideas of interrogation, torture, judicial examination, and problems (Brown, 1993, p. 2447), social scientists in the 21st century have come to much different understandings of how to ask questions of participants and for what purpose. Although questions are still a key tool for those who conduct interrogations and legal inquests, social science researchers continue to explore novel ways to generate conversations with others to *learn together* about topics of interest and understand the world.

This book presents a range of quests for those who want to learn from others through asking questions in research interviews and conversations and attending to the more-than-human aspects of the world. Authors in this book explore how to talk to people in ways that are responsive to cultural contexts and the challenges faced by people in everyday life, how to think with concepts drawn from an array of theories, including Karen Barad's (2007) concept of "intra-action," Rosi Braidotti's (2019) work on "cartographies," and Gilles Deleuze and Félix Guattari's (1987) concepts of the "fold" and "assemblage." This work troubles our understandings of interview methods, who or what might be engaged as an interview subject, and what we can draw from interview accounts. Whereas asking questions in qualitative inquiry has traditionally prioritized the generation of verbal data, authors describe how they use object, photo, and graphic elicitation and walking and mobile methods to talk to others, supplementing textual descriptions derived from interviews with images, diagrams, drawings, and maps.

Since the turn of the 21st century, methodological writing on interview methods has flourished. Qualitative scholars have a robust array of literature on different types of interviews, including those conducted with individuals, dyads, and groups belonging to specific populations (e.g., children and youth, elites, members of disability communities) and applications of different communication modalities, including in-person, synchronous and asynchronous online interviewing, and telephone interviews. Numerous topics have been explored as researchers across disciplines have discussed interactional phenomena in research interviews (Roulston, 2019) and focus groups (Gilbert & Matoesian, 2021), cross-cultural interviewing (Griffin, 2016), culturally responsive approaches to interviews (Kovach, 2010) and focus groups (Hall, 2020), and elicitation strategies using photo elicitation (Clark-Ibáñez, 2004) and photovoice (Breny & McMorrow, 2021), material (Woodward, 2016), and mobile (Kusenbach, 2020) methods.

This book adds to this literature by introducing qualitative scholars to a rich array of interview practices used by contemporary scholars—namely, how to

a. elicit verbal accounts from participants in culturally responsive ways;
b. think with theory in relation to the use of interview methods; and
c. integrate object, graphic, and photo elicitation methods and mobile and walking methods in research.

The book is designed to provoke and inspire readers' creativity to take risks and integrate different approaches to doing interviews in their research—in other words, to undertake methodological quests to experiment with the art of asking questions. Understanding the breadth of practices entailed in qualitative interview research can invigorate any researcher's practice. This volume seeks to encourage researchers to design studies that account for how they interact with others in culturally responsive ways; to consider how they can draw on theoretical concepts to re-think, re-theorize, and question conventional interview practices; and to re-imagine the generation of interview accounts using other ways of knowing, including visual, sensory, and mobile methods.

Outline of the Book

The book is organized in three parts. Part One, "Being Culturally Responsive in Interview Research," brings together scholars who have explored culturally responsive ways of working with research participants. In Chapter 1,

Lorien Jordan discusses methodological decisions that researchers can make to intentionally design and conduct studies that are culturally responsive. Drawing on fieldwork conducted in Aotearoa/New Zealand and Cambodia, she describes four principles entailed in the conduct of culturally responsive interview research that researchers might use to resist and challenge canonized Western approaches to qualitative interviewing. These are the principles of critical reflexivity, hermeneutic humility, methodological pluriversalism, and cultural and relational accountability. As another approach to culturally responsive interviews, Emma Elliott and Tim San Pedro, in Chapter 2, draw on the approach described by Jo-Ann Archibald (2008)—Indigenous Storywork—to conceptualize and model "synergistic conversations" as a way to connect with others through Indigenous storying. In this approach, "storying" involves three interrelated elements—those of story, storytelling, and story listening—facilitated by the ethical tenets of "respect, responsibility, holism, reverence, and synergy." Chapter 3 expands the application of culturally responsive approaches to interviewing and working with groups. In this chapter, Jori Hall and Joseph-Emery Lyvan Kouaho discuss the central characteristics of culturally responsive focus groups (CRFG). Their chapter provides practical questions for how researchers might decide whether CRFGs are appropriate for a study; what to do before, during, and after the conduct of focus groups; and how to design studies that demonstrate quality. Chapter 4 illustrates how one research team adapted the design of their study to attend to the particular needs of participants during the COVID-19 pandemic that caused global disruptions beginning in 2020. Although their study was initially envisioned as using in-person focus groups, Brigette Herron, Darci Bell, and Jung Sun Lee had to quickly adapt to the lockdowns and social distancing requirements that people all over the world experienced. This chapter shows how the specific contextual features of a study can inform how interviews are conducted and by what modality. In this case, focus groups initially envisioned as being conducted in person were moved online. Feminist interviewing strategies, along with a trauma-informed approach, were used to adapt focus groups' methods to respond to the emergent needs of participants in ethical ways.

Part Two of the book, "Being Inventive in Theorizing Interviews," explores how researchers have employed particular concepts and theories to bring innovation to interviews. In Chapter 5, Maureen Flint and Morgan Tate discuss their use of Rosi Braidotti's concept of "cartography" in research design. The chapter explores Flint's use of cartography in focus groups with college students and Tate's exploration of the interview method as a way to explore the natural environment. These authors provide multiple examples that examine how mapping strategies might be used to examine phenomena, thereby expanding conceptions of what an interview is and could be, and who and what can speak. In Chapter 6, Travis Marn and Jennifer Wolgemuth discuss how they used the concept of "intra-action" from Karen Barad's work to explore their on-again, off-again love affair with interview methods. This chapter illustrates how scholars can use a concept (in this case, Karen Barad's notion of "intra-action") to conceptualize the use of interview methods. A third example of scholarship is provided by Susan Nordstrom in Chapter 7. Nordstrom traces how she has used Deleuze and Guattari's (1987) concepts of the assemblage and fold to think about object interviews in her genealogical study. Nordstrom's chapter provides a bridge to the third part of the book, in which researchers discuss ways of eliciting accounts and encouraging conversations with participants that supplement verbal question-and-answer sequences characteristic of traditional forms of interviewing.

Part Three of the book, "Being Inventive in Eliciting Interview Accounts," begins with Janie Copple's exploration of how she used object interviews in a postqualitative study having to do with mothers' encounters in preparing menstruating/soon-to-be menstruating children for menarche. In Chapter 8, Janie Copple distinguishes between "object elicitation" as a way to use things to generate accounts, and "object-interviewing as an orientation to objects as lively, agential participants in qualitative interviews." This chapter provides practical strategies to illustrate another way in which researchers might think with theory (in this case, Karen Barad's agential realism) to use object interviews in research. Alison Bravington, in Chapter 9, reviews how researchers can make use of graphic elicitation and drawing to discuss topics. Her chapter shows the varied forms that graphic elicitation might take, and how researchers can use this approach to support the goals of their research projects. Researchers have also used mobile methods and walking interviews to explore people's perceptions and experiences in space and place—the focus of Chapter 10, wherein Maureen Flint and I review the history of walking interviews and mobile methods and describe examples of how researchers have used these approaches. We review questions that researchers might consider as they design studies using these methods, and Flint discusses how she used walking interviews with students on a college campus to discuss their navigation of space. The book concludes with Chapter 11, an exploration of how Nuria Jaumot-Pascual, Tiffany Smith, Maria Ong, and Kathy DeerInWater used photo-elicitation as a method to explore Native American students' experiences of STEM education. This chapter brings the book full circle, in that the authors explicitly used photo-elicitation as a culturally responsive approach to highlight the stories of Native American people. These authors asked participants to take photos and submit these along with narratives prior to conducting individual interviews. This combination of data—interview talk, photos, and written narratives—provided rich data with which to explore participants' experiences of STEM education.

Guidance for Readers

Readers are likely well acquainted with interviews in contemporary life, since people the world over engage with interviews as participants, interviewers, and audiences. Think, for example, of the ways in which interviews occur in journalism and entertainment and the mundane work of institutions (e.g., admissions interviews, clinical interviews, and so forth). Researchers use interviews for a specific purpose, however: to generate data to explore research questions. This book does not provide recipes for designing and conducting interview research. There are numerous other books that will help in those areas (e.g., Brinkmann & Kvale, 2015; Roulston, 2022; Seidman, 2012). The present book provides avenues for researchers who want to employ interviews creatively to explore research problems and think about how they might take risks in their research to press for creative methodological approaches in their fields of interest. Although the book is organized in three parts that loosely correspond to planning for interviews (i.e., who will I talk to and how will relationships be developed to foster trust and openness?), theorizing interviews (i.e., how do my ontological, epistemological, theoretical, and ethical assumptions shape my interview practice?), and conducting interviews (i.e., what forms of elicitation might I use to examine the phenomenon of interest?), readers might begin with any chapter in the book.

As numerous qualitative methodologists attest, there is no single way to conduct a qualitative study. The chapters in this volume demonstrate that there are numerous paths to integrating interviews in a study. I encourage readers to be inspired by the examples provided by the authors in this volume, and to undertake their own quests with questioning. May your quests lead you into new methodological and theoretical territories, and may your curiosities about the world be rewarded as you (ad)venture forth!

References

Archibald, J.-A. (2008). *Indigenous storywork: Educating the heart, mind, body, and spirit*. UBC Press.

Barad, K. (2007). *Meeting the universe halfway: Quantum physics and the entanglement of matter and meaning*. Duke University Press.

Braidotti, R. (2019). *Posthuman knowledge*. Polity.

Breny, J. M., & McMorrow, S. L. (2021). *Photovoice for social justice: Visual representation in action*. SAGE.

Brinkmann, S., & Kvale, S. (2015). *InterViews: Learning the craft of qualitative research interviewing* (3rd ed.). SAGE.

Brinkmann, S., & Kvale, S. (2018). *Doing interviews* (2nd ed.). SAGE.

Brown, L. (Ed.). (1993). *The new shorter Oxford English dictionary* (Vol. 2). Clarendon Press.

Clark-Ibáñez, M. (2004). Framing the social world with photo-elicitation interviews. *American Behavioral Scientist, 47*, 1507–1527.

Deleuze, G., & Guattari, F. (1987). *A thousand plateaus: Capitalism and schizophrenia* (B. Massumi, Trans.). University of Minnesota Press.

Gilbert, K. E., & Matoesian, G. M. (2021). *Multimodal performance and interaction in focus groups*. John Benjamins Publishing Company.

Griffin, G. (Ed.). (2016). *Cross-cultural interviewing: Feminist experiences and reflections*. Routledge.

Hall, J. N. (2020). *Focus groups: Culturally responsive approaches for qualitative inquiry and program evaluation*. Myers Education Press.

Kovach, M. (2010). Conversational method in Indigenous research. *First Peoples Child & Family Review, 5*(1), 40–48.

Kusenbach, M. (2020). Mobile methods. In S. Delamont & M. R. M. Ward (Eds.), *Handbook of qualitative research in education* (2nd ed., pp. 257–269). Edward Elgar.

Roulston, K. (Ed.). (2019). *Interactional studies of qualitative research interviews*. John Benjamins Publishing Company.

Roulston, K. (2022). *Interviewing: A guide to theory and practice*. SAGE.

Seidman, I. (2012). *Interviewing as qualitative research: A guide for researchers in education and the social sciences* (4th ed.). Teachers College Press.

Woodward, S. (2016). Object interviews, material imaginings and "unsettling" methods: interdisciplinary approaches to understanding materials and material culture. *Qualitative Research, 16*(4), 359–374. https://doi.org/10.1177/1468794115589647

PART I

BEING CULTURALLY RESPONSIVE IN INTERVIEW RESEARCH

ONE

Culturally Responsive Interviews: The Negotiation of Cultures

Lorien S. Jordan

QUALITATIVE INTERVIEWS ARE A CORE tool for social scientists seeking to gain an in-depth understanding of social phenomena through their interactions with the people whose lives, being, and perspectives are influenced by and influential on the phenomena of study (Roulston, 2022). Interviewing practices exist on a continuum from structured to unstructured, depending on the researcher's onto-epistemology, which informs their ideas regarding the purpose of a particular study and the methods for meeting that purpose. An interview is thus more congruent with a researcher's culture than that of the participants (Roulston, 2022).

Unless the concept of culture is purposefully engaged, it is veiled throughout the research, operating yet unacknowledged (Chouinard & Cram, 2020). In interviews, seemingly simple strategies on what questions to ask, the pacing and order of questions, and the logistics of the meeting stem from beliefs regarding what it means to design a rigorous and credible study (Roulston, 2022). At the same time, these culturally mediated decisions overtly or covertly convey to interviewees messages about their belonging and the value of their knowledge. For Westernized academics, these cultural mediations are grounded in the vestiges of Enlightenment-era onto-epistemologies, where the standard ideological assumption that inquiry is neutral, apolitical, non-cultural, universal, and objective remains (Berryman et al., 2013). These beliefs have constructed categories such as the Global North/Global South and developed/developing, which mirror the early colonial stances of civil/savage and continue to privilege those who are positioned as the majority in the Global North (Chilisa, 2020). In this chapter, I refer to these values as Westernized in order to recognize that there is no actual dividing line between the West and "the Rest," but that it is a concept that differentiates what have become scientifically "valid" and privileged modes of knowing. In creating Westernized cultural systems and knowledge, academia reflects white[1], heteropatriarchal, male, ableist, and

English-speaking hegemonic culture (Collins, 2002). Through Westernized methods, the studies created by researchers reproduce the risks and realities of epistemic violence (Fricker, 2007).

Increasingly, scholars are recognizing that research is never apolitical or value-free, and that researchers' worldviews are always central in any endeavor of inquiry (Fricker, 2007). For these researchers, there are several critically oriented, politically aligned, philosophical, and participatory methodologies from which to work, including culturally responsive frameworks. Culturally responsive research (CRR) evades simple definition; what constitutes a culturally responsive project depends on the cultural context in which it is enacted (Chouinard & Cram, 2020). A fundamental principle of culturally responsive approaches is the recognition that "culture" is crucial to the lives of both the participants and researchers. Culture is therefore a "methodologically and epistemologically relevant and vibrant construct that requires specific and focused attention" (Chouinard & Cram, 2020, p. 2). CRR asks researchers to utilize data generation methods that are culturally congruent with the study context. Across contexts, the qualitative interview has been relatively neglected as a data generation tool in CRR literature, possibly because of the concern that one-on-one interviews may enforce an individualistic lens (Roulston, 2022) within a relational culture and thus create a misunderstood and homogenous narrative of phenomena (Kovach, 2018).

The aim of this chapter is twofold. First, I orient the reader to concepts of culture and responsivity in research and data generation. Next, I explore four principles of culturally responsive interviews that flow throughout data generation, interpretation, and dissemination. Drawing on my research in Aotearoa/New Zealand, I take as my cue Stake's (2004) description of being responsive as "orienting to the experience of personally being there, feeling the activity, the tension, knowing the people and their values. It relies heavily on personal interpretation" (p. 86). The concern of "being there" and "feeling activity [and] tension" serves as the point of departure for this discussion. I thus approach the culturally responsive interview as a process of being in, at, and of a cultural dialogue and of making meaning between and within the words, actions, emotions, and thoughts both shared and withheld. This chapter is therefore not a list of instructions for creating a culturally responsive interview, but a discussion of the salient attributes for a researcher to engage ethically with their own and Other cultures.

Culturally Responsive Research

My "home" discipline, mental health, influenced my initial foray into CRR. Global mental health scholars have described how research and practice are overly dependent on Westernized worldviews, which leaves practitioners at risk of pathologizing clients and participants who do not conform to these "ideals" (Jordan et al., 2021). In confronting the normalization of white, Westernized well-being, culturally responsive therapists Seponski et al. (2013) have suggested that culture become a referent to center our understandings of the self and Other. Centering culture has two purposes: cultural competence and cultural responsivity. Culturally competent therapists focus on learning an Other's culture to "stand as an outsider expert on insider minority peoples' needs" (Seponski et al., 2013, p. 32). In contrast, responsivity is intentionally holding a balance between the therapist and client cultures to engage cultural wisdom and relevant healing.

Moving from mental health and growing as a methodologist led me to take a critical approach to CRR in order to understand how inquiry has problematized, colonized, and Othered (Jordan, 2022). From this critical lens, I view culture as a contested concept that simultaneously refers to a nation, a people, and their customs, beliefs, enactments of power, group membership, rituals, laws, and artifacts (Chouinard & Cram, 2020). Culture is produced by a people and reproductive of people. Every person has a complex cultural story that shifts and changes between contexts, time, and space. In CRR,

> the notion of culture thus moves beyond a mere demographic marker to a socially, politically, and historically vibrant and embedded construct, implicating and entwining our epistemological and ontological questions in the social, political, and cultural assumptions, norms, and values that govern our society. (Chouinard & Cram, 2020, p. 20)

Culturally Responsive Data Generation

When a researcher is from an outside, dominantly positioned group, the research techniques utilized should be minimally invasive, relevant, flexible, and reciprocal (Chilisa, 2020). These methods can be adaptations of observations and interviews so that they hold cultural relevance within the context.

They can also be new methods (or new to the researcher) that center on cultural ways of knowing and include methods that incorporate games, songs, arts, metaphors, proverbs, symbols, and artifacts to acknowledge that knowledge is transmitted through multiple dimensions (Chilisa, 2020).

Oral methods, such as storytelling, may be especially congruent for relational cultures wherein participants weave together the tangled narratives of their ancestry, self, and cosmological relationships (Berryman et al., 2013). The prioritization of oral traditions within CRR has led to the suggestion that group-oriented data generation, including focus group methods and sharing and talking circles, may be most culturally relevant (Hall, 2020). These group process approaches are highly compatible and potentially preferred, as they allow multivocality and multiple perspectives to emerge beyond the researcher's influence, thus mimicking the relational dialogic storytelling process. At the same time, scholars have suggested that group processes can decenter a researcher's power (Hall, 2020).

Given the relational component of group interviews, CRR has focused less on the individual interview as a relevant data-generation process. Within relational cultures, the one-on-one interview can potentially disconnect a person from their culture in a Westernized process that seeks to separate, isolate, and "tame" knowledge (Smith, 2012) while reproducing unequal power relations. Interviews, as Briggs (2021) suggested, risk the production of fragmented knowledge, designed to "fit the contours" (p. 955) of academia, wherein interviewers ask questions designed to shape the discourse in such a way while signaling if and when the participant's knowing is adequately complete. These one-on-one interactions can mirror societal hierarchies of power, particularly when the interviewer has a subject identity that relays power over the interviewee.

Conversely, Vázquez-Montilla and fellow researchers (2000) described CRR as an approach that embraces authenticity, affinity, and accuracy. They suggested that such authenticity relies on a cultural match between the interviewer and interviewee. Affinity is the personal connection of the participant to the data and the interviewer's guardianship of the data. Accuracy is the cultural alignment between the procedures used and the participants' understanding of the research purpose. Vázquez-Montilla and collaborators' (2000) suggestion that the interviewer is culturally congruent provokes ethical consideration of the meaning of insider/outsider research. Being a cultural insider can facilitate the process of culturally responsive interviews in recruiting, designing, and moving conversations forward. However, it can also produce feelings of distrust and tension within communities (Smith, 2012). A further problem arises when working with a culturally aligned interviewer who is not the lead researcher. At some point in the study, a translation will occur, where the researcher interprets the interview and risks superimposing their culturally biased interpretations on recorded text without participating in the meaning-making process.

Across time and cultures, what has emerged is that the connection between different modalities of culturally responsive interviews is the centrality of relationships (Wilson, 2008). The relational component contrasts with the cultural process of Westernized interviews, which follow a pattern of relatively brief encounters in which the relationship ends when the interviewer turns the recorder off. For example, the *pagtatanong-tanong* (asking questions) is an early example of culturally responsive interviewing drawn from Filipino culture (Pe-Pua, 1989). The interview is an unstructured, relational, and interactive process that does not follow a formal protocol. Instead, it works from a tentative list of topics that are revised as rich meanings are created during the interview. Throughout the process, the interviewee is central in guiding the flow and direction of the interview (Pe-Pua, 1989). Tafatolu has recently been described as a method that balances Samoan and Westernized approaches to blend the self, cultural context, and academic context within an interview. The process is rooted in the lesson found in the metaphor *fetu'utu'una'I muniao* (maneuvering a fisher's rod), wherein the interviewer and interviewee come together to mimic the rhythms and roles of partnership in co-operative fishing (Fosi Palaamo, 2018). Other interview processes, such as testimonials and witnessing, are rooted in the African diaspora as a process of countering oppression and liberation (Taylor, 2002). Here, the interviewer witnesses narratives of resistance and thus counters narratives of helplessness with stories of joy, agency, and transformation.

Positioning My Research and This Chapter

I am a White, straight, cis woman with a hidden, congenital physical disorder. I am also a daughter and an intentionally child-free wife whose ancestral connection to Land is one of settler coloniality in North Georgia and Western

South Carolina on the traditional lands of the Eastern Band of Cherokee. As an agnostic, I have a complicated relationship with spirituality that is provoked by the writings of Anzaldúa (Keating & Anzaldúa, 2015), which stimulate me to see beyond the confines of Westernized religious doctrine. As an academic in the United States, I communicate and make meaning in the colonizer's tongue (i.e., English) and live and work at a university that occupies Quapaw, Caddo, and Osage Lands. These are some of the identities I bring with me to inquiry, each holding a variety of cultural implications for myself and my participants.

I have researched in Cambodia, Aotearoa/New Zealand, and the United States on the political orientations of therapists, the neocolonialism of global mental health, and methodological whiteness and colonialism in inquiry. In this chapter, I share some of my experiences in Aotearoa/New Zealand, where I crafted my position on cultural responsivity. In 2017, I spent a year in the country, supported by a Fulbright award to work at the Family Centre, a family therapy/community development/social policy agency that had developed a holistic approach to individual, relational, community, Land, and political healing. While there, I conducted a critical ethnography of the negotiated spaces in the mental health system to understand how Māori maintain primacy in determining their healing in the face of colonial systems of power (Jordan et al., 2021).

For this project, I chose interviews over focus groups and followed the considered guidance of my cultural advisors. My primary concern about conducting focus groups is the risk of inadvertently silencing participants. For example, when meeting with elders, the transmitters of culture and knowledge, those with less status may not be comfortable sharing differences of opinion or may remain in the background out of respect. Interestingly, many elders brought others to the interviews, as will be discussed below. I also questioned my appropriateness for the interviews versus a culturally aligned interviewer. However, as one participant stated, cultural matching was "putting a veneer" on the research so that it "becomes ok to Māori." It would further potentially shirk recognition that I would still be superimposing my interpretations during the analysis. Instead, my advisors recommended that I approach interviews as *fa'afaletui* (weaving knowledge as weaving mats; Tamasese et al., 2005). Accordingly, while the interview itself may be individual, the dialogic process "shift(s) the focus and power from the researcher to the individual and allows her to speak to the collective and in a collective mode" (Taylor, 2002, p. 156).

I interviewed Māori, Pasifika (a Pacific Island-born or New Zealand-born person of Pacific heritage), *Pākehā* (a New Zealander of European descent), and *Tauiwi* (a foreigner, non-Māori), who worked within the mental health context. I also met with elders, politicians, and professors interested in engaging in culturally-just healing. I was consistently brought into and related to multiple, competing, and entangled cultures, which I understood as a negotiation of self, Other, and discipline. I therefore worked to be aware at all times of who I was in these cultural meetings, so as to better respond to my cultural biases in relation to Others. While some position CRR as a methodology (Berryman et al., 2013), I approach it as a connective tissue that stretches across researchers' onto-epistemologies, methodologies and methods, and axiological commitments and can inform deeply reflexive and justice-oriented inquiries.

Being With and Being In: Conducting Culturally Responsive Interviews

Culturally responsive interviews do not occur through prescribed processes of protocol development, meeting participants, interpreting data, and presenting knowledge (Chilisa, 2020). Instead, they mean engaging in a dynamic process of unfolding, which shifts in tone and tenor with each participant. Berryman and collaborators (2013) described culturally responsive methodologies as dialogic and requiring the researcher to embrace pluralism, the prioritization of relationships, and the deconstruction of coloniality. These dimensions are valuable touchstones and guide the following exploration of four principles of culturally responsive interviews.

Centering Critical Reflexivity

The reflexive researcher recognizes that they are a participant in knowledge reproduction and have a foregrounding awareness of the effect of their identities on all aspects of their inquiry (Finlay, 2002). To conduct culturally responsive interviews means that researchers aim to "know" and represent an-Other culture. Engaging in ethical data creation about another first requires the researcher to have a secure understanding and relationship with their own culture. Without this understanding, they risk problematic relationships and knowledge based on a lack of awareness of their cultural beliefs. They must also critically attend to the fluidity and interconnectedness of identities, which are constructions reproduced, undergirded, and determined by hegemonic systems of power. In U.S. culture, reflexivity is mostly solitarily engaged, a vulnerability only briefly shared in a subjectivity statement. A culturally reflexive interviewer approaches reflexivity as an individual and collective unfolding of self, moving away from reductive binaries of self-other to diffractively make sense of how cultural identities intersect, co-produce, and move through and around each other. This engagement is an act of becoming (see Barad's [2007] notion of diffraction).

Before my time in Aotearoa/New Zealand, I thought I had grasped the idea of critical–cultural reflexivity. However, once there, I learned how much more collaborative and vulnerable it is, with each interview beginning with a sharing of my and the interviewee's *whakapapa* (genealogy, lineage) and describing our positionality to all living things, ancestors, earth, and sky. The process is one of *whakawhānaungatanga* (establishing relationships), the foundations for trust-giving. To be able to share my whakapapa meant that I first had to learn, make visible, and be comfortable (yet not complacent) with my settler colonial culture and the ongoing violence of colonialism in my home country. By connecting my experiences of self with those of the interviewees, I learned to lean into the discomfort of questioning my right to be there and asking to be entrusted with their wisdom. This reflexive engagement continued throughout the interviews as we paused to make sense of how we were sense-making each other. This focus of shared reflexivity was of assistance in how I followed up and with what questions. I took the time to consider from which place or prior knowledge or biases these questions came and whom the questions would benefit.

While not explicitly related to the ethical protocols of *whakapapa*, I continue to open interviews with a similar sharing of self to intentionally forefront collaborative reflexive engagement. My goal is to maintain relational perspectives built on love rather than extraction. It questions who the researcher is and what identities they bring to the interview, thus encouraging openness to be questioned, challenged, and potentially refused by interviewees as they build an understanding of the researcher.

Holding Hermeneutic Humility

Rodriguez Medina (2019) suggested that native English speakers should approach the work of non-native English writers with hermeneutic humility. His call came from his experience as a Mexican man conducting his dissertation at Cambridge, where his ideas were devalued because his writing did not meet the arbitrary mark of academic English. Rodriguez Medina proposed that the central importance of scholarly work is the communication of ideas rather than linguistic stylism. The concept of hermeneutic humility is similarly relevant when conducting culturally responsive interviews. Holding hermeneutic humility means maintaining an "attitude of looking for meaning harder, of an empathetic search for what the other wants to express. It also requires interpreters to momentarily take language as a tool for communication, regardless of its cultural and geopolitical imbrications" (Rodriguez Medina, 2019, p. 3).

As a therapist, I have experienced (and been guilty of) the multiple ways in which people misinterpret others, regardless of cultural context. People communicate through culturally biased allegiances to words and the concepts they have come to symbolize, with their prejudices reflected in their questioning and beliefs about what was said. Hermeneutic humility asks that each "interpreter risk those prejudices in the encounter within what is to be interpreted" (Schwandt, 2000, p. 195).

When people from different cultures meet in an interview, hermeneutic humility reminds them not to take words for granted, regardless of the linguistic context. This reminder came to me in Aotearoa/New Zealand when, during an interview, I mistranslated a *te reo* Māori (the Māori language) word—a word that had the power to shift the conversation's focus. I misinterpreted the speaker as saying *kaupapa* (kOH-paa–paa) Māori, that is, "purposefully" Māori, the purposeful orientation to Māoridom. However, she was talking about *kūpapa* (kEW-puh-paa)—that is, Māori who purposefully act against the interests of Māoridom to better their prospects. When I transcribed the interview, I heard the difference. When speaking with the interviewee again, I asked her about this, and she laughed, saying, "I wondered why you let that drop, seems pretty sig[nificant] to me." This missed interpretation reminded me that, just as I practiced in therapy, I needed to slow down and stop myself from knowing too soon and to ask for interpretative clarification.

Beyond words and definitions, hermeneutic humility also relates to the conversation process. According to Durie (2007), Westernized thinkers operate centripetally in that they move inward and narrow knowledge into tangible bits to be labeled and isolated. Accordingly, in the United States, interviewers might be more accustomed to conversations that follow a pattern of direct questioning that results in responses that neatly align with those questions. Durie (2007) contrasted the direct question–response process with that of Māori and Pasifika thinkers, who think outwardly in a relational and centrifugal process. These conversations tend to reject linear-directness, preferring instead a seemingly circuitous pathway to answer questions through narratives that relate to self-other-ecology-cosmos. The hearer's job is to discern how a story or metaphor transmits what is to be known. As Canagarajah (2005) wrote, "it is when we acknowledge the localness of each of our own knowledge that we have the proper humility to engage productively with other knowledge traditions. The assumption that one's knowledge is of sole universal relevance does not encourage conversation" (p. 20). This acknowledgment is one of hermeneutic humility and learning to quiet the impulse to know our participants unhesitatingly, without doubt (Somerville & Hartley, 2000). In practical terms, I suggest that this means asking questions tentatively, clarifying the meanings, holding ideas lightly, slowing down, listening to hear, and experiencing the Other in their telling.

Engaging Methodological Pluriversalism

Pluriversalism recognizes that cultures' cosmologies, temporality, and spatiality are complex, fluid, and entangled in relationships of power; encouraging researchers to "dwell in the borders" (Mignolo, 2007, p. 165). Methodological pluriversality includes the methods and meanings researchers bring into their practices that encourage creative, caring, relational potentialities embedded in the diversity of onto-epistemological borders (Koro, 2022). Culturally responsive interviews approached from methodological pluriversalism invite the interviewer and interviewee to meet within their entangled cultures' borders.

In Aotearoa/New Zealand, I had devised a semi-structured interview; however, in my first meeting, I recognized how stilted and unnatural it felt. I therefore abandoned my interview guide for the unstructured, conversational method of *korero mai*. In this approach, my role as an interview guide shifted, and centrality was transferred to the participants as they guided me through their storytelling. I became a testimonial witness who followed the participants' leads and became accountable for listening "to the stories and link[ing] the stories back to the information needs" of my project (Swadener & Mutua, 2008, p. 41). Working from *korero mai* also meant that I became a participant in my research and shared my remembrances through "collaborative storying," where "the stories of the research participants (and this includes the researcher) merge to create a collaborative text, a mutually constructed story created out of the lived experiences of the research participants" (Bishop, 1999, p. 2). At the same time, it cannot be assumed that conversational, storytelling approaches are necessarily responsive.

Other entanglements emerged. My methodological mindset was stretched when interviewees invited others into our conversations, often without my prior knowledge. Bayeck (2021) termed this "conversation bombing," a take on photo-bombing, wherein someone jumps into a picture frame just as the photographer snaps the photo. "Conversation/interview bombing refers to [a] face-to-face interview with a participant that turns into an interaction with other self-selected/improvised interviewee[s] who participate in the interview without the researcher's prior invitation" (Bayeck, 2021, p. 4). In these moments, I considered whether these conversational partners were participants or supporters: Were they there to develop knowledge or protect knowledge (and the participant)? Having the support of trusted others appeared especially relevant when I met with *kaumātua* (elders), the safeguards and transmitters of sacred knowledge. These impromptu meetings were cultural entanglements that defied Westernized modes of interviewing and challenged ideas of consent, participation, and sampling, while prioritizing the value of knowledge creation as a communal and collective responsibility.

Responding to the pluriverse occurs in the small moments when a researcher and interviewees engage the cultures between them. For example, when a *kaumātua* asked me to share a poem about my relationship with Land, I sang John Denver's "When the River Meets the Sea." This engagement is the sharing of stories in sacred moments, sitting together weaving mats to prepare for a funeral, and learning from the ancestors. Methodologically, it is recognizing when a game is not just a game, or when talking through images, song, and nature is more powerful than words. It means ethically attending to protocols of gender, eldership, embodiment, and ritual, being welcomed into spiritual spaces with structured ceremonies, and sharing food. It is learning preferences for riding in a tuk-tuk or sitting under a banyan tree rather than in a closed office space. For me, it was not exoticizing or essentializing these moments, but learning to see them in my cultures, such as starting photovoice groups with music and food and closing with a grounding exercise. Conventional Westernized interview methods are linear, with a clear beginning and an end, and these culturally responsive interviews led me to a deeper appreciation of the multiple ways researchers and participants can develop knowledge.

Cultural and Relational Accountability

As culturally responsive interviewers, we are accountable to the interviewee, their community, and culture, and we need to accept responsibility for our actions within the interview and beyond. This accountability means we are intentional and critical in our attention to relational, conversational, and interpretative power. Although there are many ways we can—and should—address power throughout research, here I center Tuck and Yang's (2014) problematization of damage discourses. Research with participants who have been Indigenized, raced, or otherwise marginalized is frequently focused on "documenting damage" (Tuck & Yang, 2014, p. 226). Positioning marginalized communities as powerless and to be pitied is a "fixation . . . exhibited in eliciting pain stories from communities that are not White, not wealthy, and not straight" (Tuck & Yang, 2014, p. 227). Documenting the harm perpetrated on communities neglects to document who has enacted this harm. When researchers become damage consumers, they dig deeply into stories of pain, violence, and trauma, but neglect to see the joy, resistance, and thriving that accompany these narratives.

In Aotearoa/New Zealand, Māori clinicians shared experiences describing the complexity of their pain/trauma of working in the system and the tension of competing interests. Such narratives are "entrusted to us, stories that are told to us because research is a human activity" (Tuck & Yang, 2014, p. 233). Being entrusted with these stories means researchers should be careful about what they do with them and recognize that some stories are meant for the listener, not formal analyses. When participants share their experiences of pain, I also ask about the connected desires, values, resistances, or hopes. This process is a tenuous balance. I do not want to sidetrack the interviewee, nor do I want to evade the reality of power and violence, but I also do not want to be a trauma voyeur who only sees the participants' pain. Instead, I hope to witness them, understand the hegemonies that provoke perpetration, and, at the same time, position "the knowing derived from such experiences as wise" (Tuck & Yang, 2014, p. 231). Being accountable to the power in the interview relationship also means attending to the power of refusal. When an interviewee refuses a question or direction, it is a productive space for the researcher to redirect their gaze. In interviews, I look for these moments of hesitation, or what is called deflection in psychotherapy, as spaces to expand my focus to look at what I am being invited to see rather than what I automatically want to see.

Relational and cultural accountability in interviews with people from majoritized cultures is just as central for CRR. For example, my photovoice study with white U.S. citizens focused on cultural whiteness in inquiry. During interviews, the white participants' cultural responses were to (consciously or not) use emotionality to distance themselves from the violence and reality of white culture. Remaining accountable in these moments means I do not stay silent or lean into emotionality. Instead, these are productive moments of tension to connect the shame, guilt, or anger to their desire for transformation.

Issues of Interpretation and Representation

Positioning CRR for communities and audiences comes down to questions of how the Other is written into being. All interview interactions are moments of interpretation, and hermeneutic humility thus has ramifications for the interaction of talk in interviews, as it does for the analysis and representation of what is to become the data. Researchers translate forward by bringing something not in its context—namely, their "findings"—and making them digestible for the intended audience. When we translate/interpret, we risk distilling and dislocating the meaning from the cultural world of the participant. Ethical engagement in CRR requires a humility that understands Westernized modes of analysis and representation as aspects of this dissection, which move meaning from its context to reflect the researcher's lifeworld. As Kovach (2017) wrote, "we are re-storying through our own lens, gaze, and perspective" (p. 227).

How, then, do researchers re-story with respect and relevance for the cultural entanglements in which the stories were shared? The analytical choices made in their final interpretations of culturally responsive interviews are not prescriptive. Analysis and representation can occur through poetry, art, applications of culturally relevant theories, story-telling, performances, and songs (Chilisa, 2020; Chouinard & Cram, 2020; Kovach, 2018), as well as other artistic, written, and embodied forms (see Somerville & Hartley, 2000, for an illustration). It is also significant to remember that, as Chilisa stated (2020), "it may be counterproductive to reject applicable Western ideas simply because they originate from the West" (p. 224). The Westernized ideas that continue to dominate in my work are the analytic methods in which I was trained, including interpretative phenomenological analysis, phenomenography, and situational analysis. I appreciate these analytic styles because they encourage the double hermeneutic of recognizing that the meanings shared are interpretations bound in the moment and that analysis is a further interpretation of that interpretation. Situational analysis also encourages the visual analytic processes of mapmaking to move away from codification, homogenization, and reduction. To address the double hermeneutic in my research from Aotearoa/New Zealand, I have leaned on the theory of negotiated spaces. This theory orients the readers and writer to consider the entanglements of Māori/Pasifika science and Western science (Mila-Schaaf & Hudson, 2009). To frame my findings as developed in these negotiated spaces, I describe them as my response to my experiences within entangled cultures. At the same time, I have begun to question how I can pull away from the lure of Westernized science to engage in less extractive and more complex and artistic forms of analysis.

Ethical representation is a driving concern of CRR. When we research with Others who are or have been marginalized, we work within communities where their knowledge has been commodified, appropriated, and disinformed, a phenomenon termed epistemic violence (Fricker, 2007). Cultural and relational accountability instruct researchers to safeguard the knowledge shared with them and are clear on which stories they are allowed to re-story and share. In their final writings, researchers should focus on reporting a narrative that would be familiar to the teller and ultimately have purpose for the teller and their community (Chilisa, 2020). As a critically oriented, culturally responsive researcher, my work has focused on the hegemonic systems and cultural contexts in which mental health and research occur. In this work, I also aim for transparency with participants and audiences with respect to my alignment to power in those spaces. To give evidence of the "me" in the re-storying, I attempt to make plain my culture through critical theoretical applications, such as critical whiteness studies, critical race theory, and settler colonialism. These theories help me untangle and address how the humanization of settlers (that is, my people—white Euro-Americans) hinges on the dehumanization of all Others.

Presenting Work

Given that I have been an outsider in multiple communities, I work to bridge people (Chouinard & Cram, 2020), cultural advisors, elders, and trusted researchers and facilitators who are intermediaries within the entangled spaces of culture. They assist me by describing the work, presenting the findings, and giving back to the communities. At the same time, they generously provide critical friendship and questioning throughout my interpretative process to provoke my descriptions, understandings, and meanings. While I engage these advisors to assist in my cultural awareness and responsivity, I simultaneously acknowledge that practices such as identifying insiders to consult with places boundaries on what it means to be an insider/outsider of a culture and risks essentializing the cultures I am engaged with (Chouinard & Cram, 2020).

In academic cultures, culturally responsive interviews are not packaged easily into a cohesive meaning unit that is quickly identifiable to the audience. Given that no prescribed process of protocol development, participant dialogue, interpretation, and presentation exists, the dynamic process of unfolding that shifts and changes with each participant can be read as un-rigorous or nonvalid. The presentation of culturally responsive interviews becomes one of justifying the salience of culture and questioning the cultural function of Westernized ways of knowing and doing.

Rodriguez Medina (2019) first described hermeneutic humility to call on publishers, readers, professors, and reviewers to focus on the meaning rather than semantics in writing. Writing with hermeneutic humility has led to editorial disagreements between myself and reviewers. When citing quotations from participants, I use the terms and expressions of the participants, including the language and how it was spoken. For example, Khmer (Cambodian) is a complex, analytic, non-inflective, and non-conjugating language with many regional dialects, and the vocabulary used depends on the relationships between speakers. In interviews, I understood that the interviewees transposed

Khmer grammatical rules onto English words. In presenting quotes, I faced the choice between, as an editor advised, "smoothing over" the language versus presenting it how it was spoken. I opted to present it in the way it was spoken to me to indicate that this is the language I interpreted rather than to present a further interpretation thereof.

Language is crucial to culture, and when researchers offer linear, flattened translations of words, they lose the meanings behind them. For example, there is no direct Māori-to-English translation in many instances. Whereas English is linear, in *te reo* Māori, one word has many meanings that speak to different levels of multidimensional cosmology. Publishers have challenged my prioritization of *te reo* and asked me to put the words in footnotes, thereby suggesting that Māoridom belongs somewhere other than centered. Instead, I leave *te reo* in text, with the English in parenthesis or footnotes, while recognizing that in most cases I cannot represent the fullness of the language. For example, in this chapter, due to the necessity of word limits, I defined *whakapapa* as genealogy, an incomplete definition at best for a word that means genealogy, genealogical table, lineage, descent; recitation of genealogies or stories of the world; the ways by which people come into relationship with the world, with people, and with life. Similarly, it is the stylistic demand of APA that asks us to put into italics those words that are foreign and therefore strange.

The ethical question of identifying interviewees also arises in culturally responsive reporting. The Westernized world has long "claimed" (Smith, 2012) knowledge as its own when appropriating it from others. It is possible that publishing participants' names and place names is responsive and just. At the same time, the identification of participants risks community tension. This was apparent in Cambodia, where the number of therapists in the country are few, and the people I interviewed were concerned about being identified as critiquing a system in which they felt disempowered and constrained. Decisions such as these must be carefully determined in dialogue with the participants to represent their cultural and community experiences rather than the disciplinary culture of the researcher.

Concluding Thoughts

This chapter frames the concept of culturally responsive interviews as a relational, dialogic process that hinges on the interviewer's awareness of and security in their cultural self to ethically engage with the culture of the Other.

Fine (1994) described "working the hyphens" (p. 70) as attending to the ways in which researchers always author the Other, either transparently or not. Without purposefully attending to their role in this process, they presume that they fully know the Other, that they can describe them completely, and that they are entitled to do so. I admittedly share this view and recognize that no matter how hard researchers work the hyphen, they are the ones creating it by suggesting that research is needed, and they are the researchers to produce it. To illuminate the discursive hyphen, I have adopted a critically oriented, culturally responsive approach that focuses on the relationships, power, sociohistories, and processes of entangled cultures. Notwithstanding, I recognize that mine is not the *only way*; it is *a way*, and one upon which I invite reflection as researchers continue to evolve methodologically and epistemologically.

I have described the four principles I work to live up to when conducting culturally responsive interviews. While I have predominantly reflected on my experience in Aotearoa/New Zealand, I acknowledge that these processes are equally important when working with cultures in which I am considered an insider, and when I meet with white U.S. participants, I continue to value the confluence of our cultures. The goal is not for researchers to devalue their cultures, but to be aware of their influence over them, their research, and the communities they engage with. For Westernized interviewers, it is to divest themselves of cultural narcissism, to challenge their taken-for-granted beliefs about knowledge, value, and research. Overall, it is a shift from the Westernized canon, the approved, privileged, and valued methods of conducting and reporting research. It moves beyond calls to respect and be inclusive of diversity and to commit to the cultural transformation of how researchers create knowledge and what knowledge they privilege.

Note:

1. Throughout this chapter, I write white purposefully in lower cased format as a political commitment to problematizing onto-epistemological whiteness in research.

References

Barad, K. (2007). *Meeting the universe halfway: Quantum physics and the entanglement of matter and meaning.* Duke University Press.

Bayeck, R. Y. (2021). The intersection of cultural context and research encounter: Focus on interviewing in qualitative research. *International Journal of Qualitative Methods, 20*, Advanced online publication. https://doi.org/10.1177%2F1609406921995696

Berryman, M., SooHoo, S., & Nevin, A. (Eds.). (2013). *Culturally responsive methodologies.* Emerald Group Publishing.

Bishop, R. (1999). *Collaborative storytelling: Meeting Indigenous people's desires for self-determination.* Paper presented at the World Indigenous People's Conference, Albuquerque, New Mexico, June 15–22. https://files.eric.ed.gov/fulltext/ED467396.pdf

Briggs, C. L. (2021). Against methodological essentialism, fragmentation, and instrumentalism in times of COVID-19. *American Anthropologist, 123*(4), 954–956. https://doi.org/10.1111/aman.13653

Canagarajah, A. S. (2005). *Reclaiming the local in language policy and practice.* Routledge.

Chilisa, B. (2020). *Indigenous research methodologies* (2nd ed.). SAGE.

Chouinard, J. A., & Cram, F. (2020). *Culturally responsive approaches to evaluation: Empirical implications for theory and practice.* SAGE.

Collins, P. H. (2002). *Black feminist thought: Knowledge, consciousness, and the politics of empowerment.* Routledge.

Durie, M. (2007). Counselling Māori: Marae encounters. *Aotearoa/New Zealand Journal of Counselling, 27*(1), 1–8.

Fine, M. (1994). Working the hyphens. In N. K. Denzin & Y. S. Lincoln (Eds.), *The Sage handbook of qualitative research* (pp. 70–82). SAGE.

Finlay, L. (2002). Negotiating the swamp: The opportunity and challenge of reflexivity in research practice. *Qualitative Research, 2,* 209–230.

Fosi Palaamo, A. (2018). Tafatolu (three-sides): A Samoan research methodological framework. *Aotearoa Aotearoa/New Zealand Social Work, 30*(4), 19–27.

Fricker, M. (2007). *Epistemic injustice: Power and the ethics of knowing.* Oxford University Press.

Hall, J. N. (2020). *Focus groups: Culturally responsive approaches for qualitative inquiry and program evaluation.* Myers Education Press.

Jordan, L. S. (2022). Unsettling the family sciences: Introducing settler colonial theory through a theoretical analysis of the family and racialized injustice. *Journal of Family Theory and Review.* Advance online. https://doi.org/10.1111/jftr.12453

Jordan, L. S., Anderson, L. A., & Hall, J. N. (2021). Sowing the seeds: Sociocultural resistance in the psychological sciences. *Cultural Diversity and Ethnic Minority Psychology.* Advance online publication. https://doi.org/10.1037/cdp0000462

Jordan, L. S., Seponski, D. M., Hall, J. N., & Bermudez, J. M. (2021). "Hopefully you've landed the waka on the shore": Negotiated spaces in Aotearoa/New Zealand's bicultural mental health system. *Transcultural Psychiatry.* Advance online publication. https://doi.org/10.1177/13634615211014347

Keating, A., & Anzaldúa, G. (2015). *Light in the dark/Luz en lo oscuro: Rewriting identity, spirituality, reality.* Duke University Press.

Koro, M. (2022). Speculative experimentation in (methodological) pluriverse. *Qualitative Inquiry, 28*(2), 135–142.

Kovach, M. (2017). Doing indigenous methodologies. In N. K. Denzin & S. Yvonna (Eds.), *The Sage handbook of qualitative research* (5th ed., pp. 214-234). SAGE.

Mignolo, W. D. (2007). Introduction: Coloniality of power and de-colonial thinking. *Cultural Studies, 21*(2-3), 155-167. https://doi.org/10.1080/09502380601162498

Mila-Schaaf, K., & Hudson, M. (2009). *Negotiating space for indigenous theorising in Pacific mental health and addictions.* Le Va.

Pe-Pua, R. (1989). Pagtatanong-tanong: A cross-cultural research method. *International Journal of Intercultural Relations, 13*(2), 147-163.

Rodriguez Medina, L. (2019). A geopolitics of bad English. *Tapuya: Latin American Science, Technology and Society, 2*(1), 1-7.

Roulston, K. (2022). *Interviewing: A guide to theory and practice.* SAGE.

Schwandt, Thomas A. (2000). Three epistemological stances for qualitative inquiry: Interpretivism, hermeneutics and social constructivism. In N. K. Denzin & Y. S. Lincoln (Eds.), *Handbook of Qualitative Research* (2nd ed., pp. 189-213). SAGE.

Seponski, D. M., Bermudez, J. M., & Lewis, D. C. (2013). Creating culturally responsive family therapy models and research: Introducing the use of responsive evaluation as a method. *Journal of Marital and Family Therapy, 39*(1), 28-42.

Smith, L. T. (2012). *Decolonizing methodologies* (2nd ed.). Zed Books.

Somerville, M., & Hartley, L. (2000). Eating place: Postcolonial explorations of embodiment and place. *Journal of Intercultural Studies, 21*(3), 353-364. https://doi.org/10.1080/07256860020007575

Stake, R. E. (2004). *Standards-based & responsive evaluation.* SAGE.

Swadener, B. B., & Mutua, K. (2008). Deconstructing the global postcolonial. In N. K. Denzin, Y. S. Lincoln, & L. T. Smith (Eds.), *Handbook of critical and indigenous methodologies* (pp. 31-43). SAGE.

Tamasese, K., Peteru, C., Waldegrave, C., & Bush, A. (2005). Ole taeao afua, the new morning: A qualitative investigation into Samoan perspectives on mental health and culturally appropriate services. *Australian & Aotearoa/New Zealand Journal of Psychiatry, 39*(4), 300-309.

Taylor, J. Y. (2002). Talking back: Research as an act of resistance and healing for African American women survivors of intimate male partner violence. *Women & Therapy, 25*(3-4), 145-160.

Tuck, E., & Yang, K. W. (2014). R-words: Refusing research. In D. Paris & M. T. Winn (Eds.), *Humanizing research: Decolonizing qualitative inquiry with youth and communities* (pp. 223-248). SAGE.

Vázquez-Montilla, E., Reyes-Blanes, M. E., Hyun, E., & Brovelli, E. (2000). Practices for culturally responsive interviews and research with Hispanic families. *Multicultural Perspectives, 2*(3), 3-7.

Wilson, S. (2008). *Research is ceremony. Indigenous research methods.* Fernwood.

TWO

 Beyond Qualitative Interviews:
Toward Synergistic Conversations
as Relational and Nation Building

Emma Elliott and Timothy San Pedro

"It is a great responsibility to hear stories of another and to offer our own in return. It is beyond interviews...."

—*Emma Elliott and/or Timothy San Pedro*

As we write, the world is in a state of widespread chaos. We are collectively facing multiple and overlapping pandemics: the novel coronavirus, or COVID-19, an environmental collapse, and state-sanctioned violence against Black and Brown peoples (Ladson-Billings, 2021). These pandemics have exacerbated the existing inequalities and vulnerabilities faced by historically and institutionally underserved populations, including Indigenous, Black, Latinx, and Asian peoples, making visible the urgent need to re-center alternative approaches to qualitative research (Yip, 2020). Despite our collective efforts, the equity chasms faced by communities of color have increased across the past half-century (DePaoli et al., 2021). We have to do better; at this point, there is no alternative. As we consider the ways in which we can contribute, we hold close our academic elders who have been calling for consequential, deliberate, and transformative approaches to qualitative research (Bang & Vossoughi, 2016; McCoy et al., 2020; Paris & Winn, 2014).

The magnitude of cumulative and collective threat faced by humankind offers a distinct opportunity for scholars to re-imagine alternative approaches to research that respond to our moment in time. So, where do we go from here? What does this mean for qualitative research methodologies?

For us, Indigenous ways of knowing and being have profoundly influenced our personal and professional lives and continue to shape our every social interaction. Timothy grew up among the Salish, Kootenai, and Pend d'Oreille peoples on the Flathead Indian Reservation in Western Montana. As a Filipino-American, he was invited into the homes, lives, and stories of the Indigenous peoples there. Emma, during her early years, was raised without running water or electricity in Deerholme on Vancouver Island, British Columbia. Her parents intentionally chose this way of life to teach their children about the importance of knowledge systems, cultural practices, and ceremonies in relation to a Cowichan worldview.

We share these stories in order to give the reader a glimpse of how our experiences—that is, the stories of our lives—shape our understanding of the world. An Indigenous understanding of self involves being enmeshed within a vast system of relationships across peoples, plant and animal nations, land, and other natural world elements that are imbued with a deep sense of relational responsibility. These understandings are transmitted across generations from one person to the next and through everyday social interaction in a process of what Jo-Ann Archibald (2008)—an Indigenous studies scholar from the Sto:lo First Nation in British Columbia, Canada—calls Indigenous Storywork. Indigenous Storywork is a methodological approach that engages and highlights the powerful nature of Indigenous stories, storytelling, and storylistening. We believe that these fundamental ontologies and related commitments can offer a syncretic approach to qualitative research and practice, including how we collect, interpret, and disseminate knowledge. We also believe that, as researchers, we are never void of individual worldviews and fundamental ontologies that inform our approaches to educational research.

Drawing on these understandings and commitments, we offer an in-process conceptualization of engaging in the building with others through what we are calling *synergistic conversations*. At the heart of this understanding are the following key questions: As scholars and people enmeshed in a vast system of relationships, how do we shift our practice to respond to widespread inequity? If we are not striving to change the nature or function of the work we do in response to inequity, then what is our ultimate goal? How is our work relational, dialogic, and reciprocal with others? As we continue to grapple with these questions and enact these elements and concepts in our own dialogue and approach to research and practice, our intention is to model how our perspectives and positionalities inform our interactions and highlight the important synergetic elements that continue to transform our approaches to qualitative research and practice.

Stories carry power; they carry wisdom. Stories provide opportunities for people to define their place in the world; they shape worldviews and ethical commitments and, ultimately, inform what it means to be human and how to live a good life (Bang et al., 2016; Brayboy, 2005; Deloria, 1970; Vizenor, 1999). The root of such power lies in one's ability to shape and share stories in ways that are culturally and tribally appropriate to a community. It is a great responsibility, then, to listen closely and carefully to the stories of others, to sit with their stories, to hold their stories, and, at times, to protect their stories from harm. Yet qualitative research continues to find itself in the grips of western research practices imbued with unequal power dynamics that center on settler colonial and imperial ideals of control and exploitation (Smith, 1999).

For qualitative research in general, interviews have been the primary source of data collection—or, rather, data extraction. Often, interviewing methods reinforce cultural superiority through such extractive theories and practices that are then followed by analytical strategies that strip people from their stories and subsume control of knowledge in ways that continue to center upon the researcher's own paradigms, norms, and beliefs. If we do not deeply consider our methodological approaches as reciprocal, dialogic, and co-constitutive, then we unknowingly (or knowingly) perpetuate destructive ideals of control and exploitation. We believe there is a better way forward and argue alongside other scholars who have also been pushing the field in various ways, such as humanizing research methodologies (Paris & Winn, 2014), relational approaches to research (Kuntz, 2019), ethics of relationality (Kerr & Adamov Ferguson, 2021), narrative inquiry (Clandinin, 2006; Connelly & Clandinin, 1990), and others. In this way, we build with such scholarship while also making the conscious choice to recenter Indigenous knowledges and ways of knowing when thinking about ways to enter into ethical, dialogic, and synergistic conversations with others.

In *Storywork*, Archibald (2008, p. 33) identifies two key elements of "synergistic interactions" necessary to shape human understandings of self in the world: first, the productive interaction between storyteller, listener, and story; and second, the active participation of the listener in relationship to the storyteller. We extend these by framing synergistic conversations as requiring the following: There must be respect between those in conversation with one another—we must be open to and willing to hear the histories and contexts from which the stories of another derive, and we must offer our own in return. There must be space for stories to be shared. There must be a story. There must be a storyteller and a storylistener, and, at times and under the right circumstances, those roles can move back and forth in the generative meaning-making through story sharing. In such a back and forth, stories are strengthened, much like flour holds form and is strengthened when water is added and is folded upon itself. In this way, reciprocity—the giving and receiving of story—creates an elasticity that holds conversations together, that gives them shape and meaning and form. As one listens to the stories of the other, sits with their stories, and allows them space and time to impact us, we may become more conscious of how we are changed by their stories. We sense and can feel an alteration within us, and in a synergistic conversation, those feelings are mutual in the reciprocal nature of story sharing; we can feel that our stories are altering the other as well.

Martin and William (2018) refer to this process as an "ongoing symbiotic alliance," that is formed between people. Similarly, Archibald (2008) uses the term "synergistic interactions." We deeply connect with both terms as they move beyond witnessing or "bearing witness" to the stories of another. In Coast Salish tradition, a large part of knowledge transmission is preserved through the witnessing process. Witnesses are called to be the keepers of communal history and to share with others what they have learned, observed, heard, and felt. The process of bearing witness honors the story that is unfolding and the important contribution of the story, storyteller, and storylistener to knowledge construction. This process reflects the oral nature of Coast Salish knowledge transmission. Simon Baker of Squamish Nation shares the teaching of listening with one's heart, mind, body and spirit: "Listen with our three ears, two that we hear with and the one in our heart" (Archibald, 2008, p. 12). Lee-Morgan (2018) identifies the synergistic and social nature of synergistic conversations; our stories ". . . are intimately intertwined with our families, communities . . . and nations" (p. 156).

Synergistic conversations ask both/all peoples involved to not simply listen or witness, but also to make meaning of the stories in relation to our own experiences, and to offer our own connections, insights, and transformations. We bear a responsibility to share our own stories, either when called upon or when the moment is right, so that others can feel and sense that synergy built between us. To be in synergy means we are involved in the emergent story. With these responsibilities in mind, a final crucial ingredient in the formation of synergistic conversations is acknowledgment: we give thanks to each and every one of you, and to all of our relatives who continue to nurture and sustain us; we recognize that it is through our relational connections that we are able to develop our own sense of self in the world, and we offer gratitude to the intellectual traditions that continuously urge us, and humankind, to do better, to learn more, and to grow more fully as responsible human beings.

And so, in this chapter, we (Timothy and Emma) do the hard/heart work of not only conceptualizing synergistic conversations as a way to connect through Indigenous storying (Archibald, 2008), but to simultaneously model what that looks like and sounds like as we shared stories/ideas that eventually led to the crafting of this chapter. We do so by citing our Indigenous, Black, and other scholars of color who have offered a better way forward, an "otherwise," for building, nurturing, and sustaining good relations through the storying of our everyday lives (Grande, 2020).

Synergism Modeled: A Conversation Between Emma and Timothy

A note on this conversation: Below is a series of three recorded zoom conversations between us that took place over a two-month period as we pondered the contributions, implications, and discussion of our work. We edited the automatically generated zoom transcripts from these conversations into dialogue, with the explicit intention to create an impact upon our readers as we modeled what a synergistic conversation might sound like and feel like. We omitted multiple utterances or validations such as "mmm-hmmm" or "yes" or "that's right." However, it's important to note that those utterances gave us the awareness that our ideas resonated with one another, thus allowing us to go deeper into conversation and more in alignment with how we envision the synergy existent between us.

Tim: Welcome listeners and readers! We are so glad you joined Emma and I in this conversation. Okay, Emma, with this imagined audience that's here with us but not here all at the same time, where should we begin?

Emma: [laughter] Well, I think it's important to first draw upon the elements and principles offered by Jo-Ann Archibald's theoretical and practical framework of Storywork as our foundation. We engage these principles as fundamental tenets of Indigenous intellectual traditions broadly and, in doing so, posit that Indigenous intellectual knowledge itself is guided and informed by everyday interactions in the areas of these values and principles. The purpose of qualitative interviewing is to collect data through a scientific and methodological process. Similarly, Indigenous knowledge systems are guided by these tenets, but add to them dynamic and co-constitutive processes. Indigenous Storying offers a way to gather that information and data, but it also offers other things: it's culturally sustainable, it's ethical, it's local, and it attends to diverse and heterogeneous interpretations of knowledge. It recognizes that learning, healing, and knowledge construction (or co-construction) take place in the context of the social, cultural, and everyday interaction; it therefore leads to opportunities for transformation, because transformation takes place in everyday social interactions (Bang et al., 2018). By centering on relationality, we do these things inherently and gather the rich and important information from populations like Indigenous peoples, whose center of life hasn't always been colonization. So what can we learn from Indigenous knowledge systems to produce innovative approaches to interviewing?

Timothy: Okay! We're just gonna go there right away, dive into the deep end of the pool. Yes! [laughter]. I just love the framing and that question, Emma. We're really offering a push here, aren't we? When we're thinking about interviews, we need to push against these norms of taking without reciprocating. It should be about listening closely and carefully with another person, trying to understand what it is that their stories are offering us. Additionally, those who share their stories with us need to be a part of that analysis, of that interpretation, so that their original intentions and purposes of telling that story are included in how we share that understanding beyond us. So, in my work, the way that I've made the most sense of this idea is to get as close to the "Co" as possible—Co-authoring, Co-analyzing, collaborating (San Pedro et al., 2017)—so that it's never my story. It's a collaboration of telling that story collectively. And I think that's where the conceptualizing work I did with Valerie Kinloch on *Projects in Humanization* (PiH) helps (San Pedro & Kinloch, 2017). Through PiH, we were stating the obvious: that we, as human beings, impact and are impacted by the people and spaces and places we enter into; we are a part of that story. We can't not be. So PiH, along with Indigenous Storying, is a push against this façade of Western research, the belief that we need to extract ourselves, that we need to extract our identities for the data to be "valid." We are part of the story, and our relationships matter in the telling and shaping of those stories.

Emma: OK, thank you. I'm wondering, how does Projects in Humanization relate to storying, its purpose, and how that relates to what we're trying to offer in terms of innovative methodological strategies?

Timothy: Yeah, I mean Projects in Humanization engages storying as a relational process; we center relationships rather than turning away from them, ignoring the fact that we impact and are impacted, whether we want to believe that or not. Our presence, just being there, impacts the setting and situation. And so, PiH is, at minimum, an acknowledgment of our impact. But beyond that minimal recognition, PiH is an effort to center the relational development we have with others. And the way that Kinloch and I thought through this is to state openly that, in all this work we do, relational development is at the heart. It's a part of our collective understanding of ourselves and of ourselves in relation to those that we're working with. And by centering the heart, by centering relationships, we hope that this dissuades and prevents the heartless research, the deficit-based, and damage-based research that has hurt Indigenous, Black, and other people of color. It's not hard to find such heartless work done by researchers who did not care about those they worked with (see Mello & Wolf, 2010). Research shouldn't solely be about trying to understand a phenomenon that's external from ourselves, but really trying to understand questions of: How do we walk in this world? What do we value? What do we see as beautiful and right?

Emma: Yeah, OK. That's great! All in all, the big broad sweep is we're offering up ideas, theory, and practice related to storying and Indigenous intellectual tradition to inform qualitative interviewing, because that's the focus of this book.

Timothy: Yes. An important push we are offering is to acknowledge that qualitative interviews are often unidirectional. By that I mean that it's one person asking questions for the purposes of their research project, and the data or "stories" are extracted through the questioning of another. It's one-way because one person is asking another person to reveal themselves without any revelation of the person who's asking the questions. Instead, those who are a part of that conversation need to offer our stories in relation to the stories that are shared with us, and so in that way it's not an interview anymore. It's a dialogic conversation, and that's what I really liked about Jo-Ann's concept of synergy. What did she say? When a spark happens, it triggers a thought when we're in deep conversation. The story moves back and forth, and you sort of forget who's speaking and who's listening because both are happening concurrently, and that spiral becomes fertile and grows, and so a major component of that is to move from interviews to conversations or maybe to synergetic conversations or interactions based on synergy or dialogic conversation, something along those lines.

Emma: Wow! Is that our title? Something like "Beyond Qualitative Interviewing Toward Synergistic Conversations"?

Timothy: I love it!

Emma: Yes! Because not only do synergetic conversations gather data and information, but it is also about sustaining and strengthening relationships—something that is necessary for all living beings.

Timothy: Can you speak more on that? That's really powerful.

Emma: Yes. We started off talking about stories being analyzed and interpreted to the point that they can't be recognized. Stories themselves are actually alive because if I wasn't there to help make sure you didn't get it wrong, it was still being transformed in interaction with at least one other person. And that's why I find it so important to tell people when they share things with me that their story is theirs to keep, and you do the same thing in your work with Indigenous mothers, Tim. So, in that action, we're pushing against typical unequal power relations and demonstrating how elements of dynamic heterogeneity can create environments that facilitate learning. We need heterogeneity. We need dynamism. We're talking about reciprocity. And active listening. So how is it co-constitutive? And not just the story, but also the storyteller and the story listener, each process is actually meant to actively work together, and it's meant to be co-constitutive. By offering what I think we are calling synergistic conversations, we're saying that interviews don't always do these things. They're not always collaborative. They're not always co-constitutive, at least knowingly so. They don't push back against elements of power in the same way, and they don't attend to concepts of time and space to engage in these ideas of synergistic interactions across long periods of time.

So I think we need to point that out and say that in an oral storytelling process where knowledge is transmitted across generations, these things happen because they take place within the context of family, community, culture, ceremony, and land. I think that what we're really saying is that even before we enter into those conversations or what are typically called interviews, there's a responsibility to do the work of understanding the histories and cultural processes that are already taking place, that have been taking place for generations. If we do that, we are able to contribute to sustaining relations. We can contribute to knowledge transmission or co-construction. And we can contribute to helping others understand themselves within this vast system of relationships.

Timothy: Yes! And if the will, the intentions, and the actions of the people that we're working with aren't part of that responsibility, then it isn't a synergetic conversation. It's really just an interview because we were just asking for others to help us make sense of something we want to understand in the absence of their perspective. Our questions were already pre-assigned. We were looking for them to answer questions that they had no involvement in crafting or creating. So, in that way it is unidirectional because we're taking their stories, filtering them through our own lenses, and shaping them to our own likeness, rather than what it is that we're suggesting and offering with synergistic conversations, which is engaging in that responsibility of listening and learning with people, and recognizing that this is part of a much deeper and longer story beyond settler colonialism. Our work in those interactions is finding those alignments with the people that we're working with.

Emma: That's perfect, because what you just talked about is the censoring of not just history—social, cultural, political—but the importance of the relational, because it's the relational that subsequently guides social interaction, guides what we do or what we do *not* do, and ultimately, our fundamental purpose as educators and caretakers: to teach each other what it means to live a good and right, true and beautiful life.

The approach that we're offering is actually sustainable because it's emerging from local knowledge systems. It's ethical, sustainable, local, and culturally sustaining. This makes me think about the nature of knowledge. It doesn't assume that I understand entirely what you've been through. It allows you to interpret at any given moment based on every single social interaction you've ever participated in until this very moment. Whatever story I tell you today, even if I told you before, would be open to a brand new interpretation because of your experiences across your lifetime and beyond. So, that's the co-constitutive part. And then there's consequentiality and respect embedded within oral storytelling itself. I think about my mom and how she'll tell me a story that she thinks might have something to offer in relation to an experience or event I'm working through. I remember actively listening 'cause that actually requires an emotional engagement. So we need to make sure that we're making it known that this holistic approach is important because if we're not feeling it, our affect won't shift. Do you know what I mean?

Timothy: Yes! In that talk you sent me by Archibald, she quotes Simon Baker, who says that we listen with three ears—the two ears that we have on our head and the one in our heart.

Emma: Absolutely. Stories can connect on multiple dimensions of emotion, thereby transforming possible outcomes. And interviews, just for the sake of interviews, don't always do the same work. Something important happens when you feel a story. You'll be like "I never thought about that," and yet now it calls you into being an accomplice to a particular cause. We must stop being extractive in our methodological approaches. We must also center the needs of the community during our process while acknowledging our own part in the power dynamics, that's Projects in Humanization. The level of co-participation matters, the level of active listening matters. Do the interviewees have any say about the topic or direction? Are they asked for clarification? It's not an appropriate approach if you're trying to gather rich, descriptive, qualitative data about a cultural community that you don't know anything about.

Timothy: That's so good, Emma!

Emma: I'm so glad we're recording this! I think that that's just an important component of thinking through, you know, what interviews are about and what it is that you're collecting.

Timothy: You're offering space in order to deepen relationships. I think we're pushing against this one-way type of interview and engaging in conversations as relational building opportunities to make sense of each other and of our world (or small parts of it that are connected). Kovach (2009) uses the term "self-in-relation" to talk about how we are in relation to others. She also offers the "conversation method" that connects deeply with what we are discussing here (2019). And so these push on Western forms of qualitative interviewing, which is often extractive, which often involves taking stories and analyzing and interpreting them in the absence of those who shared them.

Emma: Right? So we're pushing on that and saying "No! In fact who we are as people, who we are as researchers, who we are as scholars matters to how we listen and how we interpret that story in the presence of others and not in the absence of others."

Timothy: So many scholars, specifically Indigenous, Black, and other scholars of color, are drawing on their community's values and way of relating to and being with one another. It's not innovative; it's what has always been, but stripped and tricked away from us through systems of coloniality, but now we're remembering that our communities have had the answers all along, and we must listen closely and carefully to the lessons they've been offering us. All of these are ways in which to get at the collaborative nature of engaging in conversations, engaging in interactions of mutuality and care, that we're not just analyzing and interpreting in the absence of others, but really centering the relationship that is created or strengthened through those conversations.

Emma: I think what you're also saying is that the actual aim of any interaction, including researcher and participant interactions, should be a Project in Humanization, or as Dr. Jo-Ann Archibald states, Indigenous Storywork, where human meaning-making and identity development is the goal. We're actually talking about contributions to human learning and human development, and we're also saying that we can contribute to the revolution and the evolution even through our research methods. We are contributing to this transformation by recognizing that heterogeneity is fundamental to human learning; it is also fundamental to social transformation. Folks often get wrapped up in the idea that "I can't make a difference. I'm just a researcher and I just do qualitative research." What we're saying is, "No, actually, of course we can! Every single one of us should be and can be a part of the revolution and of the evolution of what we offer in terms of research methods."

Timothy: So there's an actionable component to it, right? Through these conversations, there's an action element. We are aligning by listening to stories of what's happening in the community already, the things that they're thinking about, the things that are already underway. And in so doing, we are aligning with systems and processes that have been happening long before us and in the absence of formal institutions like universities. Rather than as traditional Western research practices go, you know, researchers come into particular communities and they say this is what's wrong with you and this is how you fix it based on my expertise. The latter is starting from a position of deficit. And what we're saying is we need to do the work of being invited into the community first. We need to be vouched for by others. This is a part of the relational piece. So that when we are invited, we are listening for what has been and the solutions that are already being offered and thinking about the ways in which we can align the work that we do with processes and systems that are already underway. Does that make sense? That's where the synergy occurs; it occurs in the development of relationships built through multiple opportunities to share stories.

Emma: It does, and I think in doing so, we also contribute to sustainable and ethical and local practices.

Timothy: What if we used the transcripts of our synergistic conversations as the body of our chapter contribution? You know, these are your thoughts and then I build up just as we're doing here, and then I build off that and then you build off of what I'm saying. And so within the chapter itself, we're engaging in the practice or the . . . yeah, the practice of storying. We may have a cohesive introduction that introduces the readers to our contribution, but then what comes from that is just a back and forth of a building of, "I hear what you're saying and that inspires my thinking in new ways." And then it goes back to you, just as we're doing right here. I'm getting goosebumps.

Emma: Yes! I love it! I think it would show what it looks like to move beyond interviews and toward a synergistic conversation. It's substantiated by positionality and a recognition of our relationship and position within the research unapologetically, and we describe that epistemic intersectional experience to some degree. Like what is our relationship to this community or this thing or this knowledge?

Reflecting Forward: Tenets of Synergistic Conversation

As we reflect upon our conversation that helped spur the ideas shared within this chapter, we pause to more fully define and conceptualize synergetic conversations and the many different elements that have helped us to better understand what this means. We do so fully knowing that stories are received (or not received) based on the experiences and realities of those listening. Since this is in written form, we do not have the opportunity to build with you as actively and synergistically as we've described. So, we offer the next best thing. During the remainder of our time together, we offer a deeper discussion on the following themes and ideas that emerged in our process of the development of this piece—Indigenous Storywork, Projects in Humanization, storying, dialogic spiral, extraction, and conversation method.

Indigenous Storywork

Indigenous Storywork, as theorized and shared by Archibald (2008), breaks down storying into three deeply interrelated elements—story, storytelling, and story listening—which aids in a clearer understanding of the methodological contribution. The aim of Indigenous Storywork is to provide a framework to help us understand what it means to be a human being, as guided by particular ways of knowing and being. Archibald (2008) offers ethical tenets, including respect, responsibility, holism, reverence, and synergy, that shape existential understanding of self for both the storyteller and the storylistener. Though obvious, it is important to state that those telling a story are the storytellers, while those listening to a story are story listeners. In a dialogic interaction, these roles move back and forth as ideas are connecting and constructing and weaving into a shared story (see *dialogic spiral*). Story, then, is that dialogic space between people transmitted through words (orally and written, but also through other means such as art and music) to expand one's understanding of self in relation to one's surroundings; it provides opportunities to critically examine the interactions between one's own history, culture, and life-experiences when they come into contact with another's realities, which, we believe, should be at the heart of any educational setting for all learners.

Projects in Humanization

PiH centers relational building through storytelling, story listening, and reciprocal engagements we have *with* people in ways that "on one hand, emphasize our shared desires for racial, linguistic, educational, political, and social justice in schools and communities and, on the other hand, emphasize those same desires in our professional and personal lives" (San Pedro & Kinloch, 2017, p. 374S). PiH urges us to actively consider divergent social and cultural ways of knowing, factors we believe are fundamental to knowledge co-construction and transmission, as well as human learning and development. With relational commitment at its core, PiH asks us to consider our own role, as researchers, in ways that open heterogenous possible futures toward consequential aims, and in doing so, removes the assumption of neutrality (Harding, 1995). We believe that this intentional shift pushes back against definitions of objectivity that have historically excluded particular knowledge systems and entire populations in the name of science.

Storying

Storying follows Bishop's (1997) concept of collaborative storying, whereby the boundaries between researcher and participant are deconstructed so that both are constantly serving in the capacity of listeners and learners from the stories shared with one another. Such collaborative processes highlight the importance of researcher and participant collaboration rather than individual knowledge construction. Storying involves active participation: "The story doesn't work without a participant," suggesting that those listening cannot be passive, but active in the process (Vizenor, 1987). Active listening involves grafting one's own story—lived experiences, histories, cultural truths—onto the stories offered by another. Stories serve a variety of functions, including knowledge transmission, identity development, and healing from traumatic experiences. For example, storying is the process through which knowledge is transmitted across generations; it is a pedagogical practice. The social space is intentionally cultivated so that participants can re-narrate their sense of identity based on the meanings exchanged through the storying process. In some cases, re-narrating a story in the presence of a caring other person (e.g., a mental health practitioner or a loved one) can help develop the safety and trust needed to heal from trauma. The active, alive, and emerging exchange of ideas and knowledge through stories becomes the process of storying—the action of "ing" in storying. As such, storying is an active and mutually constitutive learning process through which knowledge is shared, co-constructed, and transmitted.

Dialogic Spiral

San Pedro (2013) offered the dialogic spiral as a tool for developing effective social relations through listening to and learning from others:

> The dialogic spiral is the [social] construction of a conversation between two or more people whereby the process of listening and speaking co-creates an area of trust between speakers—the space between. In this in-between space, the speaker's discourse reveals vulnerabilities and feelings [and identities]. . . . If constructive, this dialogic spiral moves back and forth, while it also advances forward/upward by expanding prior understandings of listening and speaking. (pp. 117–118)

The spiral is thus grounded in relationship with participants giving back to the conversation, co-constructing social relations from shared ideas and stories. Insofar as it requires co-learning (that is, telling stories as well as hearing stories, as opposed to only one person sharing stories), the dialogic spiral asks both sides to take risks, to be vulnerable, and to develop trust and understanding. It is this new level of mutuality that spirals the relationship forward and upward.

Extraction

bell hooks (1990) illustrated that stories are often stripped of their context, taken by researchers, pieced apart, dissected, analyzed, and interpreted in the absence of those who told them, only to be recreated in the likeness of the researcher(s) who extracted that information through interviews. Sometimes the original story is unrecognizable to those who shared it, after it is filtered through the axiological lens of the researcher. hooks says that in interviews, the researcher shows what appears to be sincere interest, stating: "I want to know your story," then, once that story is extracted, I want to tell it "back to you [the participant] in a new way . . . that has become mine, my own [the researcher's]" and no longer yours (p. 343). hooks continues: "Rewriting you, I write myself anew. I am still author, authority. I am still the colonizer, the speaking subject, and you are now at the center of my talk" (p. 343). Unrecognizable. A synergistic approach asks us, as researchers, to listen not for extraction (Robinson, 2020) but for the broader purpose of shaping understandings of self in relation to all others.

Conversation Method

Kovach (2019) offers the conversation method as a way to rely on story to gather, share, and offer knowledge. She states that it must be in alignment with an Indigenous paradigm and "involves dialogic participation that holds a deep purpose of sharing story as a means to assist others. It is relational at its core" (p. 124). Relying on Indigenous paradigms, Kovach argues that methods used to collect data, particularly for those who are working with Indigenous peoples, must understand that such data-gathering tools, at their core, ought to rely on Indigenous understandings that knowledge is shared through oral history and storytelling traditions that are interdependent and reciprocal. Thus knowledge, she states, "is co-created within the relational dynamic of self-in-relation . . . between self, others, and nature" (p. 126).

Discussion: Building Outward With Our Readers

In conceptualizing our emergent understanding of what we mean by synergistic conversation as a method for building relations through story sharing, we use this final section to retrace our steps so as to continue a path for our readers to follow. This is a path that has long been walked before us and, we hope, long after us. Story is central. Our stories matter; our identities matter; our relations matter, just as the reasons we come to work alongside people and communities matter. We, as human beings, impact and are impacted by the people and places we enter into; we can no longer pretend otherwise. In the context of research and practice, and more specifically qualitative interviewing, we offer a framework through which to approach qualitative interviewing and, more specifically, data collection practices in ways that acknowledge how everyday social interaction informs identity development and opens up heterogeneous possible futures. So, even at the level of research, intentional shifts in methodological practice contribute to human development by engaging research approaches that specifically attend to the importance of family and community adaptation and thrivance (the combination of thriving and resistance). We do this work intentionally in our interactions with others because our conversations in the storying process allow for different relational dynamics and different disruptions to typical power relationships, and more ethical approaches that are not extractive.

We need to think about the dialogical and co-constitutive nature that attends to the ethical *and* consequential commitments we have with others. Synergistic conversations, we believe, create better opportunities and ways forward because we are centering relationships. We are *not* centering the researcher as all-knowing. We are challenging assumptions that are inherent within research fields, arguing that knowledge is not in isolation—knowledge is co-constructed through conversation, through interactions, through relationships. The interpretation and analysis of knowledge should then also be co-constructive, should be dialogic, and should be in the presence of and with others. We hope this framework pushes others to think about the ways in which storying challenges the very nature of interviews and also brings about the possibility for what these conversations can lead us to.

Because relationships are dynamic and co-constitutive, synergistic conversations focus on the process rather than the destination. Western research is often outcome-driven—researchers think about their central research question in the absence of the people and communities they intend to work with. They state their methodological intentions and form their theoretical foundation in order to generate materials to submit to the Institutional Review Board, all of which is in the absence of people and communities. Putting the destination first has the potential shortfall of performing qualitative interviews that only fit into where that destination is, as seen by the researcher, rather than centering on the journey or the process. To us, based on the lessons from our communities and families, this is backward, wrong, and even unethical. Without knowing and building relations first with people, how are we to know the questions worth seeking? How are we to know the most productive way to share stories with others when they are crafted in the absence of others? How do the stories of those I'm working with influence the ways that I'm thinking about the design, focus, and question of the research project itself? How am I changed, altered, or made more whole by their understanding and solutions to a world gone wrong?

These are questions that have been in development long before us. Indigenous scholars such as Jo-Ann Archibald, Margaret Kovach, Shawn Wilson, Eve Tuck, Megan Bang, and so many others have given us permission to be story-centered as well as knowledge- and process-driven. How are the stories that were shared with us altering and changing us? Synergistic conversations center the journey—the ways that we impact and are impacted by others. We ask of you, our readers, to think about how your journey offers expansive relational spaces to share stories that lead to emergent, adaptive, and culturally sustaining knowledges that offer solutions to a world in widespread chaos. If not now, then when?

It is important to state that we are not offering something that will directly apply to every single person; rather, we offer a framing of processes from which others can learn and observe, and then adapt that process using their own cultural and/or tribal knowledges, their own values, their own ways of knowing. This is going to look a bit different, depending on local contexts, input, and relations developed. We look forward to future opportunities to share stories, to develop relations, and to see and hear the ways in which the framing of synergistic conversations have impacted you and those with whom you have developed meaningful and reciprocal relations.

References

Archibald, J. (2008). *Indigenous Storywork: Educating the heart, mind, body, and spirit.* UBC Press.

Bang, M., Faber, L., Gurneau, J., Marin, A., & Soto, C. (2016). Community-based design research: Learning across generations and strategic transformations of institutional relations toward axiological innovations. *Mind, Culture, and Activity, 23*(1), 28–41.

Bang, M., Montaño Nolan, C., & McDaid-Morgan, N. (2018). Indigenous family engagement: Strong families, strong nations. In E. A. McKinley & L. T. Smith (Eds.), *Handbook of Indigenous Education* (pp. 1–22).

Bang, M., & Vossoughi, S. (2016). Participatory design research and educational justice: Studying learning and relations within social change making. *Cognition and Instruction, 34*(3), 173–193.

Bishop, R. (1997). Interviewing as collaborative storying. *Education Research and Perspectives, 24*(1), 28–47.

Brayboy, B. M. J. (2005). Toward a tribal critical race theory in education. *The Urban Review, 37*(5), 425–446.

Clandinin, D. J. (2006). Narrative inquiry: A methodology for studying lived experience. *Research Studies in Music Education, 27*(1), 44–54.

Connelly, F. M., & Clandinin, D. J. (1990). Stories of experience and narrative inquiry. *Educational Researcher, 19*(5), 2–14.

Deloria, V. (1970). *We talk, you listen: New tribes, new turf.* University of Nebraska Press.

DePaoli, J. L., Hernández, L. E., Furger, R. C., & Darling-Hammond, L. (2021). *A restorative approach for equitable education.* Research Brief. Learning Policy Institute.

Grande, S. (2020). After-words of the Otherwise. In A. E. Shield, D. Paris, R. Paris, & T. San Pedro (Eds.). *Education in Movement Spaces* (pp. 144–149). Routledge.

Harding, S. (1995). "Strong objectivity": A response to the new objectivity question. *Synthese, 104*(3), 331–349.

hooks, b. (1990). Marginality as a site of resistance. In R. Ferguson, M. Gever, T. T. Minh-ha, & C. West (Eds.), *Out there: Marginalization and contemporary cultures* (pp. 341–344). MIT Press.

Kerr, J., & Adamov Ferguson, K. (2021). Ethical relationality and Indigenous storywork principles as methodology: Addressing settler-colonial divides in inner-city educational research. *Qualitative Inquiry, 27*(6), 706–715.

Kovach, M. E. (2009). *Indigenous methodologies: Characteristics, conversations, and contexts.* University of Toronto Press.

Kovach, M. E. (2019). Conversational method in Indigenous research. *First Peoples Child & Family Review, 14*(1), 123–136.

Kuntz, A. M. (2019). *Qualitative inquiry, cartography, and the promise of material change.* Routledge.

Ladson-Billings, G. (2021). *Culturally relevant pedagogy: Asking a different question.* Teachers College Press.

Lee-Morgan, J. (2018). Pūrākau from the inside-out: Regenerating stories for cultural sustainability. In J. Archibald, J. Lee-Morgan, & J. D Santolo (Eds.), *Decolonizing research: Indigenous storywork as methodology* (pp. 151–166). Zed Books.

Martin, G., & William, E. J. (2018). Le7 Q'7es te Stsptekwll re Secwépemc: Our memories long ago. In J. Archibald, J. Lee-Morgan, & J. D. Santolo (Eds.), *Decolonizing research: Indigenous storywork as methodology* (pp. 56–71). Zed Books.

McCoy, M., Elliott-Groves, E., Sabzalian, L., & Bang, M. (2020). *Restoring Indigenous systems of relationality.* Center for Humans & Nature. https://www.humansandnature.org/restoring-indigenous-systems-of-relationality.

Mello, M. M., & Wolf, L. E. (2010). The Havasupai Indian tribe case—Lessons for research involving stored biologic samples. *New England Journal of Medicine, 363*(3), 204–207.

Paris, D., & Winn, M. T. (Eds.). (2014). *Humanizing research: Decolonizing qualitative inquiry with youth and communities.* SAGE.

Robinson, D. (2020). *Hungry listening: Resonant theory for indigenous sound studies.* University of Minnesota Press.

San Pedro, T. (2013). *Understanding youth cultures, stories, and resistances in the urban southwest: Innovations and implications of a Native American literature classroom* (Publication No. 3558673) [Doctoral dissertation, Arizona State University]. ProQuest Dissertations and Theses Global.

San Pedro, T., Carlos, E., & Mburu, J. (2017). Critical listening and storying: Fostering respect for difference and action within and beyond a Native American literature classroom. *Urban Education, 52*(5), 667–693.

San Pedro, T., & Kinloch, V. (2017). Toward projects in humanization: Research on co-creating and sustaining dialogic relationships. *American Educational Research Journal*, 54(1_suppl), 373S–394S.

Smith, L. T. (1999). *Decolonizing methodologies: Research and indigenous peoples.* Zed Books.

Vizenor, G. R. (1987). Follow the trickroutes: An interview with Gerald Vizenor. In J. Bruchac (Ed.), *Survival this way: Interviews with American Indian poets* (pp. 287–310). University of Arizona Press.

Vizenor, G. R. (1999). *Manifest manners: Narratives on postindian survivance.* University of Nebraska Press.

Yip, T. (2020). *Addressing inequalities in education during the COVID-19 pandemic: How education policy and schools can support historically and currently marginalized children and youth.* Society for Research in Child Development. https://www.srcd.org/research/addressing-inequities-education-during-covid-19-pandemic-how-education-policy-and-schools

THREE

 Culturally Responsive Focus Groups

Jori N. Hall and Joseph-Emery Lyvan Kouaho

INQUIRERS INCREASINGLY ACKNOWLEDGE THAT SYSTEMS of oppression in society are embedded in qualitative research (Denzin, 2006). In response, more attention is given to structural inequalities and advancing theoretical orientations that promote cultural sensitivity and social change (Johnson & Parry, 2015; Pasque et al., 2022). Against this backdrop, culturally responsive focus groups (CRFGs) have emerged as a method to pursue cultural sensitivity, advance social justice, and address power asymmetries in disciplines such as evaluation (Hall et al., 2020), health (Hall et al., 2022), and education (Lahman et al., 2011). Inquirers view focus groups as beneficial when pursuing cultural responsiveness, as they can be tailored for use with diverse groups and facilitated to reduce the inquirer's power over the data collection process (Madriz, 2000).

As Black researchers, we align ourselves with social justice–oriented methodologies and view CRFGs as valuable in honoring participants' cultures, while advancing justice. The first author, Jori N. Hall, is a professor who investigates and applies qualitative, mixed methods and evaluation designs to engage participants' cultures ethically and responsively in various contexts. The second author, Joseph-Emery Lyvan Kouaho, is a doctoral student who aims to better understand the politics of culture and democratic principles in the context of educational administration and policy. Our collaborative social justice efforts and distinct research interests guide our interest in culturally affirming perspectives and practices. In this chapter, we discuss some perspectives on and practices for CRFG inquiry. We begin by outlining our culturally relevant (CR) orientation, how CRFGs can potentially advance justice, and their central characteristics.

Cultural Responsiveness

Education scholar Gloria Ladson-Billings (1995) is credited as one of the early contributors to the conceptualization of cultural responsiveness. She defines culturally relevant pedagogy as instruction with two objectives: first, to curate spaces where students can use their culture to inform their schooling experiences, and second, to equip students to challenge inequities. Other service fields, such as evaluation (Hood et al., 2015), have advanced respect for culture and more attention to inequities. These fields share common goals: (1) to learn about clients' cultures, (2) to draw on clients' cultures when conceptualizing services, and (3) to implement culturally responsive services. Our stance on cultural responsiveness builds on these goals. Specifically, our notion of cultural responsiveness is a stance that centers on participants' cultural contexts and pursues social justice to challenge inequities (Hall, 2020). We consider focus groups a particularly generative methodological space to center participants' cultures and advance equity. In the following section, we discuss what makes a focus group *culturally responsive*.

Culturally Responsive Focus Groups

A focus group is a qualitative method designed to gather information about a particular topic through a group discussion (Hall, 2020). Focus groups are distinct from individual interviews in that they involve both discussion *and* group interaction. Indeed, focus groups produce two types of data: interview and observational data of group dynamics. While guidance on the number of participants to include in a focus group and duration varies, qualitative scholars recommend that focus groups include six to eight participants and last for 60–90 minutes (Patton, 2015).

Focus groups are not inherently culturally responsive. However, qualitative and evaluation inquirers have identified several characteristics that are central to CR methodology: (a) identifying participants' culture as an asset, not a deficit (Yarbrough et al., 2011); (b) engaging in reflexivity (Symonette, 2004); (c) addressing cross-cultural dynamics (Chouinard & Cousins, 2009); (d) using culturally relevant theories and methods (Hood et al., 2015); and (e) engaging issues of power and privilege to enhance social conditions (Hall, 2020). When focus groups are implemented with these characteristics in mind, they can be considered culturally responsive. Inquirers have used focus groups to affirm participants' cultures, facilitate participant empowerment, challenge stereotypes, include minoritized voices, and disrupt oppressive practices (Hall, 2020; Hall et al., 2022). Despite these different research purposes, there are common aspects of CRFG research to note. We consider these points in the following section.

CRFG Conceptualization and Implementation

Researcher Positionality

A key step when conceptualizing a CRFG is to consider your worldview (Holmes, 2020). A worldview is defined as a researcher's personal beliefs and assumptions about social and political contexts (Holmes, 2020). Beliefs and assumptions are important because they hold implicit and explicit biases that inform personal and research decisions. An assumption held by CR inquirers is that inequities and oppression exist, negatively impacting some cultural groups (i.e., racial/ethnic minorities, members of the LGBTQIA community, or variously disabled persons) more than others. Based on this assumption, the inquirer is positioned as a change agent, responsible for ensuring meaningful participant interactions (Rodriguez et al., 2011) and addressing issues of power and privilege.

Appropriateness of CRFG

Researchers must also determine whether CRFGs are appropriate for their research agenda. While CRFGs are a potentially powerful method, they are not appropriate for all studies. Sensitive topics might necessitate individual interviews, as participants may not feel comfortable disclosing private or potentially embarrassing information in a group setting. Therefore, considering how participants might respond to questions in a group setting and consulting with other stakeholders and/or participants about the appropriateness of focus groups is highly recommended.

Researcher Competencies

Researcher competencies are critical to CRFG inquiry, as both the character and quality of CRFGs depend on the researcher's moderation skills. Some key moderation competencies include the ability to: (a) establish trust, (b) set and implement goals, (c) encourage respectful dialogue, and (d) remain flexible.

Because moderators also function as change agents, they need the skills to facilitate group interactions toward social justice goals. Additionally, moderators must have relational skills, emotional awareness, decision-making ability, and attentiveness. Given the range of competencies needed, we recommend that moderators work with a notetaker to assist with focus group facilitation. Additionally, a notetaker can record interactions that would not be captured in a transcript (Flynn et al., 2018).

Design

After determining that CRFGs are appropriate for your study and examining your competencies, you will want to consider your inquiry design. CRFGs can be a component of a methodological design (i.e., mixed methods, case study) or serve as the overall design. Indeed, Willgerodt (2003) conducted several focus groups with Chinese immigrant families to develop a culturally appropriate questionnaire that reflected the experiences of that community. While the number of studies that utilize focus groups as their overall design has increased in recent years, scholars have yet to determine how many focus groups should be conducted to answer a research question. Guest et al. (2017) write: "Seventy years after the method was introduced, researchers must still rely on rules of thumb and personal judgment when deciding how many focus groups to include in a study" (p. 4). To inform your design decision, consider the cultural group(s) involved, the justice issues at hand, the theoretical framework used, and the evidence required for the research (Ryan et al., 2014).

CRFG Setting

Focus groups occur within two settings: physical and virtual. In-person focus groups allow researchers to respond to participants' actions in real time, but can be expensive and include, for example, travel costs. Also, participation is limited to those with access to the focus group's location (Woodyat et al., 2016). Further, unfamiliar physical settings and the visibility of recording devices can create participant discomfort (Woodyat et al., 2016).

Increasingly, researchers have opted to conduct virtual focus groups. Online focus groups are advantageous, as they can provide built-in transcription and recording tools, and increased access (Hall, 2020). For example, Shelton and Jones (2022) noted how Zoom allowed participants with no access to childcare or reliable transportation to join the focus group. However, conducting focus groups online limits a researcher's ability to capture and observe body language and group dynamics. Another criticism of online focus groups is that they are limited by the participants' familiarity with technology and their internet speed/connection. Nevertheless, online focus groups do offer options for participation (i.e., breakout rooms, chatbox) that can enhance participant interaction.

CRFG Protocol Development

Careful development of a CRFG protocol is important for two key reasons. First, the quality of CRFG data relies on the quality of questions. Second, as compared to interview protocols, CRFG protocols contain fewer questions, which allows everyone in the group an opportunity to respond to each question.

In general, there are two types of questions: closed and open-ended. Closed questions, such as *Do you consider participatory action research (PAR) a culturally responsive approach to research?* can provoke short answers (yes/no), thereby limiting participants' responses (Roulston, 2022). Open questions "provide broad parameters within which interviewees can answer in their own words concerning topics specified by the interviewer" (Roulston, 2022, p. 5). For example, during a CRFG, the following open question was posed to participants interviewed for an evaluation: *Now, based on your experiences thus far, I'd like to know what it means to you to be a co-researcher?* In response, participants described their unique experiences and definitions of a co-researcher in the context of their PAR project. CR inquirers are interested in crafting questions that elicit detailed accounts of the participants' perceptions of an experience (Roberts, 2020); therefore, open questions are preferred.

Rosenthal (2016), referencing Patton's (2002) question options, outlines six types of open questions that researchers can pose during focus groups: (a) experience and behavior questions, (b) sensory questions, (c) opinion and value questions, (d) knowledge questions, (e) feeling questions, and (f) background questions. *Experience or behavior questions* allow participants to share details about their experiences or events. For example, *Walk me through exactly how you were trained to use PAR data collection techniques for this project.*

These types of questions are responsive, as they privilege participants' experiences and allow them to give an account of actions and procedures from their unique perspectives. Researchers ask *sensory questions* to understand how participants experienced the physical elements of an event. For example, *What smells do you recall while staying in the shelter after Hurricane Katrina?* Requests like these are useful as follow-up questions to help participants recall more details or open up cultural insights that might otherwise go underexplored (Harris & Guillemin, 2012).

Opinion or value questions elicit participants' assessments of an experience: *From your perspective, what authority do you believe you have as undergraduate co-researchers to make modifications to the PAR design? Knowledge questions* seek factual details. These types of questions are culturally responsive because they position participants as experts capable of providing factual information (Lavrakas, 2008). *Feeling questions* seek the affective dimensions of participants' experiences or emotions. Because feeling questions are often confused with opinion questions, moderators should ensure that participants are discussing their emotions (i.e., happy, grateful) rather than their opinions. *Background questions* are constructed to gather demographic information (Rosenthal, 2016) and are often asked as closed questions. However, when asked as open questions, they can affirm participants' cultural backgrounds and allow them to self-identify.

Before, During, and After the CRFG

Before conducting a CRFG, researchers must receive *informed* consent from participants. Informed consent helps participants understand details about their role in the research process. If they decide to participate, they should be informed that they can decide not to answer any of the questions posed, and that they are free to stop participating at any point during the discussion. Informed consent is also imperative to support participant empowerment: the power participants have to decide how (or if) they will participate in the research.

Before the CRFG, inquirers will also want to incorporate time for reminders, participant questions, and rule-setting. Text box 3.1 is an excerpt of what was shared with participants before a CRFG for a project conducted by the first author.

Box 3.1. Guidelines for Participation.

---
1. Please turn off all mobile phones/devices.
2. This session will last about 90 minutes.
3. Before we begin, please review the consent forms.
4. Please note that the session will be audio recorded.
5. All information in this focus group will remain confidential. The final report will keep all participants' names anonymous. The audio will only be made accessible and viewed by the researchers.
6. There are no wrong or right answers; we are looking for honest responses and different points of view. We want to know your opinions.
7. We invite everyone to talk, but each person doesn't have to answer each question.
8. Please talk one at a time and in a clear voice.
9. Does anyone have any questions before we begin?

Because minoritized communities often distrust researchers, building rapport during the CRFG is critical. Facilitating icebreaker activities, asking thoughtful follow-up questions, and using non-verbal and verbal cues can help to establish rapport. Participants may experience discomfort about something that was shared or feel uncomfortable stating their opinion—even though they have consented to participate. As a moderator, you will want to be attentive to participants' feelings and their experiences, as these may shift during the discussion.

After the CRFG, Alshenqeeti (2014) recommends that the inquirer "re-express gratitude to interviewees and discuss ways of future contact" (p. 41). We agree. Expressing gratitude in a culturally appropriate way and discussing ways of future contact provide an opportunity for the researcher to be respectful and follow up with participants if needed. Also, it invites participants to discuss their questions, comments, or concerns. Following the CRFG, researchers can debrief with participants, summarizing important points from the discussion, responding to questions, and clarifying instances (Sim & Waterfield, 2019). We view debriefing as responsive and helpful to strengthen research quality.

Establishing Quality

A CR orientation enhances the quality of the research (Thomas & Campbell, 2021) by limiting ill-informed inquiry practices or biased findings. Qualitative scholars who advance cultural responsiveness or other social justice orientations (i.e., critical race theory, Black feminist thought, queer theory) suggest that quality can be established in research by addressing the following criteria:

a) Fairness: participants' different concerns, values, and perspectives are represented in a balanced way;
b) Ontological authenticity: participants' understandings of their own lives are improved/or more informed because of their participation in the study;
c) Educative authenticity: participants have a richer understanding or appreciation of how others see them as a result of their participation;
d) Catalytic authenticity: action is a result of the inquiry; and
e) Tactical authenticity: participants are empowered to act. (Johnson & Parry, 2015, p. 64)

While these criteria are important, inquirers must account for their personal biases to address them. To account for their biases, researchers typically write a position statement, delineating their worldview and how it may impact aspects of the study, including expectations for outcomes (Creswell & Poth, 2017; Qin, 2016). Explicating one's positionality is essential for responsive research, but it does not eliminate bias or abdicate responsibility to remain culturally responsive, which is why researchers must continually engage in reflective practice. Rodriguez et al. (2011) outline six questions for reflective practice (p. 405):

1. What are the participants' social and cultural identities?
2. How do the participants' social and cultural identities inform their unique communication and/or relationship characteristics that are important for me to acknowledge within this research?
3. What are the naturally occurring environments the participants already share?

4. How can I create and/or join a context that feels comfortable and affirming to participants?
5. How do I best acknowledge my own social and cultural identities and minimize the distance between myself and participants?
6. How do I best elicit the rich information these participants can share about their storied lives that, in turn, will make the research story maximally rich and representative of their experience?

Whether you decide to use the questions offered by Rodriguez et. al. (2011) or other techniques, we should point out that reflexivity is an ongoing process. Further, from a CR lens, reflexivity is imperative to establishing quality because it enables critical assessments of how you engage your role as a change agent. Further, reflexivity brings attention to how you, as a change agent: (a) confront power dynamics; (b) involve participants in decision making; (c) grapple with discomfort/failure during the inquiry as it arises (Mitchell et al., 2018); and (d) address privilege and oppressive structures relevant to the inquiry context.

Member checking is also used to establish quality. Member checking reduces research bias by involving participants in verifying CRFG results. Returning transcripts in order to enable participants to check the data for accuracy is one form of member checking (Birt et al., 2016). However, having participants review the transcript "does not enable them to make any claims on the trustworthiness of the subsequent analysis" (Birt et al., 2016, p. 1805). Therefore, Birt et al. advise having participants review synthesized data, as this allows them to validate (or refute) the results. We recommend that CR researchers take Birt et al.'s (2016) advice and use this form of member checking. See the latter source for the full discussion on various member-checking strategies and processes.

Strategies for Culturally Responsive Data Analysis and Interpretation

Johnson and Parry (2015) define data analysis as a "systematic effort toward describing, interpreting, and theorizing the data collected" (p. 63). Analyzing CRFG data requires a systematic procedure. The constant comparative method (Glaser & Strauss, 1967; Charmaz, 2014) and discourse analysis (Cowan & McLeod, 2004) are examples of systematic procedures used to analyze data.

While discussing the specific procedures for these data analysis approaches is beyond the scope of this chapter, we do emphasize a few strategies and key points to enhance cultural responsiveness. Also, we note that while qualitative data analysis software (QDAS) is popular, using software still requires inquirers to make choices about their data analysis procedures and how to implement them responsively and systematically. Therefore, we focus on strategies that deepen cultural receptivity. We think this information helps to make sense of the data, regardless of the data analysis procedures selected or whether QDAS is used.

Triangulating Sources

Triangulation offers more culturally contextualized, comprehensive, and credible interpretations. Denzin (1978) suggests four types of triangulation: method, investigator, data source, and theory. *Methodological triangulation* occurs when CRFGs are used alongside other methods—for instance, CRFGs conducted in conjunction with surveys and/or interviews. Analyzing data from different methods can confirm tentative CRFG findings, leading to broadened cultural understandings of the topic of interest.

When used, notetakers can facilitate *investigator triangulation*, as their observations and notes provide another perspective that is useful in making sense of CRFG data. Analyzing notes on non-verbal communication alongside text allows investigators to generate additional cultural insights and to detect implicit messages (Denham & Onwuegbuzie, 2013). Analyzing CRFG data with other stakeholders (participants or community members) is another form of investigator triangulation. This strategy is common in community-based and/or decolonizing research because it helps to (a) clarify cultural meanings; (b) incorporate data that participants find relevant to the topic (Massey, 2011; Stanton, 2014); and (c) attend to participants' insights that would be otherwise ignored, thereby enabling rich, culturally anchored interpretations.

Data source triangulation involves conducting CRFGs with different groups of people (i.e., parents, children). This strategy is helpful in providing a wider range of cultural perspectives, as well as additional information on the context and how inequities are experienced by different types of groups. *Theoretical triangulation* is used to analyze and interpret the CRFG data with different culturally appropriate theories, assisting with checking the accuracy of interpretations.

Memoing and Journaling

Memoing and journaling also deepen cultural receptivity, as they promote researcher reflexivity. When used alongside a data analysis technique, memoing and journaling can aid reflections on how the CRFG design is responsive and what can be done differently to enhance responsiveness. Further, memoing and journaling can be effective in gaining insight into cultural meanings, relationships, processes, contextual characteristics, and dimensions of the phenomena of interest. Rolón-Dow and Bailey (2021), for instance, used memoing to examine how race and racism are understood by racially minoritized groups organized by six questions (p. 11):

1) What racialized emotions does the storyteller name? (Bold the most prominent two and then elaborate.)
2) What racialized emotions are represented in the story, in addition to that of the storyteller (Bold the most prominent two and then elaborate.)
3) What are the two most prevalent racialized emotions that we experience as we read the story?
4) Does the story reflect a hierarchical structure of racialized emotions? (Yes/no; if yes, elaborate.)
5) How do racialized emotions expressed in stories contribute to or reflect the racialization of groups?
6) What are racialized emotions "doing" in the university context? (What behaviors are produced by racialized emotions, or what racialized emotions are produced by behaviors?)

Although interviews were used in Rolón-Dow and Bailey's (2021) study, their theoretical memo is an exemplar because the format relates each memo question to a theoretical concept—in this case, the concept of racialized emotions (Bonilla-Silva, 2019). Also, the memo parenthetically includes directions for research team members and interrogates researchers' racialized emotions. As a result, the memo permits comparisons of memos across research team members, aiding in a systematic analysis of racialized emotions. See Rolón-Dow and Bailey (2021) for more details on how this memo was developed and used.

Creative Approaches

Creative approaches to data analysis draw on visual, literary, and performative techniques. One such creative approach stems from poetry. Merging poetry with qualitative research can be culturally responsive because it "can give a voice back to scientific research that can easily get lost through the application of traditional scientific analysis" (McCulliss, 2013, p. 83). Indeed, Reilly (2013) writes that "taking words, phrases, and whole passages [from participants' own words] and reframing them as poetry" (p. 6) influences how their stories are told. An I-Poem, an example of a poetic approach to qualitative data analysis developed from Gilligan et al.'s (2003) Listening Guide, is rooted in feminist research methodology (Edwards & Weller, 2012). The I-Poem is conducted through roughly three steps: (1) reading the transcript highlighting the instances where participants use the personal pronoun "I," (2) cutting and pasting the phrase(s) that follows participants' use of the personal pronoun, and (3) arranging them in lines to eventually create stanzas (Edwards & Weller, 2012).

For further guidance, we emphasize the following points. First, careful consideration is needed to select an analytic procedure that aligns with participants' cultures and centers their voices. Second, data analysis with social justice aims demands engagement with systems of injustice (Johnson & Parry, 2015). Third, sufficient information about the cultural context, participants, and data analysis procedures is needed to solidify the credibility of the findings.

Presenting Findings in a Culturally Responsive Way

Presenting focus group findings is a contentious and complex endeavor, because researchers have historically *mis*represented Indigenous and other minoritized communities. Given this issue, we discuss *alternative* and *inclusive* strategies for presenting focus-group data to avoid further minoritizing and misrepresenting cultural groups. We do this by highlighting three areas: representation, language, and dissemination.

Representation

Alternative representations allow audiences to engage deeply with the findings, facilitating more educative, contemplative, and interactive experiences

(Johnson et al., 2013). Alternative or more creative representations include stories/narratives and visuals (i.e., photos, graphics). One alternative form of representation increasingly used by qualitative researchers is poetic representation (McCulliss, 2013). As mentioned earlier, poetry is a powerful tool for data interpretation. By extension, representing findings using poetry can be impactful. Whether oral or written, poetic (or other creative) representations are effective to convey cultural complexities, share participants' cultural experiences, provoke emotions, and help people learn about themselves and others (McCulliss, 2013).

Language

Using inclusive language when representing findings is another way to advance cultural responsiveness. Some inclusive strategies include avoiding jargon and writing at the appropriate reading level for your audience. For instance, if writing for a general audience in the United States, language should be written at the sixth-grade level (Gullion, 2022). Allowing participants to self-identify, using correct pronouns, and not presenting findings in a male-centric way (i.e., using chair instead of chairman) are other strategies critical to disrupting the historical tradition of exclusion (Madison, 2012; Sczesny et al., 2015).

Additionally, CR inquirers use anti-deficit language to avoid positioning cultural differences as deficient. For example, instead of using terms such as "at-risk" or "minorities," consider using "minoritized" communities. Using direct quotes when presenting findings also helps to avoid deficit language while credibly representing participants' voices (Eldh et al., 2020). Further, we note that linguistic adaptions or "translating findings from a source language (such as Spanish) to a target language (such as English)" (Esposito, 2001, p. 570) might be necessary to present CRFG findings. Because the target language may not have words or concepts that directly correspond to the source language, researchers are encouraged to produce "meaning-based" translations of the results rather than word-for-word translations (Esposito, 2001). To accomplish this, Esposito (2001) advises seeking the help of community members to ensure that translations of non-English focus groups convey the correct cultural dialect and connotation.

Dissemination

Publishing findings in a peer-reviewed journal or sharing findings at a conference are traditional forms of disseminating focus-group research. While used often, these forms of dissemination can reinforce the researcher–participant power hierarchy. We encourage inquirers to disrupt this power hierarchy. Collaborative approaches such as co-authoring publications and co-presenting findings with participants can be more responsive to and empowering for participants. As agents for social change, CR researchers may also consider using alternative dissemination techniques (i.e., policy briefs, blogs, podcasts, videos, and social media outlets) and reaching non-academics (i.e., practitioners, policymakers, and general consumers). As Gullion (2022) argues, "for those of us who do qualitative inquiry with a social justice mindset, cultivating a broad audience can go a long way toward advocating for social change" (p. 442). Indeed, alternative strategies and seeking broader audiences can cultivate social change by supporting collaborations between participants and inquirers, encouraging networking with others concerned with similar issues, and generating new viewpoints on and uses of findings across various social and geographical contexts (Hays et al., 2015).

While we acknowledge that CRFG findings can never fully represent the cultural dynamism and complexities of lived experience, we suggest that nontraditional forms of presenting findings can meaningfully honor participants' voices. However, we caution that alternative formats require a "considerable amount of forethought, researcher reflexivity, and creative energy" (Johnson et al., 2013, p. 501). And we advise applying alternative approaches relevant to the goals of the inquiry, using alternative approaches alongside traditional approaches when necessary, and attending to the quality standards for the alternative format applied (McCulliss, 2013).

Culturally Relevant Focus Group Research Challenges

Recruitment and Participation

Issues with child care, transportation, competing responsibilities, and lack of time are barriers to focus group recruitment and participation—particularly for non-dominant communities (Hall, 2020). Language differences, immigration status, and distrust of the research process are other possible barriers. Remaining flexible when scheduling focus groups (i.e., nights and weekends) is recommended to address some of these barriers. Other recommendations include engaging with community leaders to address barriers and ensuring the environment is culturally acceptable and non-threatening (Halcomb et al., 2007).

Confidentiality

CRFG participants' concerns about privacy and who will have access to the data may also impact their decision to participate in the study. Scholars recommend that researchers disclose data security measures to address these issues (Sim & Waterfield, 2019). Information about the context of the study or demographic details related to the participants will need to be reported to preserve confidentiality (Sim & Waterfield, 2019). Further, if pseudonyms are used to protect participants' identities, having participants approve of or suggest names or labels used for pseudonyms is recommended (Sim & Waterfield, 2019).

Disclosure

Focus groups are highly unpredictable. Discussions can go in unintended directions, and participants may intentionally or unintentionally disclose information. According to Sim and Waterfield (2019), there are three forms of disclosure. The first concerns a participant who discloses information *during* the discussion about a person in the group who did not want that information shared. The second involves a participant disclosing details of the focus group *after* the discussion has ended. The third is *over-disclosure*: a participant disclosing more information than they originally intended to share. These types of disclosures breach confidentiality and can be particularly damaging for minoritized or vulnerable persons. Although moderators are hard-pressed to control or avoid these types of disclosures, they can carefully monitor the discussion and inform participants about the potential of these disclosures occurring (Sim & Waterfield, 2019).

Technology

While using online technology broadens geographical access to focus group participants, issues remain. First, recording (video, audio) focus groups may not be culturally responsive, depending on the group or issue discussed. Recording can also raise confidentiality issues. If a recording is necessary, researchers should seek participant consent before recording and provide information on access and storage. Second, internet connectivity difficulties can limit access for those living in more rural areas. Further, losing connection during the discussion could cause participants to miss part of the conversation. Should this happen, the moderator will want to circle back to the participant either later in the discussion or afterward to enable them to contribute.

Last, we note that using Zoom features (i.e., breakrooms, chat) for online focus groups can hinder participation. For instance, Zoom features can shift on a mobile device, making them less visible on participants' smartphones. Participants might be unable to access links sent via chat when using Zoom on a smartphone, thereby limiting their ability to engage with the content provided. Recommendations for some of these issues include having another person be responsible for managing technology during a virtual focus group (Falter et al., 2022), as well as providing participants with materials and resources (links, documents) and checking participants' familiarity with online tools *before* the online focus group session.

Power Dynamics

Focus group interactions are never neutral, as they reflect the power dynamics of the larger society (Ayrton, 2019). Researchers who conduct focus groups with minoritized groups suggest sharing a cultural experience relevant to the research with group members to reduce the researcher–participant power hierarchy. Separating focus groups into different subgroups (i.e., parents, children) is another strategy for reducing the negative impact of power hierarchies within focus groups. Further, it may not be culturally appropriate to have mixed-gender focus groups in certain cultures (Halcomb et al., 2007). Seeking advice from community members on focus group composition can ensure alignment with cultural norms and avoid some power issues (Halcomb et al., 2007).

Group members who dominate the discussion or silence those who represent a voice of dissent make it difficult to manage power differentials in focus groups (Halcomb et al., 2007). Moderators can address such power dynamics by using direct eye contact, body language, interruption, and removing persons from the group (Ayrton, 2019). Yet, as Ayrton (2019) thoughtfully points out, power dynamics are not always a "problem." Participants can assert power by resisting sharing information during a group discussion. Observing the power dynamics of a cultural group can even provide valuable information about the social relations (i.e., negotiation of acceptable practices) of that group (Ayrton, 2019).

Conclusion

We have offered our stance on CRFG research and discussed its central characteristics. We have also clarified the distinction between traditional focus groups and CRFGs, emphasizing that CRFGs are unique because they center participants' culture, serve as sites for social justice, and position the moderator as a change agent responsible for ensuring that participants' lives are positively impacted by the inquiry.

We recognize that non-traditional focus group strategies are often required to ethically engage cultural diversity. Thus, we have outlined alternative strategies to enhance cultural receptivity when implementing CRFG research. We consider attending to cultural context an ethical imperative. We hope our chapter contributes to responsive and ethical focus group practice and welcome the thoughts and insights of other social justice–oriented scholars.

References

Alshenqeeti, H. (2014). Interviewing as a data collection method: A critical review. *English Linguistics Research, 3*(1), 39–45. https://doi.org/10.5430/elr.v3n1p39

Ayrton, R. (2019). The micro-dynamics of power and performance in focus groups: An example from discussion on national identity with the South Sudanese diaspora in the UK. *Qualitative Research, 19*(3), 323–339. doi:10.1177/1468794118757102

Birt, L., Scott, S., Cavers, D., Campbell, C., & Walter, F. (2016). Member checking: A tool to enhance trustworthiness or merely a nod to validation? *Qualitative Health Research, 26*(13), 1802–1811. https://doi.org/10.1177/1049732316654870

Bonilla-Silva, E. (2019). Feeling race: Theorizing the racial economy of emotions. *American Sociological Review, 84*(1), 1–25. https://doi.org/10.1177/0003122418816958

Charmaz, K. (2014). *Constructing grounded theory* (2nd ed.). SAGE.

Chouinard, J., & Cousins, B. (2009). A review and synthesis of current research on cross-cultural evaluation. *American Journal of Evaluation, 30*(4), 457–494. https://doi.org/10.1177/1098214009349865

Cowan, S., & McLeod, J. (2004). Research methods: Discourse analysis. *Counselling & Psychotherapy Research, 4*, 102. https://doi.org/10.1080/14733140412331384108

Creswell, J. W., & Poth, C. (2017). *Qualitative inquiry and research design: Choosing among five approaches* (4th ed.). SAGE.

Denham, M. A., & Onwuegbuzie, A. J. (2013). Beyond words: Using nonverbal communication data in research to enhance thick description and interpretation. *International Journal of Qualitative Methods, 12*(1), 670–696. https://doi.org/10.1177/160940691301200137

Denzin, N. (1978). The logic of naturalistic inquiry. In N. K. Denzin (ed.), *Sociological methods: A sourcebook* (pp. 6–28). McGraw-Hill.

Denzin, N. (2006). *Sociological methods: A sourcebook* (5th ed.). Aldine Transaction.

Edwards, R., & Weller, S. (2012). Shifting analytic ontology: Using I-poems in qualitative longitudinal research. *Qualitative Research, 12*(2), 202–217. https://doi.org/10.1177/1468794111422040

Eldh, A., Liselott, A., & Berterö, C. (2020). Quotations in qualitative studies: Reflections on constituents, custom, and purpose. *International Journal of Qualitative Methods, 19*, 1–6. https://doi.org/10.1177/1609406920969268

Esposito, N. (2001). From meaning to meaning: The influence of translation techniques on non-English focus group research. *Qualitative Health Research, 11*(4), 568–579. https://doi.org/10.1177/104973201129119217

Falter, M. M., Arenas, A. A., Maples, G. W., Smith, C. T., Lamb, L. J., Anderson, M. G., Uzzell, E. M., Jacobs, L. E., Cason, X. L., Griffis, T. A., Polzin, M., & Wafa, N. Z. (2022, January). Making room for Zoom in focus group methods: Opportunities and challenges for novice researchers (during and beyond COVID-19). In *Forum Qualitative Sozialforschung/Forum: Qualitative Social Research, 23*(1). https://doi.org/10.17169/fqs-23.1.3768

Flynn, R., Albrecht, L., & Scott, S. (2018). Two approaches to focus group data collection for qualitative health research: Maximizing resources and data quality. *International Journal of Qualitative Methods, 17*, 1–9. https://doi.org/10.1177/1609406917750781

Gilligan, C., Spencer, R., Weinberg, M. K., & Bertsch, T. (2003). On the listening guide: A voice-centered relational method. In P. M. Camic, J. E. Rhodes, & L. Yardley, L. (Eds.), *Qualitative research in psychology: Expanding perspectives in methodology and design* (pp. 157–172). American Psychological Association.

Glaser, B. G., & Strauss, A. L. (1967). *The discovery of grounded theory: Strategies for qualitative research*. Aldine Publishing Company.

Guest, G., Namey, E., & McKenna, K. (2017). How many focus groups are enough? Building an evidence base for nonprobability sample sizes. *Field Methods, 29*(1), 3–22. https://doi.org/10.1177/1525822X16639015

Gullion, J. S. (2022). Writing for a broad audience: Concept papers, blogs, and op-eds. In C. Vanover, P. Mihas, & J. Saldaña (Eds.), *Analyzing and interpreting qualitative data: After the interview* (pp. 431–444). SAGE.

Halcomb, E. J., Gholizadeh, L., DiGiacomo, M., Phillips, J., & Davidson, P. M. (2007). Literature review: Considerations in undertaking focus group research with culturally and linguistically diverse groups. *Journal of Clinical Nursing, 16*(6), 1000–1011. https://doi.org/10.1111/j.1365-2702.2006.01760.x

Hall, J. N. (2020). *Focus groups: Culturally responsive approaches for qualitative inquiry and program evaluation*. Myers Education Press.

Hall, J. N., Freeman, M., & Colomer, S. E. (2020). A culturally responsive, educative evaluation approach: Success and missed opportunities. *American Journal of Evaluation, 41*(3), 384–403. https://doi.org/10.1177/1098214019885632

Hall, J. N., Mitchell, N., & Halpin, S. (2022). Using focus groups for empowerment purposes in qualitative research and evaluation. *International Journal of Social Science Research Methodology*. Advance online publication. https://doi.org/10.1080/13645579.2022.2049518

Harris, A., & Guillemin, M. (2012). Developing sensory awareness in qualitative interviewing: A portal into the otherwise unexplored. *Qualitative Health Research, 22*(5), 689–699. https://doi.org/10.1177/1049732311431899

Hays, C. A., Spiers, J. A., & Paterson, B. (2015). Opportunities and constraints in disseminating qualitative research in web 2.0 virtual environments. *Qualitative Health Research, 25*(11), 1576–1588. https://orcid.org/10.1177/1049732315580556

Holmes, A. (2020). Researcher positionality: A consideration of its influence and place in qualitative research—a new researcher guide. *International Journal of Education, 8*(4), 1–10. http://orcid.org/0000-0002-5147-0761

Hood, S., Hopson, R. K., & Kirkhart, K. E. (2015). Culturally responsive evaluation. In K. E. Newcomer, H. P. Hatry, & J. S. Wholey (Eds.), *Handbook of practical program evaluation* (4th ed., pp. 281–317). Jossey-Bass.

Johnson, C. W., & Parry, D. (2015). *Fostering social justice through qualitative inquiry: A methodological guide*. Routledge.

Johnson, J., Hall, J. N., Greene, J. C., & Ahn, J. (2013). Alternative approaches for presenting evaluation findings. *American Journal of Evaluation, 34*(4), 486–503. https://doi.org/10.1177/1098214013492995

Ladson-Billings, G. (1995). Toward a theory of culturally relevant pedagogy. *American Educational Research Journal, 32*(3), 465–491. https://doi.org/10.3102/00028312032003465

Lahman, M. K., Geist, M. R., Rodriguez, K. L., Graglia, P., & DeRoche, K. K. (2011). CR relational reflexive ethics in research: The three Rs. *Quality & Quantity, 45*(6), 1397–1414. https://doi.org/10.1007/s11135-010-9347-3

Lavrakas, P. J. (2008). *Encyclopedia of survey research methods*. SAGE.

Madison, S. (2012). *Critical ethnography: Method, ethics, and performance*. SAGE.

Madriz, E. (2000). Focus groups in feminist research. In N. K. Denzin, & Y. S. Lincoln (Eds.), *Handbook of qualitative research* (3rd ed., pp. 835–850). SAGE.

Massey, O. T. (2011). A proposed model for the analysis and interpretation of focus groups in evaluation research. *Evaluation and Program Planning, 34*(1), 21–28.

McCulliss, D. (2013). Poetic inquiry and multidisciplinary qualitative research. *Journal of Poetry Therapy, 26*(2), 83–114. https://doi.org/10.1080/08893675.2013.794536

Mitchell, J., Boettcher-Sheard, N., Duque, C., & Lashewicz, B. (2018). Who do we think we are? Disrupting notions of quality in qualitative research. *Qualitative Health Research, 28*(4), 673–680. https://doi.org/10.1177/1049732317748896

Pasque, P., Patton, L., Gaston, G. J., Gooden, M., Henfield, M., Richard Milner, H., Peters, A., & Steward, D. (2022). Unapologetic educational research: Addressing anti-Blackness, racism, and White supremacy. *Cultural Studies ↔ Cultural Methodologies, 22*(1), 3–17.

Patton, M. Q. (2002). *Qualitative research and evaluation methods* (3rd ed.). SAGE.

Patton, M. Q. (2015). *Qualitative research and evaluation methods* (4th ed.). SAGE.

Qin, D. (2016). Positionality. *The Wiley Blackwell encyclopedia of gender and sexuality studies*, 1–2. https://doi.org/10.1002/9781118663219.wbegss619

Reilly, R. C. (2013). Found poems, member checking and crises of representation. *The Qualitative Report, 18*(30), 1–18. https://doi.org/10.46743/2160-3715/2013.1534

Roberts, R. E. (2020). Qualitative interview questions: Guidance for novice researchers. *Qualitative Report, 25*(9), 3185–3203. https://doi.org/10.46743/2160-3715/2020.4640

Rodriguez, K., Schwartz, J., Lahman, M., & Geist, M. (2011). Culturally responsive focus groups: Reframing the research experience to focus on participants. *International Journal of Qualitative Methods, 10*(4), 400–417. https://doi.org/10.1177/160940691101000407

Rolón-Dow, R., & Bailey, M. J. (2021). Insights on narrative analysis from a study of racial microaggressions and microaffirmations. *American Journal of Qualitative Research, 6*(1), 1–18. https://doi.org/10.29333/ajqr/11456

Rosenthal, M. (2016). Qualitative research methods: Why, when, and how to conduct interviews and focus groups in pharmacy research. *Currents in Pharmacy Teaching and Learning, 8*(4), 509–516. https://doi.org/10.1016/j.cptl.2016.03.021

Roulston, K. (2022). *Interviewing: A guide to theory and practice*. SAGE.

Ryan, K. E., Gandha, T., Culbertson, M. J., & Carlson, C. (2014). Focus group evidence: Implications for design and analysis. *American Journal of Evaluation, 35*(3), 328–345. https://doi.org/10.1177/1098214013508300

Sczesny, S., Moser, F., & Wood, W. (2015). Beyond sexist beliefs: How do people decide to use gender-inclusive language? *Personality and Social Psychology Bulletin, 41*(7), 943–954. https://doi.org/10.1177/0146167215585727

Shelton, S., & Jones, A. (2022). *Advantages of and considerations for conducting online focus groups*. SAGE Research Methods Cases.

Sim, J., & Waterfield, J. (2019). Focus group methodology: Some ethical challenges. *Quality & Quantity, 53*(6), 3003–3022. https://doi.org/10.1007/s11135-019-00914-5

Stanton, C. R. (2014). Crossing methodological borders: Decolonizing community-based participatory research. *Qualitative Inquiry, 20*(5), 573–583. https://doi.org/10.1177/1077800413505541

Symonette, H. (2004). Walking pathways toward becoming a culturally competent evaluator: Boundaries, borderlands, and border crossings. In M. Thompson-Robinson, R. Hopson, & S. SenGupta (Eds.), *In search of cultural competence in evaluation: Toward principles and practices. New Directions for Evaluation*, No. 102 (pp. 95–109). Jossey-Bass.

Thomas, V. G., & Campbell, P. B. (2021). *Evaluation in today's world: Respecting diversity, improving quality, and promoting usability.* SAGE.

Willgerodt, M. A. (2003). Using focus groups to develop culturally relevant instruments. *Western Journal of Nursing Research, 25*(7), 798–814. https://doi.org/10.1177/0193945903256708

Woodyatt, C. R., Finneran, C. A., & Stephenson, R. (2016). In-person versus online focus group discussions: A comparative analysis of data quality. *Qualitative Health Research, 26*(6), 741–749. https://doi.org/ 10.1177/1049732316631510

Yarbrough, D. B., Shulha, L. M., Hopson, R. K., & Caruthers, F. A. (2011). *The program evaluation standards: A guide for evaluators and evaluation users* (3rd ed.). SAGE.

FOUR

Recruiting For and Conducting Virtual Focus Groups and Interviews With Low-Income Populations During the COVID-19 Pandemic

Brigette A. Herron, Darci Bell, and Jung Sun Lee

QUALITATIVE FOCUS GROUPS AND INTERVIEWS have the potential to open doorways between researchers and participants. Because qualitative data collection is not easily separated from everyday life, even the most carefully designed focus groups and interviews are vulnerable to unpredictable events and human behavior. In the case of conducting virtual focus groups and interviews, a heightened closeness or vulnerability can be created when we meet participants where they are in places like homes, cars, and libraries through phones and computers. This other layer of potential vulnerability is important to consider when adapting qualitative focus groups and interviews. Contemplating the kinds of mutual responsibilities we hold for one another as humans and how these could show up in both in-person and virtual qualitative research activities is beneficial for both researchers and participants alike.

This chapter discusses an example of how one project adapted qualitative data collection in creative ways with low-income participants to support a free nutrition education intervention delivered by text message. The adaptation of these qualitative methods began with a shift from in-person to virtual qualitative data collection following the onset of the COVID-19 pandemic. However, these adaptations proved to be more complex than originally imagined, as noted in similar cases (Roberts et al., 2021). Adaptation required creative and flexible solutions to meet the needs of participants and the research project. The overall approach to conducting virtual focus groups and interviews iteratively grew to support the needs of participants, where health issues, poverty, and access to adequate nutrition and health education emerged as persistent parts of everyday life. Adaptations were accomplished through the use of a trauma-informed and a feminist approach to conducting qualitative research.

The case example discussed in this chapter was a qualitative needs assessment intended to inform the design and formative evaluation of a text messaging intervention for a nutrition education and obesity prevention program for low-income adults. Key issues encountered in adapting methods for this study from in-person to online data generation included virtual recruitment and consent, increasing access to participate online or by telephone, eliciting responses using visual and/or rich descriptions of images and content, managing various unexpected challenges with flexibility, and issues related to interpreting and sharing findings. Using virtual methods in this case had the positive result of allowing for more participatory involvement with low-income populations in a time of increased isolation. However, the virtual focus groups and interviews also required an additional layer of consideration, due to connecting with participants in their homes, cars, and other personal spaces through cell phones and computers, and the everyday trauma of COVID-19 and living with limited resources. The chapter concludes with recommendations for researchers conducting virtual focus groups and interviews with low-income populations, implications, and conclusions.

Conducting Online Focus Groups

Focus groups are typically composed of people who possess certain characteristics and provide qualitative data in a focused discussion in order to help understand a particular topic of interest. In-depth qualitative interviews serve a similar purpose, but typically involve one participant and one researcher, with less focus on the group context. Focus groups and interviews can be effective ways to develop a program or product, such as curriculum materials, logos, or social marketing messaging, sometimes using multiple phases of pre-testing, pilot testing, or evaluative focus groups (Krueger & Casey, 2009). Focus groups have the potential to be less hierarchical than other methods by centering the voices of the group rather than the researcher. The potential of focus groups to be less hierarchical can make them a desirable method when working with minoritized or vulnerable populations and is compatible with many approaches to feminist and participatory types of research (Wilkinson, 2001).

There are various costs and benefits to conducting qualitative focus groups and interviews at a distance. Early literature on the benefits and challenges of telephone and internet focus groups discussed the benefits of lowered cost and increased participation across distances, but noted the potential for physical disconnect arising from unseen body language or a diminished sense of engagement across a group (Krueger & Casey, 2009). However, the possibilities for using digital tools and synchronous online platforms for qualitative data collection have been evolving and improving over the past decade (Morrison et al., 2020; Paulus et al., 2014). Notably, synchronous video calling (also referred to as video conferencing) has continued to improve, and the use of these types of technologies has increased (De et al., 2020; Dos Santos Marques et al., 2021).

Because in-person meeting posed an increased health and safety risk, and social distancing became more prevalent during the COVID-19 pandemic, the use of various video conferencing tools such as Zoom, Microsoft Teams, Skype, Webex, Google Hangouts, and Facebook messenger became more widespread in people's everyday lives. The literature on adapting various qualitative methods to virtual methods using video conferencing software has continued to grow (Lobe & Morgan, 2020).

Adapting from In-Person to Virtual Methods During the COVID-19 Pandemic

Much of the literature has emphasized the feasibility and satisfactory qualitative data collection resulting from virtual focus groups and interviews in a variety of contexts, such as medical and health research, nutrition education, and higher education (Daniels et al., 2019; Dos Santos Marques et al., 2021; Engward et al., 2022; Jiang & Cohen, 2020; Lobe et al., 2020; Lobe & Morgan, 2021; Nobrega et al. 2021; Sy et al., 2020; Tremblay et al., 2021). In particular, virtual focus groups in health and nutrition have proven useful for investigating sensitive health topics, reaching people with disabilities, and overcoming geographic, physical, and medical limitations (Jiang & Cohen, 2020). The benefits of using video conferencing to conduct virtual focus groups and interviews to reach people during the COVID-19 pandemic and across geographic distances have been discussed frequently (Engward et al., 2022; Jiang & Cohen, 2020; Lobe & Morgan, 2021; Nobrega et al., 2021; Rahman et al., 2021; Sy et al., 2020). These include allowing participants who would not have traditionally joined due to distance or transportation issues to participate in research (Dos Santos Marques et al., 2020). Adapting methods from in-person to virtual during a crisis like the COVID-19 pandemic also allows the option for time-sensitive research projects to continue and is made possible when resilience can be built into each step of the research process (Engward et al., 2022; Rahman et al., 2021; Sy et al., 2020). As is the case with in-person qualitative research, critical reflection is a key part of research resilience in virtual settings (Rahman et al., 2021).

Recommended group size is one difference between in-person and virtual focus groups. Several studies recommended recruiting fewer participants for virtual groups to enhance rapport-building and data quality, with recommendations ranging from 2 participants (Lobe & Morgan, 2021), to 3–5 participants (Lathen & Laestadius, 2021; Lobe et al., 2020), to 6–8 participants (Dos Santos Marques et al., 2021). Some studies found that virtual participation numbers were lower than in-person focus groups, as participants struggled with technology issues such as poor internet connection or access (Dos Santos Marques et al., 2021; Rahman et al., 2021). Other challenges with conducting virtual interviews during the COVID-19 pandemic included participants seeming more distracted by interruptions at home, such as caretaking responsibilities for children or pets, work emails, being distracted by seeing oneself onscreen (Rahman et al., 2021), and other impacts of "technostress" (De' et al., 2020) or Zoom fatigue (Ramachandran, 2021). Physical distance and time constraints can also lead to difficulties developing rapport when conducting virtual qualitative research (Rahman et al., 2021; Roberts et al., 2021; Tremblay et al., 2021). Specific strategies to make virtual focus groups more inclusive for individuals with communication disabilities are also needed, and offer further support for recommendations to keep focus groups small, as Trevisan (2021) discussed in the case of in-person focus groups.

Using Virtual Methods with Low-Income Populations

Adapting qualitative research from face-to-face contexts to virtual platforms can have unexpected challenges, especially for low-income populations. The impact of the digital divide will continue to impact the ability of low-income populations to participate in virtual qualitative research (De' et al., 2020; Rahman et al., 2021; Tremblay et al., 2021). Lack of access to technology or reliable internet can make it difficult to recruit participants from marginalized populations (Roberts et al., 2021; Sy et al., 2020). Although the experience of participants experiencing low socio-economic status (SES) has been acknowledged as important in focus group research (Lathen & Laestadius, 2021), and qualitative inquiry is a key tool for identifying the needs of marginalized and vulnerable groups during times of crisis (Teti et al., 2020), only a few studies have begun to explore challenges related to conducting online focus groups and interviews with low-income and/or racial and ethnic minority populations during COVID-19.

Roberts and colleagues (2021) discussed strategies for conducting rigorous and ethical virtual interviews using a case study of student homelessness conducted during the pandemic, and emphasized the use of self-reflective memos and a guiding framework for conducting qualitative research and interviews online (see Salmons, 2011; 2016). Lathen and Laestadius (2021) offered recommendations drawn from online focus groups conducted with low SES African American adults during COVID-19, and recommended reflecting on issues of participant privacy, online connectivity, and support and time allocations. Other recommendations included allowing opportunities for participation that do not require on-camera exposure of a person's home and thinking about alternatives to facilitate safe, private, and quiet spaces with childcare provided (perhaps partnering with a library to provide private rooms with technology), and identifying strategies for providing needed technology or mobile hotspots. Considering alternative ways to address incentives lost in the transition to virtual, ways to be inclusive of various literacy levels, and ways to provide technical support ahead of and following the focus groups are also recommended (Lathen and Laestadius, 2021).

Considering Ethics of Care with Feminist and Trauma-Informed Approaches

Recommendations to carefully consider ethics when pivoting to virtual qualitative research are common (De' et al., 2020; Engward et al., 2022; Rahman et al., 2021; Roberts et al., 2021; Sy et al., 2020). While virtual methods are not inherently riskier than in-person methods, they do require reflexive and deliberate approaches to mitigate risks for participants in new virtual territory (Engward et al., 2022; Newman et al., 2021). During the COVID-19 pandemic, ethical challenges to conducting virtual research have involved issues of informed consent, privacy, confidentiality, compensation, online access to research participation, and access to resources (Newman et al., 2021). Although not widely discussed, attending to matters of care and compassion during recruitment and data collection is one specific ethical concern that could be lost in the adaptation of in-person to virtual qualitative methods. For this reason, drawing from feminist or trauma-informed approaches to qualitative data collection, which centers ethical and care-focused approaches to conducting research, may be useful when adapting methods to conduct virtual interviews and focus groups with low-income populations. For example, Tungohan and Catungal (2022) described how a transnational feminist queer methodology and ethical framework focused on flexibility and accountability allowed them to successfully adapt to virtual qualitative research methods with transnational participants during the COVID-19 pandemic. Using Zoom to conduct focus groups allowed them to enhance rapport and relationship, such as using the chat box to engage participants with sharing memes and GIFs (Tungohan & Catungal, 2022). Many feminist approaches to conducting qualitative research are compatible with supporting critical reflection that can support research resilience by adapting to various crises and participant needs (Rahman et al., 2021).

As adapting to virtual methods during the COVID-19 pandemic took place during a time of global crisis requiring research resilience fostered through critical reflection (Rahman et al., 2021), it is important to consider how the trauma of COVID-19, intersecting with everyday traumas of food insecurity, poverty, classism, racism, and sexism, might have also impacted research. In this chapter, the feminist approach to conducting qualitative interviews and focus groups is informed by myriad perspectives about feminist interviewing. Specifically, this work engages with feminist approaches in order to cultivate an ecosystem of care by using a framework for inviting stories, engaging in critical reflexivity, and avoiding dominating practices embedded in research along the lines of gender, race, class, sexual orientation, age, and ability (Herron, 2022). Literature on feminist qualitative interviews has traditionally considered one or more of the following concepts: (1) experience and voice, (2) difference and positionality, (3) power sharing and collaboration, (4) creativity, listening, and reflexivity, and (5) ethics of care and safety (Herron, 2022). For this chapter, particular attention is paid to the concept of the ethics of care and safety in virtual qualitative methods.

Drawing from trauma-informed approaches to care can support virtual qualitative research and considers the safety and well-being of participants and researchers beyond the screen. The 5 R's of trauma-informed care recommend acknowledging that trauma exists (Realize), recognizing where it takes place (Recognize), responding appropriately (Respond), resisting re-traumatizing (Resist), and fostering resilience to trauma (Resilience). These are accomplished by encouraging elements of safety, trustworthiness and transparency, peer support, collaboration and mutuality, empowerment, voice and choice, and acknowledging cultural, historical, and gender issues in all aspects of a program or project (SAMHSA, 2014). These elements overlap with the goals of many qualitative research and feminist research projects, making trauma-informed approaches a compatible framework to think with methodologically. This chapter contributes to the literature by detailing one case example of an attempt to adapt in-person qualitative methods to virtual, supported by a feminist and trauma-informed approach to conducting interviews and focus groups with low-income populations.

Background of the Project

This case example looks at the adaptation of virtual qualitative focus groups and interviews used as part of a qualitative needs assessment, the results of which were used to inform the design and formative evaluation of a text messaging intervention for a federally funded nutrition education and obesity prevention program for low-income adults. The federally funded nutrition education program is called the Supplemental Nutrition Assistance Program Education (SNAP-Ed) and provides free nutrition education and obesity programs for low-income individuals, through various implementing agencies.[1] The programming of focus in this chapter is targeted specifically for adults who are low-income or are eligible for the Supplemental Nutrition Assistant Program (SNAP), formerly known as the Food Stamps program in the United States. Of the various types of programming that can be offered, our implementing agency sought to design a text messaging intervention, where eligible participants across the state of Georgia could be enrolled and receive free text messages specifically about health and nutrition. A qualitative research design was developed that included in-person focus groups and interviews with participants who had previously participated in SNAP-Ed programming. These participants had previously indicated in exit surveys that they would like to be contacted about more nutrition education opportunities by email and/or text message. This data would then be analyzed and used to develop a pilot text messaging education intervention about drinking healthy beverages and more water. Following the pilot texting intervention, we planned to follow up with in-person focus groups and interviews with participants who received the texts. This would serve as part of the formative evaluation of the program and help continue refining and improving the messages for the texting intervention.

Our original plan was to conduct our qualitative data collection in March 2020 to support the development of the pilot texting campaign in the summer of 2020. However, after the onset of the COVID-19 pandemic, we were forced to rethink if and how we could carry on our research virtually. First, we created a plan to recruit by text and email and decided to use Zoom as our platform, and make a virtual data management plan. Next, we created virtual materials and thought about how to create virtual consent forms and a virtual consenting process, and updated our protocol for human subjects research.

We began with a series of pre-intervention virtual focus groups (4) and interviews (1), which included 13 participants. These sessions featured a moderator and co-moderator. Participants were asked about their current mobile device use, beverage consumption, and opinions about proposed content, including sample text messages facilitated through screen sharing and verbal descriptions of content. After revisions were made to content based on the participant feedback, the pilot text message intervention took place in July 2020, when 572 participants received 12 interactive and engaging text messages about drinking more water and less sugar-sweetened beverages over a period of 6 weeks. Following the text message intervention, we conducted additional virtual focus groups (4) and interviews (2) with 13 participants. The size of the virtual focus groups ranged from 2 to 7 people, with most focus groups being smaller in size. The post-intervention focus groups and interviews had only one moderator, and participants were asked to share their general reactions to the intervention, opinions about final content, ideas for improvements, and any other feedback about the intervention. Interviews were recorded via Zoom and were transcribed. Both video recordings and transcripts of audio recordings were analyzed using ATLAS.ti. The results of these post-intervention focus groups and interviews were then used to inform continued refinement and development of the text messaging intervention, which would be repeated in the summer of 2021.

One overarching concern when planning to adapt the in-person focus groups and interviews to a virtual setting was remaining accessible and inclusive for adults with limited resources. The adaptation process involved envisioning, brainstorming, and experimenting with new ways to bring a feminist and trauma-informed layer of care and safety into the virtual environment, particularly when responding to unexpected challenges that came up. Over the course of the research project, several key issues arose and are discussed in detail below.

Key Issues in Adapting Methods

Key issues encountered in adapting methods for this study from in-person to virtual included virtual recruitment and consent, increasing access to participate online or by telephone, eliciting responses using visual and/or rich descriptions of images, managing various unexpected challenges with flexibility, and interpreting, representing, and sharing findings. These key issues came up during pre-intervention and post-intervention phases.

Virtual Recruitment and Consent

Prior to the pandemic, in-person recruitment was planned at various outreach events and direct education classes. Since those were being cancelled due to COVID-19, and facilitators were struggling to pivot those classes online, an alternate recruiting strategy was developed that would not place an additional burden on facilitators and staff, or place anyone in an unsafe environment. We recruited from a pool of former participants in SNAP-Ed in-person education programs who had indicated that they would like to be contacted by text message and email regarding future programming. Since the project planned to use a text message management platform to deliver the pilot text message intervention, we decided to use the same platform to send an invitation by text message to potential participants. Additionally, participants were also sent the same invitation to participate by email. For this initial phase, the invitation consisted of a reminder of who our implementing agency was, a reminder about their participation in previous programming, a brief description of the research project, and what could be expected, including the gift card amount they would receive by mail. Participants were invited to click a link that would take them to an online survey (via Qualtrics) that included the approved consent form and multiple options to sign up for a time to participate in a focus group or interview. We quickly learned that texting was the easiest and most successful way to recruit participants. Only one participant was recruited by email in either the pre- or post-intervention focus groups and interviews. For instance, for the pre-intervention focus groups and interviews, out of 379 email invitations sent, only 2 individuals expressed an interest in participating (0.5%). Comparatively, 327 text message invitations resulted in 50 individuals expressing an interest in participating (15.3%) and resulted in 12 participants in the first round of interviewing. Recruitment for the post-intervention focus groups and interviews took place by text only. All participants in the texting intervention were invited to text a keyword "4Talk" if they were interested in participating, and this was set up to trigger an automatic response with the link to the Qualtrics consent form, survey, and sign-up options.

In the event that only one person signed up for a particular time, a one-on-one interview was held. Allowing participants to self-select times helped facilitate participants' access and participation and was accomplished by systematically rescheduling with those who missed appointments and pivoting to individual interviews if only one person were available. We found that organizing and rescheduling by text message was a non-intrusive and easy way to organize, and a process on which participants commented favorably. Participants were also encouraged to reach out if they needed to reschedule or required additional support for joining the virtual focus group or interview. In cases where participants needed to reschedule, there was a simple way to provide additional options for them by text message, with a multiple-choice option (i.e., participants could text A, B, or C to choose a specific time, or respond "more choices"). Throughout the process, ease of access for participants was continuously reflected on, self-reflexive researcher memos were written, and adjustments were made to meet the needs of participants and ensure that no participant who indicated interest in participating was left out.

Increasing Access to Participate Online or by Telephone

One concern about adapting methods to virtual formats was whether it would be accessible to participants with limited resources, varying access to reliable internet or technology, and diverse comfort levels with technology in general. One reason Zoom was chosen as our videoconferencing platform was because it would allow members to join both online or by telephone. Once the participants completed the online consent form, short online survey, and indicated which focus group session they would like to participate in, they were sent a follow-up text or email with a thank-you for signing up, a reminder of which focus group they were signed up for, and short instructions for how to join by Zoom link or call in by telephone in three simple steps. An additional message with instructions to download the Zoom meeting app on a phone was also shared, with links for downloading on Apple or android devices. This process remained the same in both pre- and post-virtual focus groups and interviews.

Eliciting Responses Using Visual and/or Rich Descriptions of Images and Content

In both pre- and post-intervention focus groups and interviews, participants were provided rich verbal descriptions of images and content related to pilot texting the intervention in order to elicit their responses and feedback. Content, such as sample text messages, infographics, images, pictures, nutrition education blogs (links shared by text message), website screenshots, and sample recipes for fruit-infused water were incorporated into a PowerPoint presentation and shared via screen share on Zoom. This material was also emailed ahead of time to participants, who were invited but not required to preview. During the post-intervention, since participants had already received the texts as part of the campaign, they were invited to revisit the content on their phones in real time if they were comfortable doing so.

We also prepared a script for reading a rich description of each content item, which was read aloud while content was shared visually. This was done to accommodate those who were joining by telephone and could not view the screen share on Zoom. This had the unintended effect of making the sessions more inclusive for one participant who shared that she was visually impaired. This also elicited important considerations about how to ensure that the text message intervention itself was also inclusive to participants who may be experiencing visual impairment and gleaning feedback that text in infographics and visual recipes should be large enough for individuals of various abilities to read, particularly on a phone.

The pacing of interview questions was also deliberate. For pre-intervention focus groups, we began by asking for information on current mobile device use, the affordability of receiving and responding to text messages, and current beverage consumption habits. For post-intervention focus groups and interviews, we began with what participants could recall from the intervention in their memory and their overall impressions of the intervention. After these verbal questions were asked, we moved to displaying or describing the content to participants to elicit their responses. In both pre- and post-intervention focus groups and interviews, this section of the talk resulted in very rich and detailed feedback from the participants, which was useful in making future adjustments to the text message intervention.

Managing Various Unexpected Challenges with Flexibility

As might be expected when adapting in-person methods to virtual settings, many unexpected challenges arose. The success of adaptation hinged on our ability to be flexible and make adjustments when needed. Challenges were sometimes technological and sometimes had to do with participants' personal life situations. A concerted effort was made at each step in the process to consider ways in which we could make virtual methods more inclusive in terms of access, abilities, and comfort level.

The pre-intervention virtual focus groups were moderated by a trained qualitative methodologist (the first author) and co-moderated by a graduate student with experience conducting interviews and who was also a registered, licensed dietitian (the second author). The post-intervention virtual focus group and interviews had only one moderator, a consequence of the relatively small size of the focus groups from the pre-intervention phase. This change was made to address the balance between participant and interviewer/moderator, due to the small sizes of the focus groups and the cases in which only one person was available and we conducted an interview. We were also mindful of having a one-to-one ratio of interviewer/interviewee and/or more focus group participants than researchers to ensure that participants would feel comfortable speaking with one another.

Unexpected challenges arose during all phases of the research process, so remaining flexible to meet participants' needs and life situations was important. For instance, during the virtual recruitment process, some participants asked for help in completing the online survey. In those cases, the researcher telephoned the participants, reading and completing the consenting process, survey, and sign-up in the Qualtrics survey. In one case, it became clear that one potential participant was uneasy when one researcher (the first author) called her on the phone. Sensing the unease in her voice, the researcher paused and asked her how she was doing and if everything was okay. It was then that the participant shared with the researcher that her daughter had unexpectedly passed away just days before, and she was having a hard time concentrating. In that case, the researcher drew upon the ethics of care, listening to her story and empathizing deeply with her experience. The participant was given the option to decline to complete the survey, and the researcher emphasized that her participation was completely voluntary and that she could still participate in receiving the text messages later in the summer. The participant agreed that she would rather not participate right then but asked if the researcher would please contact her following the texting program for the opportunity to provide feedback in future focus groups, a request that was honored.

This situation was indicative of several kinds of unexpected challenges that arose during the recruitment and consenting processes. Types of barriers to participation that participants faced included the deaths of friends and family (from COVID-19 and other causes), changing work schedules, working around children's virtual school schedules, and health emergencies. Another type of challenge arose when one participant responded to a text by asking for assistance in gaining access to food. She was an older adult who relied on public transportation to get groceries, but the bus in her rural county stopped running due to COVID-19 and staffing issues. While this was unexpected, the research and implementing agency team contacted the existing University Extension County Office in her area and was able to connect her with personnel who could link her to community services and arrange transportation. This example demonstrated how recruiting by text may become an option whereby vulnerable, hard-to-contact, or low-income individuals might reach out for assistance. It is useful to consider what kinds of plans for connecting participants to additional resources should be in place prior to recruitment.

As mentioned previously, remaining flexible in order to meet the needs of participants' access, abilities, and comfort when possible was an important part of our interviewing process. One example of this was allowing participants to choose whether or not they would turn their camera on. Choosing to share or not share video did not seem to diminish the quality of participation in interviews or interaction between participants in a focus group setting such as this. Sometimes, after becoming comfortable, participants would turn on their cameras later during sessions. This became important, as many times participants were calling in from their cars after work or in their homes, settings in which they might not feel comfortable sharing with others, or where other members of the household were present.

Interpreting, Representing, and Sharing Findings

When analyzing and interpreting the findings from the focus groups and interviews, most of the interpretation of the data was similar to the interpretation of data generated by in-person methods before a global pandemic. However, additional care was taken to contextualize the data in the environment of multiple traumas, such as adapting to COVID-19, including the stressors of social distancing, isolation, sickness, and death, and living with limited resources. Part of this process involved writing extensive memos about the context surrounding the data collection process, unexpected challenges that arose (see also Roberts et al., 2021), and the general character that particular focus groups seemed to take on. For instance, some focus groups were more resource-sharing and community-oriented, looking to make connections with one another and offer support and encouragement to each other in achieving their health goals. Other focus groups had members who were managing multiple responsibilities, such as child care, work, and health issues, so it wasn't uncommon for participants to step away from the conversation and rejoin when possible. In those groups, the moderator and participants always worked to get the participant back into the conversation, and many participants empathized with the reasons someone had to step away. Another important aspect in interpretation was noting the demographics of the focus groups and interviews, which mostly took place with participants who identified as Women, as African American or Black, between the ages of 25 and 65, and many with children and other caretaking responsibilities. Participants were given the chance to self-identify their race, ethnicity, age, and gender when completing the brief online survey before selecting which focus group to sign up for. This was helpful when interpreting additional issues arising around race and ethnicity, gender, and class. Writing memos to document these particular characteristics across focus groups and interviews helped to provide additional context when sharing these findings with others.

When representing and sharing the findings with the participants, research team, and a wider audience, providing additional context about the focus groups and individual interviews in ways that would not compromise the anonymity of participants was important. In order to represent and share findings, multiple formats were used, from a detailed PowerPoint that shared content side-by-side with participant quotes and focus group conversation excerpts. The characteristics of focus groups, including demographics and the overall "feel" or "attitude" of the focus group and interview as interpreted by the researcher, were also shared. This additional information was helpful in terms of adjusting the content for the text message campaign and thinking of how to segment the campaign to people of different ages, people with children, and remain inclusive for people with particular health concerns and abilities. Another way that results were shared was by using narrative analysis. A narrative of one participant's experience with the text message intervention and its impact, which shared many elements with other participants' experiences, was created. Narrative was a powerful way to communicate rich and complex experiences and use the participants' original words as often as possible. Short reports, shared internally and as a part of reports to funders, were also created and shared, which included demographic and contextual information about being collected virtually during the COVID-19 pandemic. Regardless of the format used to represent findings, a description and acknowledgment of the everyday trauma of COVID-19 and living with limited resources and how that impacted the data collection was always included.

Recommendations For Researchers

In drawing from lessons learned from this case example, we offer researchers interested in conducting virtual focus groups and interviews with low-income populations several recommendations. These include: (1) remaining flexible to the needs and abilities of participants, (2) embedding critical reflection into the research design to guide any necessary adaptations, (3) interpreting and representing findings with context and care, and (4) acknowledging trauma as a part of the human experience that will sometimes enter research environments.

First, remaining flexible to the needs and abilities of participants can allow for the recruitment and conduct of qualitative data collection in support of helpful programs and interventions with vulnerable and marginalized populations. Being flexible might include allowing multiple opportunities for participants to choose how they would like to engage in the research. Flexibility could involve allowing a choice in terms of whether to join a virtual focus group or interview online or by telephone, or allowing freedom of choice in terms of turning on a camera. This was helpful in our case example by allowing space for participants who were traveling to or from work, engaging in caretaking responsibilities, or had different levels of comfort with technology or internet access to join. Allowing participants to step away to attend to caretaking responsibilities and working to re-integrate them into conversations during focus groups is another example of flexibility that incorporates the ethics of care. Steps taken to be flexible in terms of access, abilities, and comfort may assist in high-quality data collection, as it did in our case example.

The second recommendation is to embed critical reflection into the research design, preferably with a compatible theoretical framework to guide any necessary adaptations. For instance, this example used a feminist approach to interviewing to guide critical reflection, with a focus on the ethics of care and trauma-informed approaches to care. This type of guiding framework can be used to clearly define and communicate expectations for researchers and participants, which can be shared during recruitment, consenting processes, and when establishing norms and procedures during a focus group or interview. Using feminist approaches to interviewing and key elements of trauma-informed care allowed us to critically reflect on the elements of safety, trustworthiness and transparency, peer support, collaboration and mutuality, empowerment, voice and choice, and cultural, historical, and gender issues (SAMHSA, 2014) at each stage of the research process and make various adaptations that might make virtual methods more inclusive for participants.

The third recommendation for researchers is to practice interpreting and representing findings with context and care. This could include incorporating memoing to fully describe the context and particulars surrounding data collection and participants' experiences. Researchers might also explore multiple ways of sharing and representing findings, even with the same audience. Using narrative, arts-based, visually appealing, and easy-to-read research briefs and infographics are a few possibilities for sharing findings in ways that can connect with diverse audiences and keep research close to the participants' voice and the context in which data was generated.

Finally, researchers should acknowledge trauma as a part of the human experience that will sometimes enter research environments. In our study, the onset of COVID-19 itself became a form of trauma that resulted in unexpected challenges and interactions with participants. It is also important to consider the potential trauma endured by researchers as well. Activities such as debriefing and sharing findings with co-moderators and co-researchers are actions that can serve as supportive activities that bring care to the research environment. Incorporating a trauma-informed approach to conducting qualitative research means carefully thinking about ways to increase the safety and well-being of participants in the settings beyond the screen and text message and is important for creating more inclusive virtual spaces for data collection. Using a feminist or trauma-informed framework is just one option for acknowledging and responding to trauma in a research context in caring and compassionate ways.

Implications and Conclusions

The experience of conducting virtual focus groups and interviews with low-income populations during a dangerous global pandemic raised important questions for researchers to ask themselves. First, as human beings, what are our mutual responsibilities to one another, and how do these responsibilities come into play during a focus group or interview? Further, virtual interviews can create a heightened closeness, even at a distance, as we are "Zooming" right into a participant's home or car via cell phones and computers. This increased level of vulnerability is worthy of careful consideration when adapting qualitative research methods.

One positive implication of using virtual methods, in this case, was that it allowed for more involvement with low-income populations in a time of increased isolation. Participants commented favorably on being able to partake in the program and also being able to provide feedback, and shared that it helped counter some of the isolation that they felt during the pandemic. Several participants also shared that the virtual focus groups and interviews allowed them to participate in sharing their feedback when they would not have been able to join a face-to-face focus group due to transportation, child care, or mobility issues.

However, virtual adaptation also resulted in many unexpected challenges, as participants faced barriers in the form of caretaking interruptions, health issues, and family emergencies. Remaining flexible and adapting to the needs of participants using a feminist approach to qualitative research, and drawing upon trauma-informed approaches in this case example, allowed methods to be adapted in ways that tended to the needs of participants experiencing low income and limited resources during a global pandemic. These adaptations allowed for an increased level of research resilience (Rahman et al., 2021) through attending to the ethics of care with reflexive and deliberate approaches to mitigate risks for participants in virtual settings (Engward et al., 2022; Newman et al., 2021) and representing findings with care to a larger audience. These approaches to adapting in-person methods to virtual settings may be helpful not only in the case of conducting research with low-income populations, but also in a variety of research contexts, as the importance of care and the presence of trauma across the human experience are relevant for everyone.

Note

1. The implementing agency for this case example is the University of Georgia Supplemental Nutrition Assistance Program Education Program (UGA SNAP-Ed).

References

Daniels, N., Gillen, P., Casson, K., & Wilson, I. (2019). STEER: Factors to consider when designing online focus groups using audiovisual technology in health research. *International Journal of Qualitative Methods, 18*, 1–11. https://doi.org/ 10.1177/1609406919885786

De', R., Pandey, N., & Pal, A. (2020). Impact of digital surge during Covid-19 pandemic: A viewpoint on research and practice. *International Journal of Information Management, 55*, 102171. https://doi.org/https://doi.org/10.1016/j.ijinfomgt.2020.102171

Dos Santos Marques, I. C., Theiss, L. M., Johnson, C. Y., McLin, E., Ruf, B. A., Vickers, S. M., Fouad, M. N., Scarinci, I. C., & Chu, D. I. (2021). Implementation of virtual focus groups for qualitative data collection in a global pandemic. *American Journal of Surgery, 221*(5), 918–922. https://doi.org/10.1016/j.amjsurg.2020.10.009

Engward, E., Goldspink, S., Iancu, M., Kersey, T., & Wood, A. (2022). Togetherness in separation: Practical considerations for doing remote qualitative interviews ethically. *International Journal of Qualitative Methods, 21* (pp. 1–9). https://doi.org/10.1177/16094069211073212

Herron, B. A. (2022). 40 years of qualitative feminist interviewing: Conceptual moments and cultivating ecosystems of care. *Qualitative Inquiry*. Advance online publication. https://doi.org/10.1177/1077800422 1139611

Jiang, Q., & Cohen, N. (2020). Use of online focus groups for nutrition and health studies: The Northeast Regional Research Project Experience. *Topics in Clinical Nutrition: Changing the Face of Dietetics, 35*(1), 9–18. https://doi.org/10.1097/TIN.0000000000000200

Krueger, R. A., & Casey, M. A. (2009). *Focus groups: A practical guide for applied research* (4th ed.). SAGE.

Lathen, L., & Laestadius, L. (2021). Reflections on online focus group research with low socio-economic status African American adults during COVID-19. *International Journal of Qualitative Methods, 20*, 1–10. https://doi.org/10.1177/16094069211021713

Lobe, B., & Morgan, D. L. (2020). Assessing the effectiveness of video-based interviewing: A systematic comparison of video-conferencing based dyadic interviews and focus groups. *International Journal of Social Research Methodology, 24*(3), 301–312. https://doi.org/10.1080/13645579.2020.1785763

Lobe, B., Morgan, D., & Hoffman, K. A. (2020). Qualitative data collection in an era of social distancing. *International Journal of Qualitative Methods, 19*, 1–8. https://doi.org/10.1177/1609406920937875

Morrison, D., Lichtenwald, K., & Tang, R. (2020). Extending the online focus group method using web-based conferencing to explore older adults online learning. *International Journal of Research & Method in Education, 43*(1), 78–92. http://dx.doi.org/10.1080/1743727X.2019.1594183

Newman, P. A., Guta, A., & Black, T. (2021). Ethical considerations for qualitative research methods during the COVID-19 pandemic and other emergency situations: Navigating the virtual field. *International Journal of Qualitative Methods, 20*, 1–12. http://dx.doi.org/10.1177/16094069211047823

Nobrega, S., Ghaziri, M. E., Giacobbe, L., Rice, S., Punnett, L., & Edwards, K. (2021). Feasibility of virtual focus groups in program impact evaluation. *International Journal of Qualitative Methods, 20*, 1–10. https://doi.org/10.1177/16094069211019896

Paulus, T. M., Lester, J. N., & Dempster, P. G. (2014). *Digital tools for qualitative research*. SAGE.

Rahman, S. A., Tuckerman, L., Vorley, T., & Gherhes, C. (2021). Resilient research in the field: Insights and lessons from adapting qualitative research projects during the COVID-19 pandemic. *International Journal of Qualitative Methods, 20*, 1–16. https://doi.org/10.1177/16094069211016106

Ramachandran, V. (2021, February 23). Stanford researchers identify four causes for "Zoom fatigue" and their simple fixes. *Stanford News*. https://news.stanford.edu/2021/02/23/four-causes-zoom-fatigue-solutions/

Roberts, J. K., Pavlakis, A. E., & Richards, M. P. (2021). It's more complicated than it seems: Virtual qualitative research in the COVID-19 era. *International Journal of Qualitative Methods, 20*, 1–13. https://doi.org/10.1177/16094069211002959

Salmons, J. (Ed.). (2011). *Cases in online interview research*. SAGE.

Salmons, J. (2016). *Doing qualitative research online*. SAGE.

Substance Abuse and Mental Health Services Administration (SAMHSA). (2014). SAMHSA's concept of trauma and guidance for a trauma-informed approach. *HHS* Publication No. (SMA) 14-4884.

Sy, M., O'Leary, N., Nagraj, S., El-Awaisi, A., O'Carroll, V., & Xyrichis, A. (2020). Doing interprofessional research in the COVID-19 era: A discussion paper. *Journal of Interprofessional Care, 34*(5), 600–606. https://doi.org/10.1080/13561820.2020.1791808

Teti, M., Schatz, E., & Liebenberg, L. (2020). Methods in the time of COVID-19: The vital role of qualitative inquiries. *International Journal of Qualitative Methods, 19*, 1–5. https://doi.org/10.1177/1609406920920962

Tremblay, S., Castiglione, S., Audet, L.-A., Desmarais, M., Horace, M., & Peláez, S. (2021). Conducting qualitative research to respond to COVID-19 challenges: Reflections for the present and beyond. *International Journal of Qualitative Methods, 20*, 1–8. https://doi.org/10.1177/16094069211009679

Trevisan, F. (2021). Making focus groups accessible and inclusive for people with communication disabilities: A research note. *Qualitative Research, 21*(4), 619–627. https://doi.org/10.1177/1468794120941846

Tungohan, E., & Catungal, J. P. (2022). Virtual qualitative research using transnational feminist queer methodology: The challenges and opportunities of Zoom-based research during moments of crisis. *International Journal of Qualitative Methods, 21*, 1–12. https://doi.org/10.1177/16094069221090062

Wilkinson, S. (2001). How useful are focus groups in feminist research? In R. S. Barbour & J. Kitzinger (Eds.), *Developing focus group research: Politics, theory and practice* (pp. 64–78). SAGE.

PART II

 BEING INVENTIVE IN THEORIZING INTERVIEWS

FIVE

 Cartographic Accounts: Qualitatively Mapping With Braidotti

Maureen A. Flint and Morgan P. Tate

WHAT COMES TO MIND WHEN you think of maps? You might imagine the brightly lit rectangle of your phone, the landscape cropped tightly to a directional arrow, unfolding before you with a blue line disappearing in the distance. Maybe you imagine a map of the weather, blobs of green, orange, and red moving across the geography. Or you might think of folded and creased atlases, tucked in the pocket of the passenger side of a car, crinkling as you open them, and trace the names of cities and towns you pass. As Deleuze and Guattari (1987) wrote, "the map does not reproduce an unconscious closed in upon itself; it constructs the unconscious. It fosters connections between fields" (p. 12). In other words, maps are not simply a reproduction of *what is*; they are a relational and open-ended construction of possibility and connection. They produce *and* are productive of how we know and engage with the world—whether it is our relationship to the destination, to the unknown, to current events, or to the weather. Engaging with a map is a simultaneous and ongoing process of locating (asking, "Where am I?" or "How am I in relation to the world?"), and navigating (asking, "How do I move through this geography?").

In this chapter, we explore the process of mapping—or thinking *cartographically*—as a methodological and theoretical practice in qualitative inquiry, thought alongside interview methods. We ground our thinking of mapping and cartography in the philosophy of feminist critical materialist Rosi Braidotti, who advances cartographic thinking as an affirmative ethical response to our present configuration. More specifically, we ask: *What does thinking cartographically do to the concept of the interview? What does using cartography or mapping do for interpreting and representing qualitative data? And how has work using cartographic thinking or mapping been presented to research participants and audiences both in and beyond the academy?* In what follows, we first provide an overview of how mapping and cartography have been taken up in the field of qualitative inquiry, before turning specifically to the writing and theorization of cartography with Rosi Braidotti, and, finally, offering examples of cartography conceptualized as interview.

Mapping in Qualitative Inquiry

The field of critical geography has long explored the practice of cartography alongside questions of boundaries, power, scale, and knowledge. Critical geographers such as Doreen Massey (2005), David Harvey (2001), Edward Soja (1989, 2010), and Katherine McKittrick (2006, 2021) have questioned our changing relationship to place and space considering the globalizing effects of capitalism and the shifting discourses surrounding race, gender, and class. Additionally, in education, Helfenbein (2010) has explored critical cartography as a practice for thinking through scale in curriculum spaces,

> broad[ening] the lens of our analysis . . . [to] take multiple scales into account—from self, the local, and place to power, the global, and space—[which] offers an explicit privileging of agency in a changing world and an ability to include the speed and impact of late capitalism in the analysis. (p. 314)

Kuntz (2018) has extended this work to consider the practice of inquiry *as* cartography that "does not dwell in the representational—the goal is to map toward a future unknown; to newly create through cartographic practices" (p. 82). In this way, Kuntz highlights how cartography and mapping are not simply tools *for* inquiry; cartography can be tools *of* inquiry.

Drawing on conceptual and material conceptualizations of cartography generated through thinking geographically, other scholars in educational research have explored the narrative potential of cartography and mapping practices. For example, Gershon (2013) noted that "maps do not necessarily have to be . . . objective sets of factual information—maps tell stories" (p. 22). Gershon offers a methodology of "sonic cartography" to think with the layered discourses that permeate a space "between community and school, school and classroom, and classroom and students—between spaces, places, and identities" (p. 24). Gershon's work with sonic cartography has also been taken up by Wozolek in her exploration of schooling spaces (2018). In her study, Wozolek asked students to engage in a sonic mapping where they "walked around the school and collected sound files to tell a narrative [they] felt exemplified their experience in schooling.... Students then drew a map that served as an accompanying data point to their recordings" (2018, p. 371). Gershon and Wozolek both incorporate mapping and cartographic practices within interview studies and ethnographies, using the concept of cartography or mapping in data generation, analysis, and as a representational frame to think with the relations between bodies, discourses, places, spaces, and time.

Other scholars within the field of qualitative inquiry have thought with the concept of cartography. For example, an edited collection by Diana Masny (2013) brings together educational researchers thinking cartography with philosophers Deleuze and Guattari (1987). Many of the chapters take up cartography conceptually, considering how spaces and places are (un)made in classrooms (e.g., deFreitas, 2013; Perry, 2013), or fields of knowledge (e.g., Semetsky, 2013). Likewise, Wooten (2018) uses cartography as a concept to think with and through how academics of science education position themselves with/in relation to their fields of science teaching and learning. Finally, others such as Ulmer (2017) and Ulmer and Koro-Ljungberg (2015) explored multimodal methods of photography and writing as mapping practices that "welcome viewers to conduct their own analysis, critique, and interpretations. The data/knowledge domain then transfers back and forth between the map maker and map user, with the cartography itself as a conduit" (Ulmer & Koro-Ljungberg, 2015, p. 139). Throughout these examples, cartography and mapping, which we use synonymously in this chapter, function as both concept and method, taking up how we make maps, how we navigate, and how we locate ourselves alongside the material processes (creating and drawing) of these mapping practices.

Thinking Cartographically With Braidotti

A challenge of reviewing the literature on cartography and how it has been approached, operationalized, and conceptualized within qualitative inquiry is how "mapping" can take on many meanings, forms, and ideas—sometimes all at once. As previously noted, maps are both virtual and actual, simultaneously real and imagined, both process and product. In this chapter, we ground our thinking of cartography in the writing of the feminist, critical materialist Rosi Braidotti. Braidotti advances cartography as a material and conceptual practice that is an affirmative and ethical response to the present.

Braidotti (2019b) characterizes this present as the "posthuman condition" wherein "'we'—the human and non-human inhabitants of this particular planet—are currently positioned between the fourth industrial revolution and the sixth extinction" (p. 2). This positioning is fraught with contradictions—we are simultaneously more connected than ever before as a global community, while also finding ourselves individually helpless in the face of globalized issues such as climate change, endemic poverty, and pandemic disease. Braidotti (2019b) argues that

> we need to learn to address these contradictions not only intellectually, but also affectively and to do so in an affirmative manner. This conviction rests on the following ethical rule: it is important to be worthy of our times, the better to act upon them, in both a critical and a creative manner. (p. 3)

Braidotti offers nomadic ethics as a way to move forward affirmatively in the here-and-now. Nomadic ethics emphasizes what Braidotti (2013) described as a "triple shift" toward: (1) an ethics of transformation that rejects the rigidity of moral protocols and instead embraces discourses about "forces, desires, and values that act as empowering modes of becoming," (2) an ontology of process and relationality, away from "unitary and rationality-driven consciousness," and (3) toward a subjectivity of affirmative otherness—or a logic of *and* rather than a logic of *either/or* (p. 343). Nomadic ethics suggest an affirmative methodology and philosophy, oriented toward positive difference, following the connections and relations between bodies and materialities.

Braidotti offers nomadic ethics as a particular kind of cartographic thinking, a way of negotiating how "*we* are in *this* together" (2006, p. 136; emphasis in original). In other words, nomadic ethics offers a way of locating oneself on the map, as well as a means of navigating the cartography of our posthuman configuration. Thus, cartography, thought with Braidotti, is both a conceptual and methodological practice that is oriented toward affirmative ethics and experimentation, based in the politics of location. A cartography makes connections between multiple timescales, spaces, and subjectivities.

Method(ologically), a cartography is invested in charting how power produces knowledge and subjectivity (Braidotti, 2006; 2019a; 2019b) in the context of space and time. Mapping, then, is a methodological practice of how we negotiate and navigate these cartographies. Mapping practices a politics of location that begins with the asymmetrical, embodied and embedded, and negotiated identities of subjects-in-becoming. As Braidotti (2019b) writes, this begins with "composing a 'we' that is grounded, or accountable and active . . . construct[ing] affirmative ethical and political practices . . . through alliances, transversal connections and in engaging in difficult conversations on what troubles us" (p. 19). Braidotti theorizes power as both "entrapment (potestas) and as empowerment (potentia)" (Braidotti, 2019a, p. 35). Thus, cartographies are situated mappings of the present, with attention to the positive and negative forces, or potestas and potentia (Braidotti, 2006, p. 252), which has several implications, metaphorically and literally, for mapping as a qualitative method.

More specifically, we consider how mapping, thought with Braidotti, offers ways of thinking about qualitative interview methods and questions of representation of qualitative data. In what follows, we offer some examples from our work and the work of other qualitative scholars to consider the virtual and actual possibilities of cartographic thinking in relation to the qualitative interview.

Mapping as Collage—Maureen

In my (Maureen's) dissertation project, guided by Braidotti's concept of nomadism and cartography, I became interested in how I might think an interview (or focus group) as cartography. How might I enter an interview as a cartographic process? How might I provoke questions about the production of space and place and memory and belonging during or through the interview or focus group? I was interested in how maps might illustrate or even engender an acknowledgment of asymmetrical starting locations and the sense of relationality that Braidotti (2019b) described as "we are all in this together but we are not one and the same" (p. 52). As I moved through my project, my process moved from a process of map *marking*—locating, orienting (disorienting) toward map *making* (toward creativity, process, and flow). In what follows, I move through three different iterations of mapping that I engaged with in my dissertation, which explored how college students navigate the sociohistorical context of race on campus. These iterations follow a series of three focus groups conducted over the course of a year.

When facilitating my first focus group, in the fall of 2016, I brought physical, printed maps of the campus to the meeting. Methodologically, this approach was inspired by a desire to locate students in the space of campus through the use of provided maps, following research by human geographers such as Kwan (2008) and Kim (2015). Specifically, I provided the maps to students and asked them to mark spaces and places they felt connected to and to trace paths they frequently traveled.

These prefabricated maps engendered particular readings of the place and space of campus. For example, one student, Steve, talking about the predominance of football culture on campus, described the stadium as the "mothership," pointing to the symbol of the stadium on his map (Figure 5.1, location B11).

Figure 5.1. Steve's Marked Map of Campus.

Through this material-discursive movement, the oval shape of the stadium immediately became recognizable and readable as a flying saucer, leading to other associations and understandings of the culture of football on campus. The physical maps, even though they were the same for each student, provoked different kinds of readings, and even engagements with the materiality of the paper and the marks that described campus. These maps sparked moments of connection and orientation, as well as disorientation. Steve, for example, circled and then crossed out a building (located at F10 on Figure 5.1), noting as he did so that he had "mislocated himself." The printed map of campus, even though it was made to help readers locate themselves in the place of campus, also made the campus unfamiliar, hard to decipher; the height and smells and sounds and affects of buildings were reduced to geometric blocks on a page. The physical maps provoked questions about boundaries and locations, about orienting and disorienting. And at the same time, thinking with Braidotti, I found the prefabricated maps snagged at mapping as a theoretical process of creating openings. In other words, the students were bound to the map, its lines and boundaries and locations.

Thinking about this in the second focus group I conducted several weeks later, I moved away from physical maps to incorporate concepts of collaging. Collage, or the process of creating a composition from multimedia (photographs, magazine images, text, and other media), has been used by qualitative researchers as a conceptual tool to gather disparate perspectives, as a process of analysis or synthesis, and as a tool for inquiry (Hanawalt, 2019; Osei-Kofi, 2013). I provided students with materials from campus resources (admissions flyers and brochures, campus magazines for faculty and staff, recent student newspapers, and alumni materials) and asked them to "draw, write, or visually describe the place of campus." This mapping, via collage, offered different points of connection and created space.

By leaving off the physical maps, the representations students created moved beyond the boundaries of "what counted" as campus as described by the physical map. After they made their collages, I asked them to describe what they had made, and asked them to tell any stories about place that the mapping had provoked. In response, students began to tell stories about affective experiences, locating themselves within the space of campus, connecting them to embedded and embodied realities. One student, Skylar, talked about what it felt like to stand in the middle of the engineering quad, a circular, green space surrounded by huge, gray buildings fronted with massive colonnades. However, the materials provided also limited the possibility of what could be considered campus. Rather than being limited by physical boundaries or the unfamiliarity of shapes on the map, place was limited by the discursive potential of the campus materials. This is perhaps best illustrated in a map made by Ryan (Figure 5.2), which features a picture of Nick Saban, the university's head football coach at the time of the study, surrounded by cut-out words, including Hazing policy; Greek Life; Kinnucan's (a local store); and UAPD (University of Alabama Police Department).

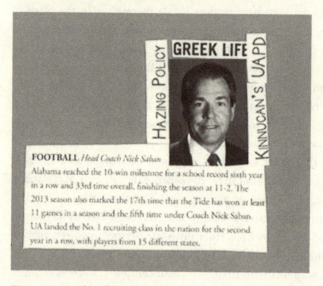

Figure 5.2. Ryan's Collage of Campus.

Rather than centering individual and personal stories, Ryan's map reproduced an image of campus told through the materials about student life in the brochures provided, centering football culture and fraternity and sorority life. We might wonder about the map Ryan would have made had the campus created materials, pictures, and phrases *not* guided or informed by how participants should think about campus. Would the interview and collages have literally centered football culture? I sat with these questions.

After leaving the focus group, I reflected on the narratives about the campus shared by students. The image of the university as produced through university materials limited and bound how students understood the production of campus. It also made me reflect on the prompt I had given students—how might their maps have been different had I asked them to critique the narratives they saw in the materials? To create counter-narratives to the place of campus? I questioned how I might provoke them to create new maps, to move beyond the maps produced for and by the campus.

Cartographic Accounts

Following these reflections, in the fall of 2017, as I facilitated focus groups for the second iteration of the study, I sought to merge the concept of mapping and collaging, asking students again to "draw, write, or visually map the place of campus, and the places and spaces they might highlight and the stories they might tell." I provided markers, glue sticks, and fashion and travel magazines. The shift in materials—away from promotional materials—and the reintroduction of the term "maps"—produced new kinds of creations. Specifically, I reflected in a memo afterward that these representations began to bridge the intents of marking maps and creating collages, *moving from marking maps to making them*. For example, Clark described her map as separated into boundaries, spaces of knowing and not knowing. Her map encompassed local knowledge and experiences, "*this is where I have most of my classes*," along with global understandings of place, "*the part that gets the most attention*." Likewise, as Leo described his map (Figure 5.3), he spoke back to what he described as the "straight line" of campus narratives, drawing curvy lines of the stories he would tell. The process of making the collaged map produces lines to other spaces and places, connections, and ruptures, enacting nomadism through dissolving generalizations toward micro-connections and transformations (Braidotti, 2006).

When I initially wrote about this series of maps in my dissertation in the spring of 2019, I presented them as a linear path, a path of making choices to become more "faithful" to my theoretical foundation (Flint, 2019). As I returned to these maps for this chapter, five years removed from the maps themselves, the maps and their stories have become infinitely more tangled, and my understandings of them are less easy. Continuing to think with the concept of cartography, I find I am no longer thinking about these earlier maps as "failures." Returning to these maps, along with the audio and transcripts of these focus groups, has challenged me to think about how each of these mappings offers particular knowledge of place—and through thinking about the process of mapping as productive and affirmative (rather than being disappointed that it did not produce the kinds of maps or stories I expected), I have opened up new kinds of questions about place and space and materiality and belonging. How might maps complicate our understandings of place and space through the process of interviewing? How might we explore the potentiality of multimodal materials used with interviews to create complicated and layered mappings of place? These questions are taken up by Morgan in the following section.

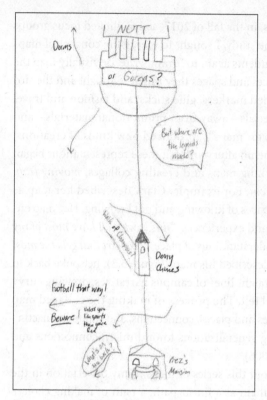

Figure 5.3. Leo's Campus Map.

Sonic Mapping—Morgan

Interviewing, from a humanist perspective, centers the voice of humans (Mazzei, 2013; Roulston, 2022). Braidotti's critical posthumanism attends to the more-than-human, bringing complexity to humanist notions of voice as sole authority in interviewing. Specifically, Braidotti's conceptualization of cartography challenges us to take "record of both what we are ceasing to be and what we are in the process of becoming" (Braidotti, 2019b, p. 37). In this context, "we" includes both human and more-than-human subjectivities. Therefore, using Braidotti's cartographic method as interview expands notions of interviewing to include the more-than-human by listening and hearing space and place. But what does it mean to listen and hear space and place? In the following section, I (Morgan) discuss how I cartographically interviewed the place of Ocoee, attending to space and place.

Cartographic Accounts

As noted earlier, a cartographic interview expands who and what can be interviewed. Thinking about mapping my (Morgan) own location, attending to limiting forces (potestas), and looking and listening for alternative, affirmative futures (potentia) (Braidotti, 2006), I think of Uwaga'hi, most commonly pronounced Oh-Co-Ee, a Cherokee Overhill settlement near the southwestern portion of the Appalachian Mountains (Schroedl, 2018). Uwaga'hi, what I will refer to as "Ocoee" as a White settler myself, is well known for its rumbling Ocoee River, deep from under the mountain, weaving its way across stones and ancient boulders, between rhododendron trees, through the leafy pine and oak gorge. The Ocoee River, which is currently dammed by the Tennessee Valley Authority (TVA), administered by the United States Forest Service (USFS), and commercialized by outdoor recreation, is a place and space I call home in the summertime and a place ripe to sonically map the present moment. (Listen here: https://bit.ly/OcoeeSoundscape).

Sitting on the bank, propped against a rock, watching bodies wander around the Ocoee Riverbed at the 1996 Olympics Slalom kayaking course, I pull out my phone and press the voice memo record button. I hear the sirens go off, a recorded voice bellows to leave the riverbed, as water is being released. The roar begins; I cannot see the water yet, but I know it is coming, and we—dogs, birds, humans, and other matter—all sit waiting for it. We are all listening, mapping our present moments as spectators on Cherokee land, awaiting the rubber rafts and rabble-rousers as they attempt to paddle through the dammed debris and turbine of rapids. The water sucks the rafts and people down and back, as the paddlers attempt to muscle forward, their guides yelling for more paddle strokes. My phone continues to record the sonic qualities of these material interactions, producing dialogue between the human and more-than-human.

Mapping these sounds offers a different way to know Ocoee and its material relations. Mapping Ocoee, guided by Braidotti's conception of a political reading of the present, I utilized Duffy and colleagues' (2016) visceral sonic mapping. Visceral sonic mapping focuses on the "gut" responses of participants (p. 52), particularly how space, bodies, and affect are interwoven. Attending to space, bodies, and affect allowed me to deconstruct the linearity of relation in mapping Ocoee. For instance, in the recording, there is the roar of the water, the voiceover, the crowd, the rafters, and a multiplicity of matter melding together, woven in a compilation of sonic resonance(s).

But practically, how does this visceral sonic mapping of sound function as an interview in qualitative research? I utilized voice memo technology on my phone to record the sonic qualities of Ocoee. Having spent a decade in this place, I had preconceived notions of what I would hear and include in this mapping. However, as Braidotti (2006; 2019b) notes throughout her works, cartography is a mapping of the *present*. Furthermore, Duffy and colleagues' (2016) visceral sonic mapping slowed my preconceptions of the sonic sensibility of Ocoee, as I listened and (re)listened. I spent days in the same spot by the Olympic slalom course. I began to chart the space and time, attending to bodies, producing a sound compilation through an audio software that attempted to evoke affects. I mixed, layered, spliced, and enhanced different parts of the sonic mappings with the audio software. Each choice allowed for some components of the sonic mapping (i.e., bodies) to be "seen," erasing or marginalizing other components (Rose, 2016). When I was (re)listening to recordings, I realized that my memory had (partially) failed me, reminding me of the infinite set of relations that are always already being constituted, in a flow, much like the river. This interview of Ocoee allowed the river and rocks to speak, to be heard. For instance, the beginning of the track sounds the damming of the water. Even after water is released, the river does not take its original course. The water moves between rocks, mediated by the engineering of the course (i.e., concrete). Humans have attempted to discipline it by moving rocks and pouring concrete. However, the water also acts on humans and other matter. Rafters count, stroke, pull, swim, fall—all of this choreography with the water, as the water exerts its own force, working with the rocks to create rapids. I came to sense this with my process for visceral sonic mapping, which included listening, recording, and more listening, as I was hearing the more-than-human offer its own account of Ocoee. Though I had intended to focus my attention on just the crowd, after several (re)listenings, the materiality of the performance of rafting began to affect me. Braidotti (2006) wrote that "... by mapping acoustically the shifts and mutations of intensities and multiplicities, rhizomic music replaces the Platonic ideal of harmony or the modernist representational model with [a] more daring quest for unlikely synchronizations with human and inhuman forces" (p. 261). In other words, within the context of using sound to map Ocoee, I found that attending to affect, bodies, and space (Duffy et al., 2016) together produced a different listening and hearing.

It was not just the verbal commands and crowd response, it was the assemblage: the intention of the commands/disciplining of rafters/paddles slicing (or not) through water/the rapids' responses to the counting, bodies, and boats/the history of the space. This sonic rendering made material some of the norms and expectations of the guide, customers, and viewers, each gathered in Ocoee for a variety of reasons. It also led me to think about which bodies get to be in this space presently, bringing up memories and the latent history of the space, producing hope, which I attend to next.

Conceptually, mapping with sound allowed difference to emerge in the interview of space and place in Ocoee. As noted earlier, Ocoee is a recreational space, where bodies can paddle and play, but the same bodies have not always and do not always have the opportunity to publicly paddle and play. This discrimination has a history across the United States (Winter et al., 2019). Based on my observations over the past decade, this space has primarily been the playground of White men, whether they be engineers on the dams, land managers for the NFS, or raft guides. However, I was able to map difference with sound. Many of the disciplining voices in the audio compilation belonged to women. Though the majority of the raft guides on the Ocoee are still men, attending to the sonic quality of space and bodies allowed me the opportunity to map different voices than the norm. For myself, this sonic mapping produced positive difference, as (re)listening opened my ears to the cracks in the foundations of a man-dominated space. For me, the qualitative affects produced promise of Otherwise—Otherwise being space for women in Ocoee again. Ocoee, predating Western colonization, always already had space for women, because women were not Other; they were spiritual and political leaders in their community (Perdue, 1998). Even after colonization, Cherokee women in the area resisted patriarchal notions of woman. For instance, Nanyehi, Anglicanized Nancy Ward, was a respected political leader and a Beloved Woman of the Cherokee Nation (McClary, 1962). Thus, listening to the voices of women, as leaders in Ocoee, reminded me that women always already lead in this space, though their political location has evolved with colonization and in the context of late-stage capitalism.

For instance, hearing women's voices, layered with the water roaring forth, produced a memory, a deep intensity of gratitude, a sense of relief, and speculation. How had my location as a photographer limited my ability to hear—even to see—the change, however slow, in the genderization of the space, of *which* bodies count? With my focus on capturing shots of customers, I had ignored the Others, human and more than human. Put differently, using sound to map Ocoee led me to engage with the partial histories told and the contingent presence of Other, as women and water were undammed in the sound map. Thus, sonically mapping produced meaning for Ocoee, opening up issues of gender, (re)mapping and (re)attaching womanness to the space. Hearing and seeing women in that space was powerful for me, and I wondered how it was empowering for customers and viewers. And as I sit with positive difference, I wonder about the many other potential ways to sonically map or interview Ocoee. What would it do to map the chirping of birds, the flapping of flags, the missing fish?

Other Mappings

In what follows, we offer additional examples of mapping to think with that take up different materials and concepts, before concluding with some considerations and future implications. In these examples, we continue to think how the concept of nomadic ethics and cartography might offer expansive readings of what constitutes an interview, and who can "speak" in an interview.

Mapping Linnentown, Georgia, through Quilting

Though you may envision a quilt as a static object on the end of your bed, the practice of quilting can be more than simply generating décor or producing warmth. It can be a practice of dialogue, a collective interview, both in its representation and creation. There is a long history of the practice of quilting that brings community members together in fellowship (Arellano, 2022; Brien, 2019). Quilting, the process of stitching together previously unconnected bits of fabric to form a whole, can produce a cartography that attends to geography, time, and space. An example that we highlight is the Linnentown Quilting Project. The purpose of this project was to story the experiences of Linnentown community members; we contend that it also maps the past's injustice on the present moment's call for reparations for Black people in Athens, Georgia. For instance, a grassroots movement for reparations for descendants of residents of Linnentown began with former Linnentown community members. They came together to (re)map Linnentown, a historically Black neighborhood and community that was forced to move from their homes in the 1960s due to eminent domain legislation and the influence of Athenian city officials and the University of Georgia (Whitehead, 2021). As a result of listening to former Linnentown resident Hattie Thomas Whitehead, art education graduate students Gabriella Victorio, Meghan Holcomb, and Sarah Livant organized a public quilting project to map memories and the present fight for reparations for Linnentown. People from across the community, including Linnentown residents, students, artists, and concerned stakeholders, constructed squares, stitching resistance, recollections, and history together. Each square produced a different piece of Linnentown, such as homes, people, congregations, and flowers—highlighting how the use of eminent domain to create dorms attempted to erase the community. This practice maps back to interviewing practices such as focus groups and collective biography. Through the process of dialoguing together, community members interview one another and the geography they inhabit. As Brien (2019) writes of her work on quilting, this work is "an example of how individuals can come together through craft and create deeper, lasting messages that can speak to researchers, collaborators and audiences in a multitude of ways" (p. 217). We find the quilt to be empowering, as its material highlights the beauty of the community, even as Linnentown members face roadblocks to recognition. This mapping is a public offering; it is an opportunity in the present to attend to the injustices of the past by stitching Black bodies back onto the map of Athens. We find that the quilt activates questions about qualitative interviewing such as: *What might a community-engaged interviewing practice look like? How might an interview move beyond text and voice to consider materials, objects, history, memories? How do we remember and through what mediums are our memories activated?* You can follow their current work on Instagram @linnentownquiltproject or learn more at redressforlinnentown.com

Wang's Linguistic Mapping through Online Reviews

Yixuan Wang's (2022) scholarship has linguistically mapped experiences, specifically customer experiences and store products and services, with three

Asian grocery stores (Achachi International Market, Fooks Foods, and Orient Mart) in Athens, Georgia, since 2019. Wang utilized Google Maps on Padlet, a web platform that allows users to create bulletin boards, to share her research and create space and conversation with the public, offering an omnidirectional and asynchronous approach to interviewing. She draws on posted reviews of grocery stores and reflections of her own experience visiting these stores to interrogate intersections of place, race, and culture. Wang's Padlet is a satellite map of Athens, Georgia, with pins that direct the viewer to other Padlet pages that include a presentation on the research, the customer experiences, and images of dishes and cooking. This asynchronous interview creates a mapping of a linguistic landscape, highlighting how insiders and outsiders conceive and relate to these grocery spaces. For example, a customer noted that they appreciated halal meat at a grocery. Another customer was miffed that an American flag was "upside down." Both reviews help to qualitatively map the clientele and their relations to the stores.

Wang's work maps the qualitative *relationship* of food, services, and people. Wang's work cartographically accounts for power, both in its limiting (i.e., xenophobia) and generative (i.e., belonging) abilities, as she attends to what the Asian grocery stores offer the Athens community, which includes a multitude of peoples who may identify as Asian, Asian American, and Pacific Islander (AAPI), or do not identify ethnically at all. Wang also includes pictures of her cooking with the food purchased at the stores. The inclusion of these images alongside the customer reviews is a cartographic practice of activating "spaces where alternative forms of agency can be engendered" (Braidotti, 1994, p. 26). Wang's work also invites the public to participate by commenting and sharing their experiences shopping at these Asian groceries, offering future mappings of relations with and made by the Asian groceries. Wang's work, then, opens up the interview to consider the community, the self, and the viewer as participants in the production of knowledge. Wang's work inspires questions about qualitative interviewing such as: *How might researchers engage in ongoing dialogue with their research sites, participants, or topics? What (beyond the human) might "speak" in an interview?* The reader can interact with Wang's work here: https://padlet.com/yxwang410/13c3u6l5othv65w3

Cartographic Accounts

Li's Mapping of the Suzhou Classical Gardens with Google Maps and Baidu Map

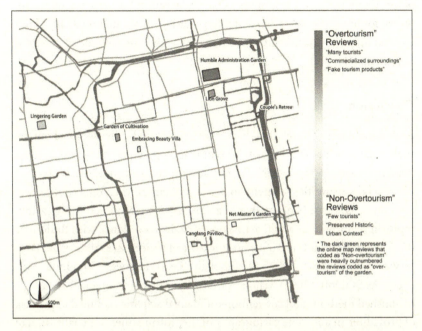

Figure 5.4. Map of the GUSU Historic District, which encompasses the old city of Suzhou.

Jingxian Li's research utilizes Google Map reviews, a web-based platform that allows users to leave responses about place, as well as Baidu Map, a similar Chinese platform, to map encounters with the Suzhou Classical Gardens in Jiangsu, China, to explore tourists' experience regarding overtourism in the gardens. Specifically, Li coded the map reviews indexing overtourism based on tourists' experiences. The map offers generative space to question who takes up space, where people take up space, and why people take up space. For example, Li's (Li et al., 2021) geo-spatial mapping makes visible frequencies, offering important implications for issues of heritage preservation. In the context of environmental design and public policy, Li's qualitative mapping offers insights that could lead to more sustainable futures.

In turn, Li's scholarship also inspired us to think about mapping's implications with interviewing. Qualitatively, Li's work with mapping reviews could be put to work in interviewing by asking participants in a research study about their own politics of location. *What places are they frequenting? What is that locating doing/producing for them? How is power at play in this space/place?* Using interview responses as data generation for mapping offers potential for both representation and interpretation, as another qualitative layer beyond interview transcription, as it makes visible the embedded locations of participants.

Conclusion

As you wandered through this chapter with us, nomadically weaving between the virtual and the actual possibilities of mapping in qualitative research, we hope that cartography—whether a physical process or conceptual tool—may offer you opportunities to attend to power and ethics when interviewing. We offer one final consideration: that of goodness or quality when using cartography in relation to qualitative interviewing. In accordance with Braidotti's thinking, there is and cannot be one measure of goodness, as that would be in service to a majoritarian regime of thought (i.e., Whiteness) (Braidotti, 2002, 2006). As Braidotti (2006) writes: "A trans-disciplinary approach that cuts the established methods and conventions of many disciplines is suited to the task of providing an adequate cartography of the shifting lines of racialization of the global labour market" (p. 61). Rather, Braidotti is invested in becoming minor, mapping anew. Goodness or the idea of quality, particularly in the context of mapping as interviewing, is determined by its ability to affirmatively attune to the processes of the interview. With Braidotti, qualitative researchers might ask: *Who-are-we-in-this-[interview]-together-when-we-are-not-one and-the-same?* Likewise, thinking cartographically means continually attending to power and potential, asking how knowledge is produced, how power circulates, how we relate to one another. These questions offer a way of living affirmatively in the present rather than a checkbox of ethical choices to make, or a predetermined set of steps to follow to produce "good" research.

Whether you are leading a walking interview on campus, analyzing reviews of Asian groceries, or mapping frequency in a garden, we offer cartography as a qualitative method(ology) that can question how to live (more) ethically in the present moment. In this way, the interview is not foreclosed as a method; instead, a cartographic iteration of the interview opens a critical conversation on who and what can speak. This has implications for considerations of voice and representation in interview and qualitive research. Therefore, thinking with Braidotti, for us, offered a reconsideration of what a qualitative interview is and what it might offer to research.

References

Arellano, S. C. (2022). Quilting as a qualitative, feminist research method: Expanding understandings of migrant deaths. *Rhetoric Review, 41*(1), 17–30.

Braidotti, R. (1994). *Nomadic subjects: Embodiment and sexual difference in contemporary feminist theory.* Columbia University Press

Braidotti, R. (2002). *Metamorphoses: Towards a materialist theory of becoming.* Polity.

Braidotti, R. (2006). *Transpositions: On nomadic ethics.* Polity Press.

Braidotti, R. (2013). Nomadic Ethics. *Deleuze Studies, 7*(3), 342–359.

Braidotti, R. (2019a). A theoretical framework for the critical posthumanities. *Theory, Culture & Society, 36*(6), 31–61.

Braidotti, R. (2019b). *Posthuman knowledge.* Polity Press.

Brien, J. (2019). Stitchery me, stitchery do. *Art/Research International: A Transdisciplinary Journal, 4*(1), 200–221.

deFreitas, E. (2013). Mapping the materiality of classroom discourse: Expression and content in school mathematics. In D. Masny (Ed.), *Cartographies of becoming in education: A Deleuze-Guattari perspective* (pp. 127–140). Sense Publishers.

Deleuze, G., & Guattari, F. (1987). *A thousand plateaus: Capitalism and schizophrenia.* (B. Massumi, Trans.). University of Minnesota Press.

Duffy, M., Waitt, G., & Harada, T. (2016). Making sense of sound: Visceral sonic mapping as a research tool. *Emotion, Space and Society, 20*, 49–57.

Flint, M. A. (2019). *Methodological orientations: College student navigations of race and place in higher education* (Publication No. 2241659855) [Doctoral dissertation, University of Alabama]. ProQuest Dissertations & Theses Global.

Gershon, W. S. (2013). Sonic cartography: Mapping space, place, race, and identity in an urban middle school. *Taboo*, 21–45. https://doi.org/10.31390/taboo.13.1.04

Hanawalt, C. (2019). At the threshold of experience: Encountering new art teachers through research as collage. *Visual Arts Research, 45*(2), 8–28.

Harvey, D. (2001). *Spaces of capital: Towards a critical geography.* Routledge.

Helfenbein, R. (2010). Thinking through scale: Critical geography and curriculum spaces. In E. Malewski (Ed.), *Curriculum studies handbook: The next moment* (pp. 304–321). Routledge.

Kim, A. (2015). Critical cartography 2.0: From "participatory mapping" to authored visualizations of power and people. *Landscape and Urban Planning, 142*, 215–225.

Kuntz, A. M. (2018). *Qualitative inquiry, cartography, and the promise of material change.* Routledge.

Kwan, M. P. (2008). From oral histories to visual narratives: Re-presenting the post-September 11 experiences of the Muslim women in the USA. *Social & Cultural Geography, 9*(6), 653–669.

Li, J., MacDonald, E., & Boley, B. (2021, March 17–20). A site-level overtourism risk assessment tool of the Classical Gardens of Suzhou UNESCO World Heritage Site. *Council of Educators in Landscape Architecture 2021 Annual Conference*. [virtual]

Masny, D. (Ed.). (2013). *Cartographies of becoming in education: A Deleuze-Guattari perspective*. Brill.

Massey, D. (2005). *For space*. SAGE.

Mazzei, L. A. (2013). A voice without organs: Interviewing in posthumanist research. *International Journal of Qualitative Studies in Education, 26*(6), 732–740. https://doi.org/10.1080/0 9518398.2013.788761

McClary, B. H. (1962). Nancy Ward: The last beloved woman of the Cherokees. *Tennessee Historical Quarterly, 21*(4), 352–364.

McKittrick, K. (2006). *Demonic grounds: Black women and the cartographies of struggle*. University of Minnesota Press.

McKittrick, K. (2021). *Dear science and other stories*. Duke University Press.

Osei-Kofi, N. (2013). The emancipatory potential of arts-based research for social justice. *Equity & Excellence in Education, 46*(1), 135–149.

Perdue, T. (1998). *Cherokee women: Gender and culture change, 1700–1835*. University of Nebraska Press.

Perry, M. (2013). Devising theater and consenting bodies in the classroom. In D. Masny (Ed.), *Cartographies of becoming in education: A Deleuze-Guattari perspective* (pp. 93–108). Sense Publishers.

Rose, G. (2016). *Visual methodologies: An introduction to researching with visual materials*. Sage.

Roulston, K. (2022). Bursting forth: Attending to the more-than-human in qualitative research. In N. K. Denzin & M. Giardina (Eds.), *Transformative visions for qualitative inquiry* (pp. 65–84). Routledge.

Schroedl, G. (2018). Overhill Cherokees. In G. Schroedl (Ed.), *Tennessee Encyclopedia*. Tennessee Historical Society. http://tennesseeencyclopedia.net/entries/overhill-cherokees/

Semetsky, I. (2013). Learning with bodymind: Constructing the cartographies of the unthought. In D. Masny (Ed.), *Cartographies of becoming in education: A Deleuze-Guattari perspective* (pp. 77–91). Sense Publishers.

Soja, E. J. (1989). *Postmodern geographies: The reassertion of space in critical social theory*. New Left Books.

Soja, E. J. (2010). *Seeking spatial justice*. University of Minnesota Press.

Ulmer, J. B. (2017). Writing urban space: Street art, democracy, and photographic cartography. *Cultural Studies ↔ Critical Methodologies, 17*(6), 491–502.

Ulmer, J. B., & Koro-Ljungberg, M. (2015). Writing visually through (methodological) events and cartography. *Qualitative Inquiry, 21*(2), 138–152.

Wang, Y. (2022, April 21–26). "Welcome," "Thank you," and "Come again" [Virtual structured poster session]. American Educational Research Association 2022 Convention. San Diego, CA.

Whitehead, H. T. (2021). *Giving voice to Linnentown*. Tiny Tots & Tikes, LLC.

Winter, P. L., Crano, W. D., Basáñez, T., & Lamb, C. S. (2019). Equity in access to outdoor recreation—Informing a sustainable future. *Sustainability, 12*(1), 124.

Wooten, M. (2018). A cartographic approach toward the study of academics of science teaching and learning research practices and values. *Canadian Journal of Science Mathematics and Technology Education, 18*, 210–221. https://doi.org/10.1007/s42330-018-0029-9

Wozolek, B. (2018). In 8100 Again: The sounds of students breaking. *Educational Studies, 54*(4), 367–381. https://doi.org/10.1080/00131946.2018.1473869

SIX

 Intra-Action is For Everybody! (Re)Thinking the Qualitative Interview

Travis M. Marn and Jennifer R. Wolgemuth

IN THIS CHAPTER WE DESCRIBE how the concept of *intra-action* (Barad, 2007) shapes our conceptualization of the interview method. We consider how intra-action prompts us to examine everything we have taken for granted in research, as researchers, as interviewers, and as scholars. It attunes us to a world that is much more than "human" (Braidotti, 2013). We think through these issues in this chapter through a rhapsodic styling to show that we, as scholars, and the interview itself are not still, static, unchanging. Rather, we show that we are active agents always already in flux, and our relationship to the interview is likewise in a constant state of change. These changes to our relationship with the interview have not always been pleasant or welcome, causing us to fall in and out of "love" with the interview method. We present below our "love story" to show that while this chapter is explicitly new materialist, the insights offered by intra-action are for all scholars as they grapple with the interview method.

Intra-Action: A (Brief) Primer

Intra-action is a concept within Karen Barad's (2007) larger project of *agential realism*, a dominant framework within the new materialism constellation. This framework contends that matter and discourse are not separate but rather mutually constitutive. Agential realism enables an "understanding of the role of human and nonhuman, material and discursive, and natural and cultural factors in scientific and other social-material practices" (2007, p. 26). Agential realism focuses on the material-discursivity of phenomena, holding that human and non-human (material) agency are both mutually produced in *intra-actions*. This clever neologism distinguishes itself from the more common word "interaction"—interaction is the belief that two elements brought in proximity are wholly separate from each other and devoid of connection beyond their meeting. Intra-action is the acknowledgment that no elements are disconnected from each other—that all agents are in an entangled state long before any proximate meeting. For example, Western discourses, science culture, capitalism, popular culture, and globalism are always active on various agents, and, as such, these agents are not truly separate; they act within an entangled state; they intra-act rather than interact.

This is a significant insight for the interview process. It means, for example, that interviewer and interviewee are entangled with each other long before any data collection occurs. Interviewers and researchers typically share common languages, knowledge of social discourses, and exist within similar or the same social worlds. In this way, intra-action demands that we examine the interview process from this mutually entangled state—that scholars are constantly intra-acting with the interview process long before any study even begins to be planned. It is through the intra-action of co-constituting material and discursive elements that meaning and material arise. That is, any "truth" and "matter" of people and things do not precede the intra-action, but are made possible within it (Kuntz, 2015). In (qualitative social) science, this means that research processes and outcomes are entangled—neither can be "known" or "experienced" without the other. Through Barad (2007), a research study is best thought of as an apparatus—a boundary-making force in which materials and discourses intra-act, are (in)separable and (un)knowable, what Barad terms "agential cuts." These boundaries mark what is possible and impossible in the research process, "what matters and what is excluded from mattering" (p. 148). For example, "the researcher" and "the participant" do not precede interviews in any natural way. Rather, these positions are the result of agential cuts. They become available, performable, intelligible within the interview intra-action, but at the same time are always intra-acting with other, mutually constitutive interview elements: setting, design, interview guide, recorders, bodies, and so on.

It is with/toward this understanding of intra-action that we write this chapter. We seek to show that intra-action transcends the moments between participant and researcher—that intra-action occurs before planning an interview study, during data collection, during data analysis, and even in the consideration of what it means to ethically conduct an interview. Our "love" stories are, then, how we have accounted here for our constant intra-action with the interview method—how at times the method has seemed vital and full of possibilities, while other times it seemed intrusive and voyeuristic, even tyrannical (see, for example, Barlott et al., 2020). We offer these stories in hopes of demonstrating that intra-action is always already in process, and rather than run from these intra-actions, we embrace them as necessary to evolve our (mis)use of the interview method.

Love Story 1

Good books find you. Kathy Roulston (2010) wrote an excellent book on interviewing that I didn't know about until I interviewed for my current position at USF. (I love my job.) One of the search committee members mentioned the book, Reflective Interviewing, *and pointed out that I was cited in it. Glee! A prominent scholar at a top university . . . took me seriously! Good books find you through good people. Librarians know this, of course. Connecting people to texts is caring, made possible by both knowing and appreciating someone. Barad's* Meeting the Universe Halfway *met me this way, too. "You would love Barad," said colleagues (friends, companions, scholars, workout buddies). If I would love Barad, then surely Travis, a doctoral student with a penchant for theory, would, too. A gift! To read, digest, discuss, and build a collective (mis)understanding of new (to us) theory was exciting. Digging into a new theory, a new text, a new way of theorizing the interview—introduced and supported by people who know and appreciate you—rocks your world (Bridges-Rhoads et al., 2018) . . . it's almost like falling in love.*

A Theory (love) Story . . .

Falling in "love" with the interview method was seemingly easy—it offered us the means by which we could become scholars, the method of our dissertations, something to learn and "master"—the method for our stock-in-trade; we enthusiastically pored over methodological texts and were "seduced" (Wolgemuth & Marn, 2022) by the revelatory "power" of the interview method. The "romance" (Roulston, 2010) with interviewing was intense, like the thrill of discovering for the first time something others had long known. Staying in love has proven more difficult. The "romantic" interview style views the subject as stable and knowable (2010), as something to understand and be understood in turn. It was easy to fall in "love" with the narratives, the stories the interview elicited. As the concept of intra-action seeped into us, these "romantic" notions were tested. Like all love stories, like all those that pursue the thing they cannot not want, our relationship with the interview did not remain static. As we continued to intra-act with the interview method, we experienced the exaltation of new possibilities and the disappointment of failure—seemingly falling in and out of love with the interview.

This somewhat/largely tongue-in-cheek description of our becoming-with the interview, our "love" story, is a lighthearted way to look at the long years spent in graduate school, in the "publish or perish" fire, dealing with the COVID-19 lockdowns, Black Lives Matter protests, and the always-already uncertainty of the future. We do not "love" the interview, but perhaps we are enamored by it, compelled by the possibilities it offers—a way to "play" with fraught concepts and feelings (Wolgemuth et al., 2018). The interview method has been vital to us as researchers, teachers, and in our very becomings—a way to understand the world, a method to discovering things important. And yet we have doubted the need for the interview in the world at times, been driven to think that what the world needs is not prolonged conversations in quiet rooms but something else—perhaps something unknowable so long as we remain in "love" with the interview. Our "love" story is an affective way to analyze our intra-activity with the interview, the intra-activity with our use of it, and the intra-activity that precedes our story and what may happen subsequent to it.

You Make Me Feel Brand New (Materialism)

Call it an "old" materialist, pragmatic, maybe a somewhat anti-theoretical and anti-ideological impulse, or even middle age. Whatever the label, we (once again) find ourselves confronted by a world begging for new perspectives, a world that is/feels vastly different from the one we inhabited when we giddily read Barad in 2015. We've written that post-structuralism's radical uncertainty, for example, may be inadequate for moving qualitative researchers toward justice in anti-democratic times (Wolgemuth et al., 2022). More broadly, we worry that our readings, training, philosophies are failing us entirely (Van Cleave et al., 2022). Maybe they always will. At the same time, of course, we cannot (or maybe do not want to) turn our backs on theories, methods, and theorists that made us, and continue to make us. What we can (and want to) do is repurpose them, render them practical, useful, helpful to meet the demands of inquiry—now. And what we see in the now is a world that expects more from us. We live in precarious times that demand capacious thinking and caring (Care Collective, 2020); in a world that screams us off our ideological "high horses" (Killam, 2022); an apocalyptic world that cannot be inquired into without creative, responsible, fluid methodologies (Koro & Wolgemuth, 2021). Maybe we cannot return to romantic notions of the interview, but we can certainly appreciate that many, many interview approaches and theorizations are required. We continue to explore Barad's insights not because we advocate a Baradian revolution in interview research. Rather, we do so because we have found and expect that Barad's theories have something to offer interviewing *in general*, no matter how theorized, and help us to an account of interviewing that is responsive and responsible to contemporary demands that our inquiries (and interviews) matter.

So, in this chapter, we think through the qualitative interview method using Barad's (2007) concept of intra-action, providing examples along the way that demonstrate its broad remit (mattering). We analyze the interview method through the concept of intra-action to examine, re-examine, and articulate differently processes of generating knowledge through interview methods and through our affective "love" story with interviewing. We examine how participants and interviewers intra-actively reconfigure the interview space, explore how researchers intra-act with the resulting interview data and similarly reconfigure that data, and showcase the possibilities afforded by conceptualizing the interview as an intra-action. The purpose of this chapter, then, is to demonstrate how the interview method is not simply a preexisting set of procedures, but rather a constantly evolving sea of possibilities—that each interview intra-action renders possible novel ways of being, thinking, and doing *in* the interview process. We do not reject "romantic" (interpretivist, humanist) interview methods but, through the purposeful lens of intra-action, we do employ them differently. In doing so we suggest that thinking with intra-action may inspire new possibilities for the generation of knowledge about human experience as enmeshed with the things and ideas, the processes and products of research, and for which the researcher is more keenly responsible. We show that no matter the philosophical orientation researchers adopt for their broader inquiries, insights made available by thinking of the interview as intra-action are widely insightful and broadly applicable—intra-action, in this sense, is for every(interview)body in qualitative research.

Key Interview Intra-Actions

While intra-actions do not simply start and stop, for the interview method some key interactions yearn to be accounted for. An intra-active analysis of the interview must examine the materiality of the interview and the specific arrangements of that materiality. Whenever possible, these arrangements should not be accidents but rather purposefully (Marn & Wolgemuth, 2017) accounted for and articulated together. The materiality of the interview is a principal element to any intra-active analysis, and we will describe three common agents in any interview: participant and researcher bodies, the interview materiality, and the interview phenomenon.

Bodies

The interview is a space wherein bodies are brought into proximity—whether virtually or physically, the body is an inescapable, essential, and active agent within the interview space. The researcher "body," the "researched" "body," and coming into being "researcher-researched" body all serve to iteratively intra-act in the interview space (Marn & Wolgemuth, 2020), producing effects not readily understood. Bodies are produced by discourses and are themselves refusals of other discourses (Butler, 1993, 1997)—the "male" body, the "female" body, the "trans" body, the "queer" body, the bodies "of color," all instantiations of certain discourses and degrees of disavowals of others.

Physically, materially, the body is a stylization of discourses—a way to make itself intelligible as a "type" of body (Butler, 1993). For example, a "biracial" individual may wear certain kinds of clothing associated with White culture, cut their hair, and employ language to be performatively recognized as White (Marn, 2018). In the interview, this materiality is a prime site of analysis and intra-acts with the body-materiality of the researcher to affect the interview space itself. The researcher, similarly embodied and performative, intra-acts with the participant's body enacting agential cuts (Barad, 2007) that reshape the interview process. Taking the previous example further, "biracial" participants could assume a researcher to also be "biracial" based on their body (e.g., curly hair, light brown skin). This could have the effect of participants more readily performing a "biracial" identity if they assume the researcher to be "biracial," and this could further render impossible monoracial "White" or "Black" identity performances (Marn, 2018). This intra-action would likely be different if the researcher had a "White" body and performed a White identity in the interview. This material-discursive intra-activity is then always-already implicated in the interview data—two different researcher bodies intra-acting with the "same" participant body produce two different datasets. Bodies and their intra-activity must be conserved and analyzed together with the data, transcripts, and memory (Marn & Wolgemuth, 2021). Analyses without taking bodies into consideration are partial, decontextualized, and far less revealing of the discourses that drive interviewing and the social world.

The meaning of a "body" can also shift radically; for example, the ongoing COVID-19 pandemic has produced bodies as pestilential, vulnerable, and under siege. Conducting an in-person interview now carries new risks to both participant and researcher. The COVID-19 pandemic could even call into question the separateness of bodies—that "health" is no longer a strictly personal, individuated matter but dependent on the bodies of all people. Other social and material changes similarly alter discourses of the body—the body is never just one thing (Mol, 2002). These social and discursive alterations of the body demonstrate that bodies are not static but active agents reconfiguring what is possible, knowable, thinkable in the interview process.

(Out Of) Love Story 2

I asked her, as I did with all my "Black-White" biracial participants, about "interactions" with the "Black" side of her family. She tried talking but just started sobbing. She told me through tears that her father told her directly that she was "not Black enough." I stopped the recording. She asked if I had encountered the "not Black enough" sentiment. I told her I had and have had similar feelings to her. I got her tissues and attempted to console her, my "researcher" persona shattering, giving way to my "biracial" performativity. She insisted that she could pull it together and continue the interview. I had misgivings and told her that we could stop at any time. It was not long before I ended the interview. The interview method did not feel like some passive form of data collection, but rather it felt vulgar and voyeuristic—my study was IRB approved and under the supervision of professors, but that seemed little comfort in that moment. My "biracial" researcher intra-acted with my participant's "biracial" body to instantiate discourses of "not enoughness" common in biracial experiences (Marn, 2018). It felt like I leveraged this intra-activity without realizing it could enable my participants to revivify these unpleasant discourses and memories. The interview felt like something for my benefit at the expense of my participants.

Interview Materials and Space

Just as bodies intra-act in the interview space, other materiality is likewise an active agent within the interview process. This materiality includes computers, questionnaires, pictures, or videos brought to the interview, documents, and any other element that alters the boundaries of the interview. For example, Nordstrom (2015) analyzed how recording devices intra-actively reconfigure the "data" they collect and directly affect the interview process—that "recording devices never were innocent and mute tools that can be taken for granted" (p. 397). Recording devices then need to be analyzed through their agency and intra-activity; for example, participants know they are being recorded, and the material presence of a recording device may lead them to espouse socially desirable sentiments rather than what they might possibly say absent the materiality of the recording device. The intra-activity of the recording device leaves lasting marks on the interview data that must be conserved in any analysis.

Each material-discursive intra-action leaves entangled traces during the interview that offer pathways for analysis—no interview materials can be simply discarded or ignored without careful consideration. The interview setting itself, a quiet room in a university building, a walk on campus, a noisy coffee shop, all intra-actively reconfigure what is possible in each interview moment—setting plays a power role in the intra-activity in each moment (Aagaard & Matthiesen, 2016). These materials intra-act with bodies and all other kinds of materialities in ways that are not always easy to see or analyze. While seemingly a daunting task, researchers must carefully attend to material agents and analyze their intra-activity within the interview process.

The Purposeful Use of Intra-Action in the Interview

While intra-action is always occurring, it is possible for interviewers to leverage this to fuel their interviews and enact desired material-discursive intra-actions. Researchers can plan these desired intra-actions in advance to potentially produce effects within the interview. The material-discursive configuration of the interview, the interview "phenomenon" (Barad, 2007), is mutable and, to some extent, purposefully controllable—researchers can largely select the materiality present in the interview phenomenon and plan alterations to that materiality. We will describe how we have used the concepts of agential cuts and the "hailing" of subjects as ways to purposefully employ intra-action in the interview.

While not the sole agent in the interview, the researcher has the capacity to predict (Manning, 2016) the potential outcomes of intra-activity with materials during the interview; while seemingly complex, this ability to predict relies on careful consideration and familiarity with the discourses at hand more than extensive introspection skills or other esoterica. For example, Latour (2005) suggested that adding a speed bump to a road will slow traffic—that is not to say that every driver would be slowed by a speed bump, but rather that the vast majority of drivers would not risk damage to their vehicle by ignoring the materiality of the speed bump. While not every material-discursive intra-activity would be so simple to predict, especially in an interview setting, prediction need not be perfect to be useful.

Intra-active materiality can be altered during the interview process. These changes reshape the boundaries of the interview phenomenon and enact what Barad (2007) termed "agential cuts." These agential cuts mark the changes between different material-discursive configurations and intra-activity. As in the previous example, the presence or absence of a speed bump will alter the driving conditions on that road—the presence of the speed bump would likely have the effect of both slowing drivers and cueing them that there may be a reason why traffic needed to be slowed on that road (e.g., a nearby school, unsafe road conditions). The addition of the speed bump marks a reconfiguration of what is possible on that road. As in the interview, enacting agential cuts will likewise reshape what is intra-actively possible in the phenomenon as they cue certain discourses.

Introducing computer programs and questionnaires, altering the "interview style" (Roulston, 2010), changing interviewer vocabulary, and other material alterations will reconfigure the interview space through agential cuts (Marn, 2018). These agential cuts may enable interviewees to draw upon novel discourses during the interview and prevent the use of others. These changes offer researchers insight into the process by which intra-activity functions in social settings, as well as investigative space for analyzing how and why these material alterations produced these effects—what the materiality rendered possible or impossible.

While material-discursive intra-activity is itself a productive space of analysis for any topic, researchers can further leverage intra-activity to instantiate certain desired identity performances. Identities are not latent elements of an individual; rather, they are a series of gestures and signs termed "performativity" (Butler, 1990; 1993; 1997). Identity is then material-discursively produced (Chow, 2010) rather than something one simply "has" (Foucault, 1995). Researchers can use this intra-activity to attempt to prompt or "hail" (Butler, 1997) identities into being. This seemingly complex process, similar to the above speed bump example, relies on the same material-discursive intuition as previously described. For example, "Black–White" biracial individuals can rapidly shift between "Black," "White," and "biracial" identity performances during an interview (Marn & Wolgemuth, 2020). In order to examine these identity performances individually or serially, researchers can enact agential cuts (e.g., employing questionnaires on identity) to hail particular identity performances and thwart others. These hailed identities intra-act with the interviewer and interview phenomenon as new avenues for investigating identity. Intra-activity is not simply something that happens, but is rather something sought, courted, and partially directed by researchers in the interview settings.

Love Story 3

One of my participants sent me an email and thanked me for letting them participate in my interviews—I felt I should be thanking them. She then said that I "changed her life." As a teacher, I had heard those words before, but I had yet to hear them as a researcher. I had intended to change my participants with my interviews—I had hoped our intra-actions would leave them with, to my belief, a better understanding of race in the United States. I purposefully choose the intra-active tools, the interview materiality, the agential cuts to hail the racialised subjects and then provide my participants with the tools and language to deconstruct them. It worked. Beyond anything I had ever felt in research, the interviews succeeded (to whatever degree) in reshaping my participants through intra-action as they themselves reshaped me through those same intra-actions. Interviews felt powerful again, a source of emancipation, a source of change, something beyond a purely academic, staid, publish-or-perish affair. My love for the interview never burned brighter.

The Intra-Active Interview Refrains, Reframes, Rewrites

Theory undermines taken-for-granted assumptions, destroys world(view)s, and ruins us (Marn & Guyotte, 2022). Theory makes things (un)thinkable and lives (un)livable (Butler, 1997). Theory matters. It matters what matters we use to think matters with (Haraway, 2016). And this is why, when we read Karen Barad's (2007) *Meeting the Universe Halfway* together seven years ago, whatever "romantic" (Roulston, 2010) notions we may have (still) held about

- the natural separation of interview researcher and participant
- the truth(iness) of interview data
- the neutrality of interview spaces, encounters
- our ability to gather data about and represent people's experiences
- what it meant to do good (ethical, quality) research

were entirely undone, available perhaps only as useful, if naive, fantasies. Theory can carry you away, but it dumps you somewhere. And here we are, again, wrestling with intra-action, the interview, and ourselves. Such is our refrain.

What is clear is that intra-activity demands we reframe how we conceive concepts underpinning the interview. When the interview is an intra-action, ethics, truth, subjects, and . . . are deterritorialized, reconstituted. Barad uses the term *ontoethicoepistemology* to make the point (possible). Responsibility, truth, and reality are co-constituted in the interview. We are responsible for the worlds we make manifest, including what we can "know" about and do with those worlds, within interview encounters. In this way *ethics* cannot be fully predetermined—both what constitutes an ethical dilemma (e.g., a participant cries) and whatever might be a right thing to do (e.g., stop recorder, hand participant a tissue) emerges within the interview intra-action, often in aporetic moments when the "right" thing to do is not obvious (Koro-Ljungberg,

2010). Researcher responsibility is not given, but emerges as response-ability (Haraway, 2016), ethical sensitivity, becoming-with, collective responsibility for rendering one another capable. Response-ability means it matters how researchers theorize and act within the interview, theorize and ask questions, theorize and configure the interview spacetime, theorize and assemble resources required to conduct the interview. *Truth* is also something that cannot be predetermined or understood as something separate from the interview. Truth is intra-active, a product of the interview, as opposed to something the interview might un/discover. What is possible to know, what counts as knowing, what constitutes "voice" (Mazzei, 2013), what is included or excluded from mattering as knowledge (or data) all emerge within the interview. Interview *subjects* similarly do not "exist" outside the interview—rather the interview hails subjects, and cooperative participants embody/perform them. Other subjects and materials intra-act in interviews to make the embodied performances possible—the recording device signals the start and end of the performance, questions asked focus the performance, the interviewer and interviewee subjects contain the performance and make clear its boundaries and expected responses. The interview, as such, is an accomplishment—it produces truth and reality to and within which the researcher is response-able.

This reframe of the interview has many implications we think are important, regardless of the extent to which researchers share our passion for intra-action, our love of the interview. If truth, reality, and ethics are all a product of the interview intra-action, then what happens in interviews, how the researcher theorizes the interview, and how the research does ethics within the interview all matter (greatly) to understanding how the interview generated data. As Barad (2007) articulates, the details of the research (interview) apparatus—the inputs, outputs, configurations—should be described in vivid detail. As methodologists and methodological scholars, it is probably no surprise that we would advocate for more attention and space to be given to describing and theorizing methods. Our entangled experiences (born from our theories, methodologies, methods, scholarship, teaching, desires to remain relevant and employed, and . . .) confirm for us that methods and methodologies matter (a lot, for everyone). Through Barad and intra-action, it is difficult to think otherwise.

As such, we advocate rewrites of interview research, the crafting of lively write-ups that not only attend to the vivid details that generated interview data, but also make visible the *interview-as-entanglement*. An entangled interview cannot be easily parsed, with methods separated from findings, and we urge interview researchers to experiment with writings that avoid pain(fully/stakingly) separating methods from results from interpretation—that is, getting creative (Koro-Ljungberg, 2012) and exploring ways of writing about qualitative interview data that include what happened (materially and discursively) to generate *that* piece of data. What question prompted that particular response? What material, moment, affects were involved, caught-up, in the prompting and that response? To be clear, we are not arguing for the lengthy inclusion of spurious details in research write-ups (see, for example, Wolgemuth et al., 2022). Alongside others (e.g., Aagaard, 2021), we caution against hyper-reflexive research writing that, in its abstract/ed attention to detail and process, risks losing sight of the matter (material-discursive) it seeks to analyze. The researcher is ultimately responsible/response-able for reporting what matters/ed. All the same, we encourage creative, responsible rewrites exemplified, for example, in accounts of writing slow ontology (Ulmer, 2017a), writing as/with/through paralysis (Bridges-Rhoads, 2015), rebuilding worlds (Schadler, 2019), and collaborative writing (Taylor, 2014), which privilege process over product, presentation over representation, and attune to the entanglements of language and material in the generation and representation of inquiry. (See also Carlson and colleagues' [forthcoming] edited collection of examples and reflections on theoretically driven, creative qualitative writing.) Slow ontology, for example, evokes careful, patient attending and crafting required for writing the materiality of research environments (Ulmer, 2017a). After all, the interview is more likely a complex accomplishment within a particular material-discursive environment than a neutral encounter eliciting pre-existing, latent, true data, and should be written(-up) accordingly, patiently, lovingly.

Love Story 4

I agreed to be interviewed by a friend/colleague/#qualeague about my experiences as an academic and mother during the COVID pandemic. Academic. Mother. Interviewee. I have varying degrees of (dis)comfort with the subjects hailed. Nevertheless, I agreed, happily. I really like my #qualeague. We chatted a bit and then the interview began. She embodied The Interviewer very well. She explained the study, went over the consent form, and I happily consented.

"Recording started," says Zoom, and off we go.

She asks questions and I answer, maybe self-consciously. Some questions resonate, others I can't or don't care to answer. Some I've never thought of before; I am not sure they matter. But they are being asked. Surely, they matter. I talk too much. I say things I'm not sure I mean. I mean things I'm not sure I say. I get distracted by my own uncertainty—is this quality data? Do I like how I am representing myself (as mother, as academic)? Is the recording working? I don't want my #qualeague to think less of me. I am conjuring up ideas, impressions, experiences I'm not sure I had, not sure I care about, not sure I understand. I wonder whether I will ever say or think these things again. Does that matter? Writing now, I don't remember what I said.

"Your recording has stopped," says Zoom.

The interview ends and we chat again. She shares her experiences, what was brought up for her while listening to me. We connect, we relate. I feel validated and process my experience through hers, with her. I/my recounted experiences make more sense. I revise or clarify what I said, what I might have meant. The conversation is rich, connecting, affirming—it does not represent anything—it solidifies our friendship, a becoming together. It is not data. Writing now, I remember a story she shared with me.

I often tell students that good interviews are more like conversations. Yet what is required to produce conversation seems revolutionary or maybe make-believe: non-representational dialogue, ideas and thoughts that swirl in the moment (pastpresentfuture), manifest kinship and "data" that may or may not matter or endure beyond the encounter. At the same time, The Interview—the time between the pressing and releasing of the record button—heightens our attention, makes us aware of things we may more easily ignore in "natural" conversation. Things like who we are supposed to be (subjects), how those subjects should make account of themselves (data), and. . . . And maybe this heightened attention is precisely the point. It makes manifest the material-discursive configurations that make meaning matter. And in this sense maybe The Interview produces good data. For me, the interview may always be strange, puzzling, discomforting, unknowable.

However Far Away, I Will Always Love You

The interview method is seductive, reshaping us into "better" users in subtle ways. That's the power of good methodology, good theory. It makes what is familiar and comfortable seem strange. We have not fallen out of "love" with the interview, but instead we seek to come to terms with our relationship with it. Like any relationship, at times we have matched well with theory, our becomings and its becomings a strength to both. New intra-activity changes us, our becomings, and the ways in which we relate to what was once familiar. At times this has meant that we were no longer good for the interview method and the interview method no longer good for us. Our knowledge of and continued becoming with theory continues to provide the constant, irresistible push and pull with the interview method—the churn of constant intra-activity with a world in chaos. Theory is not an intermediary between us and the interview; rather, it is the old friend who knows us both separately and together—it whispers to each of us about the other.

Embracing theory as an old friend or even lover, we have come to appreciate the broader (intra-active) process of thinking-with theoretical concepts (e.g., Jackson & Mazzei, 2012). We read Barad, and our together–apart engagement with her work shifted our thinking, but not just thinking. Barad shifted all possibilities for the researchers and interviewers we could be and become, and the interview projects we could create. Philosophical reading (Van Cleave, 2018) is an excellent strategy for confronting and rethinking taken-for-granted assumptions about methods and methodologies and for inventing new ones. If we can offer any lessons from our engagements with Barad (and other scholars), and if anything we have described can be figured as at least in part an intentional process of human agents, we highly recommend selecting, reading, and discussing philosophy and theory texts with peers, colleagues, scholars, and friends. Surely (some of) these readings will rock worlds (Bridges-Rhoads et al., 2018). From these readings, pick up concepts like we did with intra-action and ask, "What does this concept differently help me/us think/believe/know about . . . ?" Pursue that question tirelessly, but slowly with passion and love (Ulmer, 2017b). Observe how the once-obvious becomes unthinkable/unlivable in the wake of the new. Laugh. And begin to build new worlds amidst the ruins. Rinse. Repeat. Perhaps we cannot not think without intra-action, conceptualizing as we have this recommended philosophical reading as an ongoing intra-active process. We do not know what will emerge in the ruins of intra-activity, but if we understand anything about ourselves (debatable), anything about intra-action, we would be safe to say that what we write about interviewing next will not—cannot—be the same.

Intra-activity extends far beyond the interview space—it is a constant process always-already in actions and in reconfigurations. Intra-action is not wielded by researchers, but it can be leveraged, predicted, and purposefully employed (Marn & Wolgemuth, 2017). Intra-action is a complex and layered concept leaving little or nothing of certainty. Yet this is not a call for interview paralysis or eternal reflexivity. We've offered our rhapsody, our love stories, to show that intra-activity brings us to a constant state of flux (as researchers, as people). Bodies, interview spaces, and research materials all intra-act to produce an iteratively unique interview phenomenon in which something entirely new may be possible, something not yet thinkable. It is these moments that make our "love story" with the interview continue. While rethinking ethics, subjectivities, and our own entanglement with our interviews is fraught, we see these as necessary reconfigurations to evolve the interview method past its humanistic, "objective," passive origins—that the intra-active interview is worth the "price" of uncertainty. Intra-action reminds us that we are inextricably "part of the nature we seek to understand" (Barad, 2007, p. 26).

References

Aagaard, J. (2021). Troubling the troublemakers: Three challenges to post-qualitative inquiry. *International Review of Qualitative Research*, 15(3), 311–325. https://doi.org/10.1177/19408447211052668

Aagaard, J., & Matthiesen, N. (2016). Methods of materiality: Participant observation and qualitative research in psychology. *Qualitative Research in Psychology*, 13(1), 33–46. https://doi.org/10.1080/14780887.2015.1090510

Barad, K. (2007). *Meeting the universe halfway: Quantum physics and the entanglement of matter and meaning*. Duke University Press.

Barlott, T., Shevellar, L., Turpin, M., & Setchell, J. (2020). The dissident interview: A deterritorializing guerrilla encounter. *Qualitative Inquiry*, 26(6), 650–660. https://doi.org/10.1177/1077800419859041

Braidotti, R. (2013). *The posthuman*. Polity Press.

Bridges-Rhoads, S. (2015). Writing paralysis in (post) qualitative research. *Qualitative Inquiry*, 21(8), 704–710. https://doi.org/10.1177/1077800414566690

Bridges-Rhoads, S., Hughes, H. E., & Van Cleave, J. (2018). Readings that rock our worlds. *Qualitative Inquiry*, 24(10), 817–837. https://doi.org/10.1177/1077800418767202

Butler, J. (1990). *Gender trouble*. Routledge.

Butler, J. (1993). *Bodies that matter*. Routledge.

Butler, J. (1997). *The psychic life of power: Theories in subjection*. Stanford University Press.

Care Collective, The (2020). *The care manifesto: The politics of interdependence*. Verso.

Carlson, D. L., Vasquez, A. M., & Romero, A. (Eds.) (Forthcoming). *Writing and the articulation of qualitative research.* Routledge.

Chow, R. (2010). The elusive material: What the dog doesn't understand. In D. H. Coole & S. Frost (Eds.), *New materialisms: Ontology, agency and politics* (pp. 221–233). Duke University Press.

Foucault, M. (1995). *Discipline and punish: The birth of the prison* (A. Sheridan, Trans.). Vintage Books. (Original work published 1975.)

Haraway, D. J. (2016). *Staying with the trouble: Making kin in the Chthulucene.* Duke University Press. https://doi.org/10.1215/9780822373780

Jackson, A., & Mazzei, L (2012). *Thinking with theory in qualitative research: Viewing data across multiple perspectives.* SAGE.

Killam, R. K. (2022). My high horse is dying: Agitating internalized neoliberalism in higher education with(out) compassion. *Cultural Studies ↔ Critical Methodologies, 23*(1), 35–61. https://doi.org/10.1177/15327086221107050

Koro, M., & Wolgemuth, J. R. (2021, April 8–April 12). *Methodologies for the apocalypse: Unthinking the thinkable.* [Paper presentation]. American Educational Research Association Annual Meeting, Virtual conference.

Koro-Ljungberg, M. (2010). Validity, responsibility, and aporia. *Qualitative Inquiry, 16*(8), 603–610. https://doi.org/10.1177/1077800410374034

Koro-Ljungberg, M. (2012). Researchers of the world, create! *Qualitative Inquiry, 18*(9), 808–818. https://doi.org/10.1177/1077800412453014

Kuntz, A. M. (2015). *The responsible methodologist: Inquiry, truth-telling, and social justice.* Left Coast Press.

Latour, B. (2005). *Reassembling the social: An introduction to actor-network-theory.* Oxford University Press.

Manning, E. (2016). *The minor gesture.* Duke University Press.

Marn, T. M. (2018). *Performing the Black–White biracial identity: The material, discursive, and psychological components of subject formation.* [Unpublished doctoral dissertation.] University of South Florida.

Marn, T. M., & Guyotte, K. W. (2022). Ruinous mentorship. In K. W. Guyotte, & J. R. Wolgemuth, (Eds.), *Philosophical mentoring in qualitative research: Collaborating and inquiring together* (pp. 84–104). Routledge.

Marn, T. M., & Wolgemuth, J. R. (2017). Purposeful entanglements: A new materialist analysis of transformative interviews. *Qualitative Inquiry, 23*(5), 365–374. https://doi.org/10.1177%2F1077800416659085

Marn T. M., & Wolgemuth, J. R. (2020). Qualitative interviews as purposeful entanglements. In M. K. E. Thomas & R. Bellingham (Eds.), *Post-qualitative research and innovative methodologies* (pp. 35–50). Bloomsbury Academic.

Marn, T. M., & Wolgemuth, J. R. (2021). Applied qualitative data analysis after the ontological turn. *The Qualitative Report, 26*(6), 2094–2110. https://doi.org/10.46743/2160-3715/2021.5014

Mazzei, L. A. (2013). A voice without organs: Interviewing in posthumanist research. *International Journal of Qualitative Studies in Education, 26*(6), 732–740. https://doi.org/10.1080/09518398.2013.788761

Mol, A. (2002). *The body multiple: Ontology in medical practice*. Duke University Press.

Nordstrom, S. N. (2015). Not so innocent anymore: Making recording devices matter in qualitative interviews. *Qualitative Inquiry, 21*(4), 388–401. https://doi.org/10.1177/1077800414563804

Roulston, K. (2010). *Reflective interviewing: A guide to theory and practice*. Sage.

Schadler, C. (2019). Enactments of a new materialist ethnography: Methodological framework and research processes. *Qualitative Research, 19*(2), 215–230. https://doi.org/10.1177/1468794117748877

Taylor, C. A. (2014). Telling transitions: Space, materiality, and ethical practices in a collaborative writing workshop. *Cultural Studies ↔ Critical Methodologies, 14*(4), 396–406. https://doi.org/10.1177/1532708614530312

Ulmer, J. B. (2017a). Writing slow ontology. *Qualitative Inquiry, 23*(3), 201–211. https://doi.org/10.1177/1077800416643994

Ulmer, J. B. (2017b). Critical qualitative inquiry is/as love. *Qualitative Inquiry, 23*(7), 543–544. https://doi.org/10.1177/1077800417718298

Van Cleave, J. (2018). Engaging uselessness: Philosophical reading and dwelling in the excess. *Qualitative Inquiry, 24*(9), 681–686. https://doi.org/10.1177/1077800417732092

Van Cleave J., Marn T. M., & Wolgemuth J. R. (2022, May 18–May 21). *Philosophical readings and failure*. [Paper presentation]. International Congress of Qualitative Inquiry Annual Meeting, Virtual conference.

Wolgemuth, J. R., & Marn, T. M. (2022). Contagious sapiosexuality: Dreamy conference seductions as ethics of qualitative research. *Reconceptualizing Educational Research Methodology, 13*(1). https://doi.org/10.7577/rerm.4928

Wolgemuth, J. R., Marn, T. M., Barko, T., & Weaver-Hightower, M. (2022). Radical uncertainty is not enough: (In)justices of post-qualitative research. *International Review of Qualitative Research, 14*(4), 575–593. https://doi.org/10.1177/19408447211012658

Wolgemuth, J. R., Rautio, P., Koro-Ljungberg, M., Marn, T., Nordstrom, S., & Clark, A. (2018). Work/think/play/birth/death/terror/qualitative/research. *Qualitative Inquiry, 24*(9), 712–719. https://doi.org/10.1177/1077800417735860

SEVEN

 Past, Present, Futures of Assembling Object-Interviews

Susan Naomi Nordstrom

MEMORIES OF STUDIES LONG SINCE completed tend to haunt researchers in the most beautifully generative ways. In a way, these memories can become our dearest intellectual friends. Moments in an interview—a particular turn of phrase, a doing, an object—return to us like dear friends, hugging us with their familiar warmth as they check in on us and soothe our tired thoughts into new and different ones. These moments are so precious, so loved, and many times so powerful that their importance is sometimes difficult to explain to others. For me, so many memories are about object-interviews, a conversational interview in which both humans and nonhumans are primary producers of knowledge. I developed the method in 2009 for my dissertation study about the objects (e.g., photographs, documents, and other artifacts) that family history genealogists use to construct their ancestors. I could not have anticipated the memories of object-interviews and how they would come to shape my scholarly life in articles about object-interviews themselves (2013b), a data assemblage (2015a), transcription (2015b), and antimethodology (2018), for example.

In this chapter I follow how object-interviews have shaped my career and how they have moved my thinking in different ways. First, I explain the Deleuzoguattarian (1987) assemblage that served as a guiding concept in my study and set the stage for the object-interviews. From that assemblage, I share stories from my study about the object-interviews similar to how they happened during the object-interviews. Participants would many times excitedly share objects with me, jumping from object to object, leaving me to make connections between objects. I engage a similar practice in this chapter, jumping into and from stories, allowing the reader to make whatever connections they may (or may not). In this way, the stories, the memories, are more like trajectories shooting off from the assemblage I call my study. My tone, at times, is informal—as if I am speaking to the reader in a mentoring session about the method and how I developed it. I situate each story within the time frame in which it happened. For example, in the dissertation proposal, I reference only what I had available to me at that time. I gently remind the reader that I began this work in 2009, and, since then, nonhuman object work has gained quite a bit more traction. The stories, the memories, of the object-interviews and study presented in this chapter aim to generate even more traction.

Assembling Assemblages

When I first read about the Deleuzoguattarian (1987) assemblage, the concept felt right in my body. I felt that I could breathe a bit easier, even though I felt as though I barely understood the words on the page. It was then that I came to believe that our bodies know the theoretical frameworks well before we encounter them. Our bodies many times have been waiting for those words that hollow out some space for us to exhale all those suffocating discourses we have consumed. The ability to breathe with ease is most welcome. I finally had a word, assemblage—a language with which to think the world, as I understood it. The term assemblage—a dynamic, ongoing, and mysterious entity—offered me the air I needed.

Venn (2006) described the assemblage as "a relay concept . . . [that] focuses on process and on the dynamic character of the inter-relationships between the heterogenous elements of the phenomena" (p. 107). In other words, the assemblage is always arranging itself, always creative and surprising. It is an affirmative concept that studies what something is doing, how something is living. The assemblage is not about testing life with preconceived notions or transcendental categories. It is about affirmatively and slowly attending to life and thinking about how something came into being and the ongoing processes that made something possible. Because the assemblage is dynamically arranging itself, a study puts parentheses around whatever one is studying. It is never about arresting movement. It is about temporarily holding with soft hands what is happening in an assemblage to study its processes. Colebrook (2005) explained:

> Any assemblage such as a philosophical vocabulary (or an artistic style, or a set of scientific functions) faces in two directions. It gives some order and consistency to a life which bears much greater complexity and dynamism, but

it also enables—from that order—the creation of further and more elaborate orders. (p. 3)

As a study puts parentheses around an assemblage, one can study the consistency of it and then learn what that consistency can do. Specific to my study, I wanted to put parentheses around the objects of family history of genealogy to study the life, the order of them in genealogy, and what that order may generate.

Proposing Within an Assemblage

As part of the design process of my dissertation study, I studied the objects in my family's genealogy books and artifacts in my childhood home to better think about their importance in genealogical work. In particular, I studied a framed collage of my grandmother Naomie that I made when I was a teenager. After being told how much I look like her and being gifted her engagement ring, I put together the collage to honor a woman whom I had never met, but only knew through objects. I searched the basement of my house and found three pictures of her in our family photo collections: the first, her confirmation photo taken in 1927 when she was 15; the second, her high school graduation photo taken in 1930 when she was 18; and third, a copy of a photo taken of her with my father and uncle in 1942, when she was 30 years old, that she sent to my Grandfather Norris while he was serving with the Navy in the Pacific Theatre during World War II. I also found an announcement for her wedding to my grandfather on Wednesday, August 7, 1935, as well as her and my grandfather's wedding certificate. I carefully put her photographs and the wedding documents into a small frame so that I would have something tangible about a woman I never knew face-to-face. Using that collage and the family history books, I began to think how objects materialize the deceased, invitations to "speculation... [where I gave] myself over to phantomatic or phantasmatic reconstructions" (Derrida, 1989, p. 55). I wanted to know more about those reconstructions in my study about the objects of family history genealogy.

To my knowledge, I asked very different questions about family history genealogy than the existing literature that focuses on family history genealogists' identities (e.g., Hackstaff, 2009, 2010; Nash, 2002; Tutton, 2004; Tyler, 2005), family history genealogists' research practices (e.g., Bishop, 2008; Duff

& Johnson, 2003; Lambert, 1996; Veale, 2004), the work of memory in family history genealogy (e.g., Harevan, 1978; Lambert, 1996, 2002, 2003; Parham, 2008), and family history genealogy and its relation to the field of history (e.g., Rosenzweig & Thelen, 1998; Stearns, 1982). Within those bodies of work on family history genealogy and those who accomplish it can be found provocative fragments about objects (e.g., documents, photographs, and artifacts) shared by study participants that researchers left unexplored. For example, Hackstaff (2009) shared the following from her interview study about ethno-racial identities of 11 family history genealogists living in the San Francisco area:

> Participants wanted to show me photographs of ancestors, gravestones, and houses, certificates of marriage, births recorded in Bibles. . . . Clarissa showed me a lock of hair that had been an ancestor's; others, like Heather, described walking on the land that had once been their ancestors' land, and Katie described how she wept upon seeing the signature of a grandfather who had eluded her research. (p. 182)

Immediately following this evidence, Hackstaff suggested that her participants might have been engaging in a form of Altheide and Johnson's (1998) analytical realism, meaning that the objects are symbolically constructed from the perspectives of their owners. In other words, the owners of the objects, the family, imbue objects with meaning(s) based on their experiences. More specifically, family history genealogists infuse objects—gravestones, houses, and signatures on documents—with meaning(s), because these objects are yoked to particular ancestors they study. Though Hackstaff does not develop this idea beyond what I have summarized, nor does she share her participants' constructions about the objects and the ancestors who owned them, her suggestion about her participants' use of analytical realism opens a space to explore the interconnectedness of nonhuman objects and humans in family history genealogy work.

Altheide and Johnson (1998) suggested that "analytical realism rejects the dichotomy of realism/idealism, and other conceptual dualisms as being incompatible with the nature of lived experience and its interpretations" (p. 292). While Altheide and Johnson do not list the other conceptual dualisms that analytical realism rejects, one dualism that is preserved throughout their piece is presence/absence and, by extension, living/dead, as is evidenced by their constant references to "lived experiences." However, Hackstaff (2009) offered that her participants might have engaged in a form of analytical realism—infusing those objects with constructions about presumably deceased (absent) ancestors associated with the objects. Hackstaff's suggestion can be analyzed as a troubling of the presence/absence and living/dead dualisms, because the constructions—part of the "lived experiences" of her participants—are about deceased (absent) ancestors—as such, the absent, the present, the living, the dead, the human, and nonhuman objects muddled together in an assemblage.

I was operating in a different ontological space and needed to figure out how to study that space. I used the Deleuzian concepts of the fold and assemblage to help me engage that space. The fold helps me to re-describe the work between binary terms as relational and in movement and the ontology of the study as rhythmic folds (Deleuze, 1993). The fold permeated the study as folding, refolding, and unfolding binary terms formed innumerable pleats in the study. Those pleats, or folds, then created linkages that formed assemblages—principally, family history genealogy assemblages that are governed by Deleuze and Guattari's (1987) logic of the "and." That logic conceptualizes a horizontal rather than hierarchical relationship. In such a relationship, non-human objects and humans (both living and nonliving) constantly arrange themselves in sometimes novel configurations. While I called my study a "qualitative" study, it marks a shift from conventional interpretive qualitative research in which non-human objects and humans are treated in a binary fashion (c.f., Nordstrom, 2013b; 2018). Conventional qualitative research is human-centered in that it primarily uses methods such as interviews and observations to draw information from people. I, however, was interested in both nonhuman objects and humans and the ways in which their configurations produced knowledge. To do this work, I needed to interview family history genealogists, but I had to interview differently to better engage that ontological space. I had to slow down and carefully read to figure out how to do these interviews differently.

I rethought it as an object-interview in which the binary terms, such as nonhuman objects and humans (both living and nonliving), could move in horizontal and relational ways. Specifically, I defined it as a conversational interview in which participants bring objects to share with a researcher. In 2009, I theorized objects as blurry incendiary objects, which contrasted to the existing literature in which objects were theorized as stable, mute entities that are secondary to humans (e.g., Collier, 1957; Collier & Collier, 1986; De Leon & Cohen, 2005; McCracken, 1998). Following Scheurich's (1997) critique of the interview, the objects and what was said about them could never be known in their entirety, even though they would be photographed and discussed. I anticipated that transcription would be a prominent act of text and photos working together. And that was it: around two pages about object-interviews in a dissertation proposal. The guide itself was an open-ended list of three questions that asked about the object, the ancestor, and how the object helps the genealogist know the ancestor. I successfully defended the proposal and then received IRB approval. I was ready to go.

Tater Tots

However, one can never be ready for what happens in an ever-arranging assemblage and what it generates. Prior to the first object-interview in early 2010, I stopped for lunch at a café across from the public library, where the interview would take place. During my lunch, I studied the interview guide, because that is what I thought researchers should do—study the guide to be prepared for what was to come. However, the café, a converted Quonset hut (a steel or tin hut usually used for equipment storage), and its customers had different plans for me. Four ranchers sat next to me, and I overheard them talk about the cold weather and snow. One rancher related how the county asked him to help remove snow from the many graveled roads in the area. He described how an upturned piece of frozen manure shredded one of his tractor tires, a costly shredding resulting in a new, $500 tire. Another group of men came in to meet friends for lunch. One particularly loud man asked, "Where is that big guy?" as they waited for a presumably big man to join them for lunch at the café. He did, and he was quite big, crouching to fit himself into the Quonset's door. As I finished my grilled cheese sandwich with tater tots, an older woman walked by my table and winked at me—perhaps a small-town welcome. Life was happening all around me—a shredded tractor tire, friends meeting for lunch, and a friendly wink. I put my guide in my bag and tuned in to the life happening around me. I realized that no interview guide could anticipate the conversations I would have with participants. While I did put the guide on the table in the library and on other tables at other interviews, I never used it. Our conversations were circumnavigating and flowing discussions about the objects participants brought to the interviews. I learned that it was my job to softly yield to the assemblage and facilitate space for humans and nonhumans and living and nonliving to endlessly move together.

The assemblage is truly more of a verb than a noun, a constantly arranging constellation of people, things, nature, and ideas, and ... and ... and .... The above example, then, has two, if not more assemblages being introduced to each other. The first is the assemblage in which I was situated, the assemblage of a late-stage doctoral candidate doing research. The other is the café assemblage. There is significant ethical work to be done when assemblages meet. As assemblages assemble together, unanticipated ethical moments occur. One must attempt to be worthy of the moment when it happens (Deleuze, 1990). In the moment described above, I believe the ethical moment asked me to allow space for the two assemblages to move together more freely. I could have easily attempted to wrestle the café assemblage into a way of knowing and being that better aligned with more conventional ways of doing research. I, however, made the ethical decision to slow down, soften, and let the assemblages mingle and create something different. This decision shaped the remainder of that study and so many others.

The decision to listen and attend to how assemblages meet up, assemble, and move together is critical to my work in qualitative research. In this way, qualitative research is a set of research practices grounded in ongoing series of ethical moments that ask me to respond to assembling assemblages in ways that free up movement between them. Qualitative research is responsive, not transactional. It is about attending to the assemblages that have so graciously allowed us to enter, and doing the ethical work of responsively tending to the movements of those assemblages.

To articulate that responsiveness, I published "Object-interviews: Folding, Unfolding, and Refolding Perceptions of Objects" (Nordstrom, 2013b). In that article, I attempted to describe what I did to attend to the assemblages in which I found myself. I described how I designed the interview using the fold, a Deleuzian ontology that makes the relationship between nonhuman objects and human subjects as relational rather than fixed in binary fashion. I then use the fold to rethink the existing literature about objects in interviews (e.g., Collier, 1957; Collier & Collier, 1986; De Leon & Cohen, 2005; McCracken,

1998). This rethinking allowed me to create a relational interviewing method that positioned both nonhuman objects and human subjects as primary producers of knowledge in interviews. Such a repositioning prompted that I ask connective questions, questions that attempted to strengthen the linkages between nonhumans and humans initiated by the questions in the open-ended guide. Connective questions respond to the assemblage. They cannot be known in advance and materialize from the assemblage as it is assembling. For example, in this study, connective questions included (but were not limited to) questions about the connections between ancestors or objects and sometimes between interviews (i.e., "I saw something similar in another interview..."). These kinds of questions shifted the more traditional questions that aim to clarify interpretations. Connective questions sought to create spaces for connections in assemblages to proliferate. These proliferations allowed ideas to connect within object-interviews and, sometimes, to other object-interviews. I also discussed how the participants used pronouns to talk about the objects and how that usage created a grammar that blurred the supposed boundaries between humans and nonhuman objects. For example, participants used "she" to refer to a tea cup associated with a female relative. In effect, that article attempted to explain what I did while I was entangled in the ever-arranging assemblages.

A Motley Crew

The object-interviews created many connections. Participants wanted to know about my genealogical work, which I shared with them. They shared novels that helped them think about their ancestors. They shared their research about larger historical events that I then studied on my own. I dreamed about the data (St. Pierre, 1997). The dead became lively in my study through spectral data (Nordstrom, 2013a). An unusually cold and snowy winter created weather data. Response data (St. Pierre, 1997; Nordstrom, 2015c) figured prominently as I presented the research to the participants and other genealogists. And so much more. I was not working with a data set. I was working with a data assemblage (2015a).

My research journal materialized the elements of the assemblage. While a data set is usually conceived of as a neat and tidy entity, the data of my study was an assemblage. Each of those elements moved and shifted together. I wrote through, with, and against those elements as they made connections and, sometimes, did not make connections. I understood the data of the study to be an assemblage, which I described in 2015 as a moving entity of a variety of kinds of data. In that article, I claimed that I did not collect or gather data; rather, I assembled it. The term assemble suggests that the assemblage was not out there waiting for me to put the parentheses around it. It was and is moving. My parentheses just paused the assembling.

Butts and Corduroy

Transcription was unlike anything I had ever done. I had to manage hundreds of objects that were shared with me during interviews that lasted well over 100 minutes. Those objects needed to be inserted at the right place, given that many times participants would refer to objects as she, he, or they. As I transcribed, I took notes as objects linked to other objects in the interview or objects in other interviews. For example, a document may link to several ancestors. I wrote about the ways the participants' hands held precious objects. I included my research about the larger historical events that situated an object (e.g., a battle, an immigration wave, and so on). I also wrote about what I later learned were affects, movements within interviews that shape what is said and how it is said. The transcripts became lively entities with proliferating connections.

One moment has always stood out to me. A participant was visibly unnerved by the recording device. Of course, I asked her several times if she was okay with recording the interview. She said she was, but as she took me on a tour of her home, which was filled with family history objects, I felt her gaze on the recording device. Consequently, I kept moving the recording device around my body as I repeatedly asked her if it was okay to record. I moved the recording device around my body that also was managing a camera, a notebook, and a pen. I didn't think much of it at the time . . . until transcription. I heard all the movements of the device in the recording. I heard the recording device move from my hand to the crook of my elbow to a thick sweater pocket to the corduroy pants pocket. I laughed it off as I put notes about the movement of the recording device in my transcript.

I honestly did not think that much of the movements, except for thinking that it was a really good story and made me laugh, until I read Karen Barad's

(2007) *Meeting the Universe Halfway*. While reading it a few years after completing the study, that story and others came back to me: the participant who was so excited that she could not wait for me to set down my backpack or take off my coat, much less turn on a recording device; the participants who asked to go "off the record"; and others. After all the objects I studied during object interviews, I realized that I had yet to think about the work of one of the objects that was doing such valuable work for me in my study—the recording device. The attention I devoted to the objects of the object-interview eclipsed the recording device and camera that made my research possible. That moment created a space for me to consider the work of those objects in my research and qualitative research in general.

In my article "Not so Innocent Anymore: Making Recording Devices Matter in Qualitative Interviews" (2015b), I examined those moments in which the recording devices I used during the object-interviews came to matter. I first did a material-discursive reading of recording devices in qualitative research. That reading generated an argument that recording devices have become so ubiquitous but still are burdened by post-positivist discourses about capturing reality. Drawing on instances in the object-interviews, I then offered disruptions that situate recording devices within new materialism. I suggested that recording devices ask researchers to ethically attune themselves to the contingent worlds that contain culturally and socially situated meanings that they and the participants make.

Ensembles of Life

I wanted to do my best by and with the data assemblage. I wanted to show off what the participants were doing rather than placing them in existing categories. I began the arduous task of reading and writing with the assemblage. Deleuze and Parnet (2002) wrote, "The writer invents assemblages starting from assemblages which have invented him" (pp. 51–52). I just had to listen and attend to those assemblages that invented me, invented the study. I knew that whatever I invented from that which had invented me, invented the study, had to be affirmative and generative. Whatever I would do had to match the intensity of those vital assemblages.

Assemblages ask researchers not to latch onto transcendental categories in the hope that they might help me make sense of a study. Assemblages ask researchers to experiment with the assemblage to consider what it might do and become. Working with the object-interviews became about experimenting, not interpreting the assemblages (Deleuze, 1995). Experimentation is experiencing an assemblage, studying its parts and seeing what those parts can do and the potential of those doings. There is no blueprint for such work. It becomes a playful space of creation, whether that creating be writing, reading, making, and so on. In such a space one does not ask "What is it?" (which signals transcendental categories). Instead, one asks, "What is it doing already?" "What is living and breathing there?" "What is giving it life?" "How do I foster more life?" After five months of reading and writing with the data assemblage, an affirmative concept began to emerge: the ensemble of life.

The ensemble of life is a loose grouping of objects associated with a deceased person that is open and connectable to other people, objects, and social, historical, and cultural milieus. This concept is a product of the data assemblage and Deleuzoguattarian concepts of events, the fold, and a life. The participants told verb-rich stories during the interviews. The objects materialized an action, or event, in an ancestor's life (e.g., a land purchase and a marriage). Because the object materializes an action, the object is defined by processes, or actualizations, which occur in various times and places. For example, a purchase of land occurred in a specific time and place, and that event can be actualized again whenever anyone interacts with that land deed. In this way, the event, or object, is always open to potential connections. Those events are connected to ancestors. The event of death (to die) in an ancestor's life "makes them rise, descend, and rise again" (Deleuze, 1993, p. 74). As a result, the ancestors are in movement, "infinitely folding upon [them]selves" (p. 74). A productive force, a life, moves in those infinitely folding events. A life is "a resource or reserve of other possibilities, our connection" (Rajchman, 2000, p. 84) that can be actualized in different times and spaces. Deleuze (2006) wrote:

> A life is everywhere, in every moment which a living subject traverses and which is measured by the objects that have been experienced, an immanent life carrying along the events or singularities that are merely actualized in subjects and object. (p. 387)

A life is an atmosphere that penetrates the objects of family history genealogy and opens them up to potentials and possibilities. I began to understand the verb-rich stories and all those objects as ensembles of life, collections of nonhuman objects, humans, and events that are animated by a life. In effect, the ensembles of life proliferated from the object-interviews. The rich Deleuzoguattarian concepts lived in the verb-rich stories. In my 2019 article, I articulate each of the concepts—events, folds, and a life—with verb-rich stories from the data assemblage, as well as explain the ethical and affirmative work of generating concepts.

Generating affirmative knowledge about what is happening, what is being lived by participants, is ethical work. Braidotti (2011) wrote that "the ethical ideal is to increase one's ability to enter into modes of relation with multiple others" (p. 286). In other words, affirmative ethics seeks to open up becomings, new ways of being. Intensive concept development does this work. Colebrook (2017) argued that educational research should be active in the generation of new concepts rather than taking existing concepts and applying them to educative spaces. Kuntz (2015) argued for practices that engage in a "determination to simultaneously be other than we are and other than we have been" (p. 91). The ensemble of life seeks to do such experimental and creative work. The open-ended and affirmative ensemble of life shifts understandings about family history genealogy and those who practice it into a space of becoming, which the 2019 article attempts to articulate.

Peeling Away the Parentheses

Earlier I discussed how I placed parentheses around the objects of family history genealogy to design the study. Assemblages are ever assembling themselves. They do not stop. They just keep going. This begs the question: How does one know when to stop? When does one peel away the parentheses and let that arranging keep on keeping on? Unfortunately, there is no tidy rule I can provide at this time. Something happens when it becomes clear that it is time to say "Enough. Time to let it just assemble on."

In the 2019 article about the ensemble of life and dissertation, I dabbled in what might now be called multispecies inquiry. In those spaces, I explored some of the nonhuman animals I encountered in the data assemblage. Most of the participants lived in rural areas, where farm life dominates culture. Animals were always a part of the study. For example, in an interview, I said "Wow, that is the largest hog I have ever seen!" upon seeing an exceptionally sized hog that a participant's ancestor showed at a county fair. County fairs are social gatherings but also places to show off one's abilities in animal husbandry. One such fair-goer even had a chicken ranch where he kept and bred his prize-winning chickens.

I began work to further develop the animals of the ensembles of life, but always seemed to lose interest. I'm not sure how to explain it, but it felt forced. I felt it in my body. It just did not feel right. Still, I tried to do something with it, and I failed every time. The recurring failures suggested to me that maybe it was time to part ways. The assemblages that met in 2009 needed to move away from one another. While both of us remain forever changed, it is time for us to take those changes into other assemblages. This chapter will probably be the last I will write about this study. While I currently do not know exactly what the next assemblage is or where it lives, I know there is another assemblage, many more assemblages that I have yet to encounter. There is more affirmative and generative work to be done.

More Inventions

Back in 2009, when I designed the method, I wanted the object-interview to be affirmative and generative. Since then, I have focused on how my writing can create more affirmative assemblages. I have attempted to write open-ended, process-based methodological pieces that are open and connectable to other studies. Simply put, over the past 10 or so years I have attempted to write methodological pieces that do not offer a prescriptive way of doing object-oriented qualitative research. Such a manner of writing is about creating assemblages, activating lines that I hope researchers can use as lines of flight for their own work.

Even though Deleuze and Guattari (1987) claim that things pick up speed in the middle, assemblages ask researchers to slow down so that they can study how an assemblage functions, to examine its elements and how those elements are connected (Deleuze & Guattari, 1987). To write an assemblage asks the writer to slow down and first study the elements of the assemblage in which she is caught. For me, this meant slowing down my dissertation and studying each of its elements. Then I attempted to write that element in an open configuration so that others might be able to plug it into their study. For example, I began with the object-interview (2013b), spectral data (2013a; 2017), response data (2015c), data assemblage (2015a), recording devices (2015b), antimethodology (2018), the ensemble of life (2019), and, finally, this chapter. Each of these elements is a part of the assemblage I call my study. Each element required a slowing down to see how it worked so that I could write about it for others. Such work allowed me to write open-ended invitations to do research differently. Each invitation attempted to include stories from the assemblage I call my study, a frank openness about the assemblage process as I encountered it, and a theoretical argument for the element. Each element aimed to contain lines of flight that opened to others so that they could put them to work in their study. In effect, each element, each article, attempts to serve as both an invitation and a justification to do research differently.

From those lines of flight have come some of the most exciting work from object-interviews. When someone who has read the 2013 article asks me how to do an object-interview, I ask them to share the assemblage in which they are caught, and then we think together about how object-interviews might work in their assemblage, their study. Many times I am asked about what counts as a "good interview." To help them through what constitutes "good," I ask them to reflexively consider the following questions only they can answer. How did they move with the assemblage? How did they yield to the assemblage assembling rather than attempt to control it? What is the assemblage generating? What new thoughts were created? How did the interview and assemblage change them? Challenge them? Inspire them? I then follow up with them and ask about the work of object-interviews in their study. I am always so excited to see how the object-interview worked in another assemblage and how other researchers have made the object-interviews something otherwise. I am not much interested in the number of citations; I am interested in how people take that open-ended invitation, that line of flight, and make it groan and twist by doing research differently. That is where the interesting work lives. It is where the assemblage proliferates.

Soft Proliferations

As my assemblage moves me to an elsewhere that is yet to be known, I close this chapter with generative hope. The work of following the memories generated by the object-interview has created a new memory. The work of the object-interviews themselves, returning to the transcripts, the journal, the past publications, and the stories that bring a smile to my face have created a scholarly history. History, as Deleuze and Guattari (1987) remind us, is always a past, present, and future. As I consider the study yet to be done, the tater tots, the corduroy, the hundreds of objects, and the other memories will always find their way into my thinking. They're never gone. They're always memories of a future to come, of assemblages that I have yet to (or may not ever) encounter.

When I said yes to assemblages and the process ontologies that constitute them in the dissertation research, I said no to thinking that there was some kind of "I" that precedes the process. This means trusting the process, yielding to it. It means not knowing what will happen next. It means being okay with that. It means uncertainty. There is a softness to such work, a soft, gentle flow in assemblages that generate lines of flight. Some of these lines are creative, others less so. Even in the latter, there is something always happening. One must be open and soft to those happenings to allow them to be. To just be in process. What a lovely way of being. While such a way of being rubs against the academy that expects that there is an "I" that precedes the process and values certainty, the softness is too delightful, too affirmative, too generative to walk away from. So I try very hard to stay with the softness.

One of the fondest memories I have of the object-interviews is how they rode with the undulating foldings, unfoldings, and refoldings of the ancestors and the nonhuman objects. Those undulations create softness. No matter how long those interviews were, I lost a sense of time. I rolled with those objects, became one with them, as I came to know the participants' ancestors. The memories of that warm and soft rolling help me now. As I consider the elements of the failed multi-species work, I remember an object I collected during a research walk for that project in the summer of 2021. To help me think about the topic, I took walks in which I collected items and put them into glass jars. I did not plan which items I would collect on the walk. Instead, I went on the walk and collected whatever appealed to me and wrote about it later. On one such walk, I felt compelled to find soft things on my hike through a local state park. I knelt to the ground and explored it through my sense of touch. I attended to the connections between my skin and the items: a feather, a piece of moss, and an ear (the fuzzy, seed-bearing part of grasses). I return to those items now and consider how they folded me into their softness. As they folded me into that softness, I thought of the object-interviews. I remember the ways in which the participants touched the objects. I remember the softness of their touch as they eagerly showed me the objects of their family history work, the objects that materialized their family. I remember the softness I had to cultivate for their objects and families. A soft responsibility to them, myself, and the study. A lesson materialized.

Find softness. Find the folds that cradle you. Let them cover your body. The assemblage is always working. Be soft. Let it work. Let it work you. Become otherwise. Become soft with others. Trust the softness, for when you land in it, you will land in its pillowy folds. Becoming soft may be the most radical thing you do.

References

Altheide, D. L., & Johnson, J. M. (1998). Criteria for assessing interpretive validity in qualitative research. In N. K. Denzin & Y. S. Lincoln (Eds.), *Collecting and interpreting qualitative materials* (pp. 283–312). SAGE.

Barad, K. (2007). *Meeting the universe halfway: Quantum physics and the entanglement of matter and meaning*. Duke University Press.

Bishop, R. (2008). In the grand scheme of things: An exploration of the meaning of genealogical research. *Journal of Popular Culture, 41*(3), 393–411.

Braidotti, R. (2011). *Nomadic theory: The portable Rosi Braidotti*. Columbia University Press.

Colebrook, C. (2005). Introduction. In A. Parr (Ed.), *The Deleuze dictionary* (pp. 1–6). Edinburgh University Press.

Colebrook, C. (2017). What is this thing called education? *Qualitative Inquiry, 23*(9), 649–655.

Collier, J., Jr. (1957). Photography in anthropology: A report on two experiments. *American Anthropologist, 59*(5), 843–859.

Collier Jr., J., & Collier, M. (1986). *Visual anthropology: Photography as a research method*. University of New Mexico Press.

De Leon, J. P., & Cohen, J. H. (2005). Object and walking probes in ethnographic interviewing. *Field Methods, 17*(2), 200–204.

Deleuze, G. (1990). *The logic of sense*. In C. V. Boundas (Ed.), and M. Lester & C. Stivale, (Trans.). Columbia University Press.

Deleuze, G. (1993). *The fold: Leibniz and the baroque*. (T. Conley, Trans.). University of Minnesota Press.

Deleuze, G. (1995). *Negotiations: 1972–1990*. (M. Joughin, Trans.). Columbia University Press.

Deleuze, G. (2006). *Two Regimes of Madness*. (D. Lapoujade, Ed.; A. Hodges & M. Taormina, Trans.). Semiotext(e).

Deleuze, G., & Guattari, F. (1987). *A thousand plateaus: Capitalism and schizophrenia* (B. Massumi, Trans.). University of Minnesota Press.

Deleuze, G., & Parnet, C. (2002). Dialogues II (H. Tomlinson, B. Habberjam, & E. Ross Albert, Trans.). Columbia University Press.

Derrida, J. (1989). *Rites of inspection.* (D. Willis, Trans.). *Art & Text, 32,* 19–97.

Duff, W. M., & Johnson, C. A. (2003). Where is the list with all the names? Information-seeking behavior of genealogists. *The American Archivist, 66* (Spring/Summer), 79–95.

Hackstaff, K. B. (2009). "Turning points" for aging genealogists: Claiming identities and histories across time. *Qualitative Sociology Review, 5*(1), 130–151.

Hackstaff, K. B. (2010). Family genealogy: A sociological imagination reveals intersectional relations. *Sociology Compass, 4*(8), 658–672.

Harevan, T. (1978).The search for generational memory. *Daedalus, 107*(4), 137–149.

Kuntz, A. (2015). *The responsible methodologist: Inquiry, truth-telling, and social justice.* Left Coast Press.

Lambert, R. D. (1996). The family historian and temporal orientations towards the ancestral past. *Journal of Time and Society, 5*(2), 115–143.

Lambert, R. D. (2002). Reclaiming the ancestral past: Narrative, rhetoric and the "convict stain." *Journal of Sociology, 38*(2), 111–127.

Lambert, R. D. (2003). Constructing symbolic ancestry: Befriending time, confronting death. *Omega: The Journal of Death and Dying, 46*(4), 303–321.

McCracken, G. (1988). *The long interview.* SAGE.

Nash, C. (2002). Genealogical identities. *Environment and Planning D: Society and Space, 20,* 27–52.

Nordstrom, S. (2013a). A conversation about spectral data. *Cultural Studies ↔ Critical Methodologies, 13*(4), 316–341.

Nordstrom, S. (2013b). Object-interviews: Folding, unfolding, and refolding perceptions of objects. *International Journal of Qualitative Methods, 12,* 237–257.

Nordstrom, S. (2015a). A data assemblage. *International Review of Qualitative Research, 8*(2), 166–193.

Nordstrom, S. (2015b). Not so innocent anymore: Making recording devices matter in qualitative interviews. *Qualitative Inquiry, 21*(4), 388–401.

Nordstrom, S. (2015c). Unfinished, fragmented, shifting, and folding slips toward the political possibilities of response data. In A. B. Reinersten & A. M. Otterstad (Eds.), *Metodefest og øyeblikksrealisme (Methodfestival and Realism of the Moment).* Fagbokforlaget.

Nordstrom, S. (2017). Spectral data experiment n-1. In M. Koro-Ljungberg, T. Löytönen, & M. Tesar (Eds.), *Disrupting data in qualitative inquiry: Entanglements with the post-critical and post-anthropocentric* (pp. 151–160). Peter Lang.

Nordstrom, S. (2018). Antimethodology: Postqualitative generative conventions. *Qualitative Inquiry, 28*(4), 215–226.

Nordstrom, S. (2019). Ensembles of life: Developing an affirmative and intensive concept in educational research. *Educational Research for Social Change, 8*(1), 14–40.

Parham, A. A. (2008). Race, memory and family history. *Social Identities, 14*(1), 13–32.

Rajchman, J. (2000). *The Deleuze connections.* MIT Press.

Rosenzweig, R., & Thelen, D. (1998). *The presence of the past: Popular uses of history in American life.* Columbia University Press.

St. Pierre, E. A. (1997). Methodology in the fold and the irruption of transgressive data. *International Journal of Qualitative Studies in Education, 10*(2), 175–189.

Scheurich, J. J. (1997). *Research method in the postmodern*. Routledge.

Stearns, P. N. (1982). Summoning the wandering tribes: Genealogy and family reunions in American history. *Journal of Social History, 16*(2), 21–37.

Tutton, R. (2004). "They want to know where they came from": Population genetics, identity, and family genealogy. *New Genetics and Society, 23*(1), 105–120.

Tyler, K. (2005). The genealogical imagination: The inheritance of interracial identities. *The Sociological Review, 53*(3), 476–494.

Veale, K. H. (2004, Spring). A doctoral study of the use of the internet for genealogy. *Historia Actual Online, 4*, 7–14.

Venn, C. (2006). A note on assemblage. *Theory, Culture, & Society, 23*(2/3), 107–108.

PART III

 BEING INVENTIVE IN ELICITING INTERVIEW ACCOUNTS

EIGHT

 Object Lessons:
Considering Object-Interviews
and Narrative Representation in
Qualitative Research

Janie Copple

THIS CHAPTER IS A PARTIAL account of what occurred when I incorporated object-interviews in my dissertation study on mothers preparing children for menstruation. Between the fall of 2019 and January 2021, I interviewed 10 mothers about their experiences preparing children for menstruation. As I conducted my first interviews, I noticed how encounters with objects (e.g., informational materials, menstrual management items) entangled with the stories mothers shared. The framework guiding my study drew on concepts from Karen Barad's (2007) theory of agential realism. This theoretical perspective argues for an understanding of the world as materializing through the entanglements of humans and non-humans. Following Barad, I asked: *How do subjectivities of supportive motherhood materialize in mothers' narratives of preparing children for menstruation?* As I considered how objects showed up in mothers' stories, I wondered what might happen if I invited mothers to bring an object to share in their interviews. Like many novice researchers, I was excited by the possibility of trying something new!

In what follows, I begin with a brief overview of the literature on object methods in the social sciences, noting how different approaches to object methods rely on particular epistemological and theoretical assumptions. Next, I provide a brief overview of my interview study, focusing specifically on my interview with a participant named Sara[1] to illustrate how orienting to objects as lively, vibrant (Bennett, 2010) co-participants became intertwined with my interviewing practices (e.g., establishing rapport), my sensemaking with data, and my approach to constructing narratives from interview data. I conclude with suggestions and guiding questions for qualitative researchers new to object methods in qualitative interviewing.

Objects and Interviewing

Anthropologists and material culture scholars have long been interested in the relationship between humans and objects (Collier, 1957; Hoskins, 1998; Hurdley, 2007; Miller, 1994; Pink, 2001; Woodward, 2020). Since the early 2000s, qualitative researchers have adopted creative approaches to incorporating object methods in interview studies to elicit participant responses and even disrupt traditional approaches to interviewing. In this overview of object methods in social science research, I begin with the question: *What is an object?* The word "object" may seem self-explanatory, yet the presence of objects all around us makes defining objects difficult. Is an "object" the same as a "thing"? How does the definition of "object" matter when we orient to the role of objects in research settings?

What Is an Object?

In her book *Material Methods*, Sophie Woodward (2020) writes, "Whether you write about things, objects, or constellations of materials is not just a question of terminology, but these words imply that you are taking a particular ontological position" (p. 12). Some material scholars have argued that the term "objects" implies closed-off entities, separate from the world (Hicks, 2010). For instance, Henare and colleagues (2007) note that while objects might be comprised of various materials and are capable of multiple iterations over time, the term "object" locates an entity in a particular time and space. Others have emphasized the importance of understanding things in relation (Law, 2004), while some scholars opt for the term "thing" over "object," because "thing" connotes an entity that is unfinished, in process, and open to possibilities (Ingold, 2012). Whether scholars refer to objects or things, considering these distinctions is helpful for engaging questions of epistemology and ontology when considering object methods in social science research. In other words, how researchers understand things/objects engages with epistemological assumptions about how knowledge is produced, and this matters for the questions we ask (e.g., research questions, interview questions, or questions of data). Let's turn now to some examples of how social science researchers incorporate object methods in qualitative interview studies.

Object Lessons

Object Elicitation, Interviewing with Objects, Object-Interviews

Most qualitative studies using object methods are elicitation interviews. In elicitation interviews, the interviewer may either invite participants to respond to a text, photo, or object stimulus, or ask the participant to engage in an activity in which they create images or text to guide the interview (Roulston, 2022). The earliest mention of interview elicitation methods is John Collier, Jr.'s (1957) writing on photo elicitation methods in his work with French Canadian Maritime and U.S. Southwestern Navajo communities. Working with a team of researchers, Collier used field photographs to elicit participants' experiences with industrial labor and its impact on mental health. Collier was struck by the response photographs produced from participants, noting how photo elicitation created a "language bridge" for participants who may "lack fluency of words to make clear statements about complex processes and situations" and how photographs triggered "latent memory to stimulate and release emotional statements" (p. 858). John Collier, Jr., writing with Malcom Collier (1986), noted how photographic interviewing "elicits a flow of information about personalities, places, processes, and artifacts" (p. 106). They described how photographic interviewing offered "a detachment that allows the maximum free association possible within structured interviewing" (pp. 106–107). In other words, photographs function as a conduit for meaning-making that occurs outside the participant and interviewer. Collier (1957) and Collier and Collier's (1986) writing on photo elicitation methods provides a basis for understanding the function of stimuli in elicitation interviews more broadly. In the decades that followed, social science researchers built on Collier's work to expand visual methods to include other forms of imagery (Banks, 2001; Bissell, 2000; Pink, 2001) and methods for generating elicitation images (Harper, 2002; Latz & Mulvihill, 2017; Pain, 2012).

Likewise, studies using object elicitation have contributed to the growing body of literature on visual interview methods. One notable example is de Leon and Cohen's (2005) use of "object probes" in ethnographic life history research, in which participants were asked to bring an object of significance to share. de Leon and Cohen argued that "object probes" were useful to "generate verbal responses" (p. 201) and keep participants "focused on a topic" while "providing a trigger for memories" (p. 202). Further, they noted the potential for object probes to put participants at ease when talking about uncomfortable or sensitive topics. A more recent example from qualitative psychology studies is Willig's (2017) discussion of object elicitation methods in a study with patients living with a terminal illness. Willig noted the potential of object elicitation to "facilitate unrehearsed, in-the-moment reflections" and "allow a phenomenon to show itself" (p. 220). There are numerous examples of qualitative studies in which objects are used to elicit memories of past events (Abildgaard, 2018; Holmes, 2020; Pahl, 2012; Sheridan & Chamberlain, 2011; Thomson & Østergaard, 2021) and prompt descriptions of complex relationships or difficult emotions (Bird & Jensen, 2022; Fuller & Kuberska, 2022; Gondwe & Longnecker, 2015; Notermans & Kommers, 2013; Pottinger et al., 2022; Romano et al., 2012). What ties these studies together is the emphasis on objects as external loci for meaning making—as mechanisms for getting at a particular phenomenon or experience. In many of the studies cited here, scholars use terms such as object elicitation, object-centered interviews, or object interviewing to describe how objects provoke responses, memories, or stories. In some instances, scholars may use these terms interchangeably. In this chapter, I distinguish between object elicitation as "researching with things (using things as a way to generate responses and data)" (Woodward, 2020, p. 12) and object-interviewing as an orientation to objects as lively, agential participants in qualitative interviews.

Susan Nordstrom (2013) described object-interviewing as "a qualitative method that uses poststructural theories to understand the confused and confounded relationship between objects and subjects (both living and nonliving)" (p. 238). Drawing on Appadurai's notion of methodological fetishism and the Deleuzian concept of the fold, Nordstrom developed object-interviewing in her study with 11 Midwestern family genealogists to engage "a theoretical attention to objects and how those objects enliven and illuminate subject-object relationships" (p. 238). Nordstrom's object-interview approach troubles conventional qualitative elicitation methods in that it begins in entangled subject–object relations. Objects are more than triggers to get at a phenomenon of inquiry. In object-interviews, objects co-constitute the phenomenon. Thus, in object-interviews the researcher attunes to connections made with/through objects and to the materiality of the object (e.g., how an object looks, feels, sounds, smells). In this way, object-interviews facilitate an understanding of objects that "allows us to recognise entities which are at times bounded and distinct, but also explore how these entities are themselves relational" (Fowler & Harris, 2015, p. 133). In object-interviews, objects do not exist "out there," waiting to be invited in. Objects are already lively agents in the interview. Thus, in object-interviews the researcher considers how stories about an object entangle with its material qualities (e.g., the way it looks, sounds, feels). Likewise, an understanding of objects in relation and unfolding disrupts the stability and permanence of objects and considers the "many trajectories that material items can take through shifting meanings" (Hodder, 2000, p. 709).

Although there are few examples of qualitative interview studies adopting Nordstrom's object-interview method explicitly, there are numerous examples of qualitative interview studies in which object encounters/methods disrupt subject–object duality (Adams & Thompson, 2011; Allen, 2015; Caronia, 2015; Flint, 2019; Guyotte et al., 2020; Hannan et al., 2019; Hultin, 2019; Taylor, 2013). In their study on the experiences of women doctoral students, Guyotte and colleagues (2020) drew on Sara Ahmed's concept of objects as "affective and desiring materials" (p. 5) to examine how the objects participants discussed not only represented their experiences but how they "connected . . . bodies in the world" (Guyotte et al., 2020, p. 5). In one instance, they noted how a participant's chipped, empty cup "(re)oriented her to her struggles" during her interview and created a "willful archive of her negotiations as a multiracial Black woman-mother-daughter-scholar" (p. 8). In another example, Woodward (2016) used object interview methods to explore women's relationship with old jeans to better understand how people "speak the material" (p. 359). As she argued: "Changes in both the garment and fibres enact relations between people and encode memories, as the material and social are entangled and co-constituted" (p. 360). In this way, object-interviewing becomes more than asking participants to reflect on a memory about an object or to describe the qualities of an object; it is an orientation to the way objects and participants encounter one another both in memories and in the interview.

For researchers new to object-interviewing, you will want to think about the relationship between object methods and the theoretical framework guiding your inquiry. In my overview of object methods in qualitative interviewing, it is not my intention to advocate one approach over another by drawing distinctions between object elicitation and object-interviewing. Rather, I point to the ways in which different scholars have approached object methods in qualitative interviewing to draw your attention to the epistemological and ontological implications of using various approaches. For instance, if your research engages critical perspectives, you might be interested in how objects participate in counter narratives of marginalized groups (see, for example, Guyotte et al., 2020). If you are guided by social constructivist theories, you may be interested in the symbolic role objects play in constructing social identity (see, for example, Romano et al., 2012). Regardless of how you are incorporating object methods, you will want to consider how your methods align with your theoretical and conceptual framework. I turn now to a discussion of how object methods—specifically, object-interviewing—entangled in my interview with a participant named Sara.

Overview of Research Study and Theoretical Framework

I interviewed Sara as part of a qualitative research study exploring mothers' experiences preparing children for menstruation. I conducted interviews between the fall of 2019 and January 2021 and recruited participants using purposive network sampling (Schwandt, 2015). My inquiry was guided by Karen Barad's (2007) concepts of entanglement and intra-action to inform my thinking on the role of objects in interviews. Barad's concept of entanglement troubles Cartesian dualism (e.g., subject–object, nature–culture, human–non-human, space–time). As opposed to autonomous entities possessing agency and enacting agency upon an*other*, Barad argued that agency is produced as entities materialize. She noted: "To be entangled is not simply to be intertwined with another, as in the joining of separate entities, but to lack an independent self-contained existence. Existence is not an individual affair" (Barad, 2007, p. ix). Likewise, interviewing is not an individual affair consisting of interactions among autonomous selves. Reconceptualizing interviewing practices as entangled matters for how we understand encounters/experiences/stories materializing among humans and non-humans. Barad described the process of materialization among entangled entities as *intra-action*. Just as entanglement troubles subject–object duality, intra-action troubles conventional notions of agency as something that is possessed and enacted from one autonomous entity upon another. Object-interviews thus become human-object-space-time entanglements in which encounters, subjectivities, rapport, and narratives materialize.

After my initial three interviews, I began inviting mothers to bring objects to their interviews. The invitation was open-ended: Bring an object of significance in preparing your child for menstruation. Of the ten mothers I interviewed, five mothers brought objects to their interviews. My interview with Sara was the first online object-interview I conducted in my study. Although I discuss the online entanglements of our object-interview, my focus here is not on online interviewing per se, but rather on the affordances of orienting to objects in qualitative interviewing. I turn now to a partial account of my object-interview with Sara—the object-interview I assumed was doomed to fail from the beginning and the one that probably taught me the most about how "matter comes to matter" (Barad, 2003, p. 801).

Encountering and Sensemaking With Sara

Online Jitters

It was a chilly Saturday morning in January 2021 when I finally met Sara. She had been referred to me by another mother in my study several months earlier. Sara, a mother of four, worked part-time as a doula and also as a tutor at a private college at the time of our interview. I initiated an email exchange with Sara prior to the initial COVID-19 lockdown in March of 2020. Unsure how long the pandemic would continue, we postponed our interview several times over the next few months. My previous interviews had been in-person, and I hoped I could "wait out" social distancing guidelines with enough time to conduct my remaining interviews in person. *Face-to-face is better, especially with object-interviews*, I thought. How do I follow objects around through a webcam? After a few months into the pandemic, it became clear that I would need to conduct any remaining interviews for my study online. I mourned this decision. I worried about my ability to conduct object-interviews in a virtual space and wondered how to establish rapport, to be(come) in communion (Ezzy, 2010) the way I had with mothers during in-person interviews.

Qualitative scholars have noted how technology (Adams & Thompson, 2011), recording devices (Caronia, 2015; Nordstrom, 2015) and field notes become part of the interview apparatuses (Barlott et al., 2020). *Indeed*, I thought on that January morning, as I surveyed the laptop-recorder-Smartphone-notebook-interview protocol apparatus in front of me. I considered how the global COVID-19 pandemic entangled with this interview apparatus. Sara would likely be home with her spouse and children during our conversation.

My family—a toddler, two teenagers, and my spouse—were on the other side of my bedroom/office door. Before our interview, I double-checked the bedroom door and situated my recording devices as close to my computer speaker as possible.

I chose to audio record Sara's interview just as I audio recorded in-person interviews, using a digital audio recorder and a backup Smartphone recording app. Although Zoom software embeds audio/video recording capabilities, I was sensitive to interviewing Sara in her home with her family and wanted to ensure her comfort during our conversation. I wanted to avoid potential ethical issues with video footage of family members, even as I was aware of the ways in which audio recording also entangles with associated others during interviews (Mazzei, 2013). As for encountering Sara's object, I would be unable to hold it, touch it, and photograph it the way I had done with in-person object-interviews. Instead I would have to rely on Sara for photos and my ability to take descriptive field notes and memos. *"Here goes nothing!"* I thought as I opened the Zoom room.

The following is a vignette narrating the beginning of my interview with Sara and my initial poetic representation of this encounter.

Mother-mess

A few minutes pass and Sara appears in the Zoom room. We exchange smiles, hellos, and I thank her for being willing to talk with me—especially on a Saturday! I notice Sara is sitting at what appears to be a table in a bedroom. Behind her is a closet and dresser with drawers and door ajar. A clothes basket topped with shoes sits in the closet doorway. On a cold Saturday morning in a house with four children, this is likely the most privacy Sara can hope for. As we settle into our interview, Sara fiddles with her earbuds as if locking them in place.

Janie: Talk about the object you brought to share.

Sara: I'm sorry, one of my children *(glancing over left shoulder)*—Hey, can you not do the robot by the door? *(turns to computer)* Can you hear it over the recording?

I hope you can't. (Interview with Sara, January 8, 2021)

Object Lessons 155

I assure Sara that I can't hear the robot, although I'm curious what it sounds like. Her earbuds are doing their job. The padded carpet on my bedroom floor and the door securely closed are doing their job... mostly. Occasionally, I hear someone yell, laugh, or cry.

Before telling me about the object Sara brought to share (a book on puberty), Sara begins our conversation describing the reusable menstrual pad her aunt gave her at the celebration of Sara's first period:

Sara: I have—let's see.... I can... they're nearby. *(Gets up, looks in dresser drawer)*

Janie: If you're comfortable. If you're not—totally, I mean, it's totally fine.

Sara: Yeah. That's—that's one thing.... I'm like, I'm not very shy. *(laughter)* Like, I'm all about what happens... and all of those things. I also think, I wonder if *(looks through another drawer)*. Okay, typically it's easier to find stuff, but my kids have also gone through all of my drawers. *(laughs)*

Janie: That's okay.

Sara: Okay. And it may be actually *(looks through a laundry basket by the closet)*. I just, um, I can't find them. *(laughs)*. Okay, I'm sorry. *(sits down at computer)*

Janie: No, no, that's fine. (Interview with Sara, January 8, 2021)

Following our interview, I read my pre-interview memo and reflect on my initial concerns about building rapport. Before I join my family on the other side of my bedroom door, I draft the following poetic memo in my research notebook:

I met Sara today
in her bedroom.
While we talked, she rummaged dresser drawers
sifted through unfolded laundry,
Looking for a twenty-year-old maxi pad.

I sat in my bedroom.
   Inches from a trash can overflowing with last week's life scraps
      Q-tips, tissues and empty toilet rolls.
I ask about the first-period celebration her mother gave her.
As toddlers wolf-howl in the distance
Begging off sleep
—Can you hear that?
   —No, don't worry!
—I'm so sorry.
   —No, it's ok!
Kids need pencils, need headphones, need a hug, need to slide past the referee
   called dad who forgot his whistle.
The noise mess, the clutter mess
The mother-mess that distracts,
Detracts,
Disarms,
And enDears.
Makes us laugh together.
Who are we kidding? We know our conversation has a limited shelf-life.
And aren't we kind of here to talk about our messy shit, anyway?
After a "sorry to bother you, Mom," we pick up where we left off.
I ask a question and Sara answ——
We startle.
Look over our shoulders.
Turn toward our Zoom room squares and ask:
"Is that mine or yours?" (Poetic memo, January 8, 2021)

Orienting to Disruptive Objects

I was instantly struck by the way objects materialized (unexpectedly!) in my interview with Sara, how they produced our "mother mess," and how they enacted rapport. In the encounter described above, Sara has not yet introduced the object she brought to our interview, and yet objects (a robot and a reusable menstrual pad) are already producing stops and starts in our conversation. These stops and starts matter for the way Sara and I encounter this interview space, for the way rapport materializes. Writing about unexpected object encounters in walking interviews, Flint (2019) noted that "examining what object encounters produce emphasises the importance of the researcher's awareness and intention behind the cuts and connections made through methodology" (p. 134). As I linger with these unexpected object encounters, I notice how rapport becomes materially enacted, produced in relation among humans and objects. I am not establishing rapport; rather, it is materializing through intra-actions among toy robots, reusable pads, dresser drawers, and mothers.

Sara's search for a reusable pad was both "on topic" for an interview on preparing children for menstruation, even as Sara's search interrupted the flow of conversation. This disruption enacts a point of connection. Eventually Sara returns to her seat and says, "My children have been in all my drawers, I cannot find it." This moment tugged at me as I stared at my own pile of unfolded laundry in the corner and the overflowing trash can by my feet. It tugged at me in the poetic memo I wrote following our interview and of my representation of this moment in my dissertation (Copple, 2022). These unexpected object encounters became "moments that glowed" (MacLure, 2013) in my research study, moments that mattered methodologically for my understanding of objects becoming material. As I thought with the robot and the reusable pad encounter, they shifted my conceptualization of rapport. The very notion of rapport becomes a more-than-human intra-action, materializing in the lively relations among things and people.

Following "The Bodies Book"

"This is actually what I brought to share," Sara laughed, holding up a paperback book entitled *It's perfectly normal: Changing bodies, growing up, sex, and sexual health*, by Robie H. Harris and Michael Emberly (2009). When I asked Sara to talk about why this book is significant in her discussions about puberty and menstruation, she replied:

> This has been like our house go-to, um . . . for talking to–talking to the kids about puberty. . . . When I started [having] kids, I was like, "How do I disseminate this information to kids in a way that they're also, you know, going to understand, and it's going to be meaningful, and something that they want, they can hold on to?" And that's when I started looking for books. And this wasn't the first book

that I came across. I went through a few other ones, got rid of some *(laughs)*. But I really liked the representation in this one, because they're all *(turning pages)*– Oops! This page is a little ripped up *(laughs)* but you can see here, like *(holds up book to show pages)* different kinds of bodies, all different, family orientations *(turns pages)*. It's not just mom and dad. It kind of goes through a really nice, all-inclusive way of talking about bodies and family. The kids like this page with all the bodies on it. That's the ripped one *(laughing, turns pages, showing illustrations)*. They, um *(laughs)* call it the bodies book. (Interview with Sara, January 8, 2021)

In this excerpt, Sara describes how inclusive representation becomes information her children can "hold on to." Later in our conversation, Sara talks about her experiences as a bi-racial child in the United States in the 1980s. She turns to the double-page spread of naked bodies, pointing to the illustrations as she talks about how her mother tried to find books with "bodies that looked like mine." When Sara describes conversations about reproduction, she opens the book, pointing to pages covering these topics. In this way, the book offers Sara something to "hold on to" as she describes conversations with her children. She talks about how she and her children "pull the book off the shelf" when her children have questions. When I follow up with a question about the ripped pages, Sara cannot recall how the pages got ripped. Instead she describes the creased cover and loose binding, how the book falls open to the ripped pages of naked bodies. She goes on to talk about how the book gets lost in the house, gets tucked away under her daughter's bed, or left under piles of toys on the living room floor.

In the weeks following our interview, I read the transcript and my notes from our conversation, listen to the audio recording, and linger over the images Sara emails me. As I follow "the bodies book" encounter in my conversation with Sara, the book's contents become inseparable from its sights and sounds. The sounds of flipping pages, the shuffle-slide of the book picked up and laid down, "Oops!" as Sara discovers a ripped page, the way the book falls open to the double-page spread of naked bodies. I examine the photograph of the book cover (see Figure 8.1[2]), attuning to the creases and tears, wondering about each wrinkled intra-action.

Object Lessons

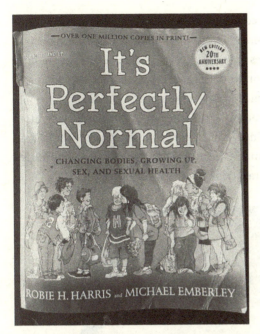

Figure 8.1. Book Cover.

Illustrations, ripped pages, loose binding, Sara's childhood, her children's fingerprints—all these entanglements and more mattered for the materializing narrative of this object-interview encounter (Tamboukou, 2008). As Donna Haraway (2016) wrote, "It matters what stories we tell to tell other stories" (p. 12). Object-interview methods mattered in my sensemaking with Sara's data and in my representation of our interview encounter, just as they mattered in our conversation. As I wondered how I might construct a narrative representation of Sara's data, I resisted a hurried approach to emplot my "findings." Rather than "excavating for stories" (Kim, 2016, p. 274), I followed Nordstrom's idea of tracing connections. Nordstrom (2013) wrote of tracing "connections" in object-interviews to get at the multiple, unknowable ways people "read objects" (p. 244). She argued that tracing connections engages the unstable, non-linear way participants described multiple, unfolding relations. Unlike Nordstrom, I did not refuse the notion of stories altogether. Rather, I thought with Nordstrom's (2013) tracing alongside Maria Tamboukou's (2008) notion of materializing narratives. Tamboukou, drawing on Baradian concepts, described materializing narratives as the intra-active process of stories becoming among infinite possibilities. Materializing narratives disrupts notions of stories as inevitable, fixed, stable. Bringing object-interviewing methods in relation with narrative representation situates materializing narratives as unfolding, bundles of human-object relations.

Rather than reading and coding Sara's interview looking for narrative elements (e.g., characters, setting, conflict, plot), making sense with the data required an orientation to human-object encounters as I listened to the recording and read notes and a transcript of our conversation.

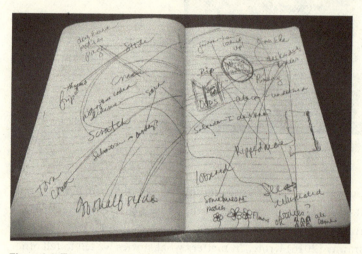

Figure 8.2. Tracing connections.

Woodward (2020) argues that object methods entangle ontologically, epistemologically, and methodologically with qualitative inquiry. Understanding objects as entangled with researchers and participants in interviews matters for the ways researchers conceptualize what counts as data and how they make sense with data. Tracing human-object connections provoked questions for the bodies book. How is the bodies book being held on to? How does the book circulate in Sara's house? Among Sara's children? As I consider the book in motion—changing hands, becoming worn, becoming creased, sliding under a bed, becoming lost, becoming found—the narrative materializing becomes a story of following the book across space and time.

Takeaways and Suggestions

In this chapter, I have focused on my encounters during an object-interview to explore how object methods entangled with sensemaking and representation in my study on mothers preparing children for menstruation. I provided an overview of the literature on object methods and object-interviewing, situating my approach to object-interviewing as a sensory mode of knowing—a way to think with narratives materializing as participants, objects, and researchers intra-act. Through my encounters with Sara, I illustrated the methodological implications of orienting to objects as always already entangled with interview practices and consider how these entanglements continue mattering beyond the interview. I conclude with suggestions and guiding questions for researchers new to object methods in qualitative interviewing.

Why Objects?

As you consider using object methods in your interview study, you will want to think about how object methods align with your research questions and theoretical framework. In my inquiry, I noticed how objects entangled with mothers' stories and wondered how object-interviews might make these entanglements more explicit. For me, incorporating object-interviews became a way to follow Barad's (2003) notion of "matter coming to matter" (p. 801). Ultimately, my decision to incorporate object-interviews was a response to my initial interview data and informed by the theoretical, epistemological, and ontological assumptions guiding my study. Likewise, you will want to think about the relationship between object methods and the assumptions guiding your inquiry. As with any qualitative study, making clear connections between methods, research questions, theory, and epistemology provides a justification for how object methods add quality to your study. You might consider questions such as:

- How will objects help me understand particular phenomena, experiences, or events related to my inquiry?
- How do my theoretical, epistemological, and ontological assumptions inform my approach to object methods? Are objects external stimuli? Co-participants?

Which Objects? And Where?

When designing an interview study using object methods, you will want to think about the types of objects related to your inquiry and the criteria for selecting objects. Given my interest in the relationship between mothers' experiences and encounters with objects, it was important that mothers select their own objects. My invitation to "bring an object of significance in your experiences preparing children for menstruation" served as the criteria for selecting an object. Mothers brought objects ranging from informational materials to menstrual management materials to personal journals and letters. Due to the sensitive topic involved and the potential for sharing private and personal objects, I asked mothers to select the location for in-person interviews prior to the COVID-19 lockdown. The shift to online interviewing due to the COVID-19 pandemic situated me inside participants' homes and vice versa. Although unexpected, conducting online interviews in participants' homes produced ethical and methodological insights regarding the entanglements of space, objects, participants, researchers, and family during interviews. As you think about the types of objects, object selection criteria, and potential interview settings, you might consider the following questions:

- What types of objects might relate to your inquiry?
- Will participants select objects? If so, what criteria will participants use?
- Will you select objects for participants? If so, what criteria will you use to select objects for interviews?
- What ethical issues might arise as you ask participants to engage with objects in particular interview settings?

Asking Questions About Objects

As with any qualitative interview study, object-interview questions should be guided by your research questions. Your research questions should help you determine what you want to know about objects. Since my study focused on the ways in which narratives materialized in relation to objects, I used open-ended questions to invite participants to "describe in as much detail as possible" the object's physical characteristics, as well as their experiences with the object. An open-ended approach allowed space for participants to wonder and wander in their responses to questions about how objects mattered in their experiences. As a researcher, this approach created space in which to witness narratives materializing. As you develop interview questions, consider what you want to know about objects. For instance:

- Are you interested in the physical qualities (e.g., sight, sound, taste, touch, smell) of objects?
- Are you interested in stories about objects?
- Are you interested in the symbolic value of objects?
- Are you interested in the ways participants use objects for daily activities or special occasions?

Final Thoughts

Whether you consider the role of objects as the primary phenomenon of interest, an elicitation tool, a co-participant, or some combination of these, your decision to use object methods will influence the data in your study. The data, in turn, will shape your analysis and ultimately your findings. As Woodward (2020) aptly noted, "Methods produce understandings of the world" (p. 28). I couldn't agree more. For me, object-interviews entailed both a method conducting interviews and an orientation to the lively potential of non-human actors as co-participants in generating knowledge. Listening to objects, looking at them, thinking *with* them required me to return over and over again to many of the questions posed in this section. Although I offer these questions to guide your thinking as you design your study, it may be important to return to these questions throughout the research process, knowing that you will likely have more questions along the way! I have found that one of the most exciting things about object-interviewing is the opportunity to think with different questions about what it means to generate and make sense with interview data. I encourage you to experiment with object methods in your own interview study, even if it's risky and you're unsure where objects might lead you. Follow them around and see what happens.[3]

Notes

1. I use pseudonyms in referring to participants.
2. Photograph by Sara (pseudonym).

3. I offer a note of acknowledgment to Dr. Maureen Flint, Assistant Professor in the qualitative research program at the University of Georgia. Thank you for introducing me to Susan Nordstrom's work and for encouraging me to "follow objects around and see what happens."

References

Abildgaard, M. S. (2018). My whole life in telephones: Material artifacts as interview elicitation devices. *International Journal of Qualitative Methods, 17*(1). https://doi.org/10.1177/1609406918797795

Adams, C. A., & Thompson, T. L. (2011). Interviewing objects: Including educational technologies as qualitative research participants. *International Journal of Qualitative Studies in Education, 24*(6), 733–750. https://doi.org/10.1080/09518398.2010.529849

Ahmed, S. (2010). *The promise of happiness*. Duke University Press.

Allen, L. (2015). The power of things! A "new" ontology of sexuality at school. *Sexuality, 18*(8), 941–958. https://doi.org/10.1177/1363460714550920

Banks, M. (2001). *Visual methods in social research*. SAGE.

Barad, K. (2003). Posthuman performativity: Toward an understanding of how matter comes to matter. *Journal of Women in Culture and Society, 28*(3), 801–831. https://doi.org/10.1086/345321

Barad, K. (2007). *Meeting the universe halfway: Quantum physics and the entanglement of matter and meaning*. Duke University Press.

Barlott, T., Shevellar, L., Turpin, M., Setchell, J. (2020). The dissident interview: A deterritorializing guerrilla encounter. *Qualitative Inquiry, 26*(6), 650–660. https://doi.org/10.1177/1077800419898590

Bennett, J. (2010). *Vibrant matter: A political ecology of things*. Duke University Press.

Bird, T., & Jensen, T. (2022). What's in the refrigerator? Using an adapted material culture approach to understand health practices and eating habits in the home. *Social Science & Medicine, 292*. https://doi.org/10.1016/j.socscimed.2021.114581

Bissell, S. (2000). In focus: Film, focus groups and working children in Bangladesh. *Visual Anthropology, 13*(2), 169–183. https://doi.org/10.1080/08949468.2000.9966796

Caronia, L. (2015). Totem and taboo: The embarrassing epistemic work of things in the research setting. *Qualitative Research, 15*(2), 141–165. https://doi.org/10.1177/1468794113517392

Collier, J., Jr. (1957). Photography in anthropology: A report on two experiments. *American Anthropologist, 59*, 843–859.

Collier, J., Jr., & Collier, M. (1986). *Visual anthropology: Photography as a research method*. University of New Mexico Press.

Copple, J. (2022). *Making menstrual knowledge through multi-genre methodologies: Exploring mothers' encounters with children at menarche*. (Publication No. 29063604) [Doctoral dissertation, University of Georgia]. ProQuest Dissertations and Theses Global.

de Leon, J. P., & Cohen, J. H. (2005). Object and walking probes in ethnographic interviewing. *Field Methods, 17*(2), 200–204. https://doi.org/10.1177/1525822X0527473

Ezzy, D. (2010). Qualitative interviewing as an embodied emotional performance. *Qualitative Inquiry, 16*(3), 163–170. https://doi.org/10.1177/1077800409351970

Flint, M. A. (2019). Hawks, robots, and chalkings: Unexpected object encounters during walking interviews on a college campus. *Educational Research for Social Change, 8*(1), 120–137. http://dx.doi.org/10.17159/2221-4070/2018/v8i1a8

Fowler, C., & Harris, O. J. (2015). Enduring relations: Exploring a paradox of new materialism. *Journal of Material Culture, 20*(2), 127–148. https://doi.org/doi.10.1177/1359183515577176

Fuller, D., & Kuberska, K. (2022). Outside the (memory) box: How unpredictable objects disrupt the discourse of bereavement in narratives of pregnancy loss. *Mortality, 27*(1), 1–17. https://doi.org/10.1080/13576275.2020.1783221

Gondwe, M., & Longnecker, N. (2015). Objects as stimuli for exploring young people's views about cultural and scientific knowledge. *Science, Technology & Human Values, 40*(5), 766–792. https://doi.org/10.1177/01622439155

Guyotte, K. W., Flint, M. A., & Shelton, S. A. (2020). Giving up as a willful feminist practice. *Gender and Education, 33*(2), 202–216. https://doi.org/10.1080/09540253.2020.1743821

Hannan, L., Carney, G., Devine, P., & Hodge, G. (2019). "A view from old age": Women's lives as narrated through objects. *Life Writing, 16*(1), 51–67. https://doi.org/10.1080/14484528.2019.1521259

Haraway, D. (2016). *Staying with the trouble: Making kin in the Chthulucene*. Duke University Press.

Harper, D. (2002). Talking about pictures: A case for photo elicitation. *Visual Studies, 17*(1), 13–26. https://doi.org/10.1080/14725860220137345

Harris, R. H., & Emberley, M. (2009). *It's perfectly normal: A book about growing up, changing bodies, sex, and sexual health* (3rd ed.). Candlewick Press.

Henare, A., Holbraad, M., & Wastell, S. (Eds). (2007). *Thinking through things: Theorising artefacts ethnographically*. Routledge.

Hicks, D. (2010). The material-cultural turn: Event and effect. In D. Hicks & M. Beaudry (Eds.), *The Oxford handbook of material culture studies* (pp. 25–98). Oxford University Press.

Hodder, I. (2000). The interpretation of documents and material culture. In N. Denzin & Y. S. Lincoln (Eds.), *Handbook of qualitative research* (pp. 703–715). SAGE.

Holmes, H. (2020). Material relationships: Object interviews as a means of studying everyday life. In H. Holmes & S. M. Hall (Eds.), *Mundane methods: Innovative ways to research the everyday* (pp. 66–83). Manchester University Press.

Hoskins. J. (1998). *Biographical objects: How things tell the stories of people's lives*. Routledge.

Hultin, L. (2019). On becoming a sociomaterial researcher: Exploring epistemological practices grounded in a relational, performative ontology. *Information and Organization, 29*, 91–104. https://doi.org/10.1016/j.infoandorg.2019.04.004

Hurdley, R. (2007). Focal points: framing material culture and visual data. *Qualitative Research, 7*(3), 355–374. https://doi.org/10.1177/1468794107078516

Ingold, T. (2012). Toward an ecology of materials. *Annual Review of Anthropology, 41*, 427–442. https://doi.org/10.1146/annurev-anthro-081309-145920

Kim, J.-H. (2016). *Understanding narrative inquiry*. SAGE.

Latz, A. O., & Mulvihill, T. M. (2017). *Photovoice research in education and beyond: A practical guide from theory to exhibition*. Routledge.

Law, J. (2004). *After method: Mess in social science research*. Routledge.

MacLure, M. (2013). The wonder of data. *Cultural Studies ↔ Critical Methodologies, 13*(4), 228–232. https://doi.org/10.1177/1532708613487863

Mazzei, L. A. (2013). A voice without organs: Interviewing in posthumanist research. *International Journal of Qualitative Studies in Education, 26*(6), 732–740. http://dx.doi.org/10.1080/09518398.2013.788761

Miller, D. (1994). Artefacts and the meaning of things. In T. Ingold (Ed.), *Companion encyclopedia of anthropology* (pp. 396–419). Routledge.

Nordstrom, S. N. (2013). Object-interviews: Folding, unfolding, and refolding perceptions of objects. *International Journal of Qualitative Methods, 12*(1), 237–257. https://doi.org/10.1177/160940691301200111

Nordstrom, S. N. (2015). Not so innocent anymore: Making recording devices matter in qualitative interviews. *Qualitative Inquiry, 21*(4), 388–401. https://doi.org/10.1177/1077800414563804

Notermans, C., & Kommers, H. (2013). Researching religion: The iconographic elicitation method. *Qualitative Research, 13*(5), 608–625. https://doi.org/10.1177/1468794112459672

Pahl, K. (2012). Every object tells a story: Intergenerational stories and objects in the homes of Pakistani Heritage families in South Yorkshire, UK. *Home Cultures, 9*(3), 303–327. https://doi.org/10.2752/175174212X13414983522152

Pain, H. (2012). A literature review to evaluate the choice and use of visual methods. *International Journal of Qualitative Methods, 11*(4). https://doi.org/10.1177/160940691201100401

Pink, S. (2001). *Doing visual ethnography*. SAGE.

Pottinger, L., Barron, A., Hall, S. M., Ehgartner, U., & Browne, A. L. (2022). Talking methods, talking about methods: Invoking the transformative potential of social methods through animals, objects, and how-to instructions. *Geo: Geography and Environment, 9*(1). https://doi.org/10/1002/geo2.107

Romano, D., McCay, E., & Boydell, K. (2012). The use of material objects in understanding the process of recovery from a first episode of schizophrenia. *Arts & Health: International Journal for Research, Policy & Practice, 4*(1), 70–82. https://doi.org/10.1080/17533015.2011.584882

Roulston, K. (2022). *Interviewing: A guide to theory and practice*. SAGE.

Schwandt, T. (2015). *The SAGE dictionary of qualitative methods*. SAGE.

Sheridan, J., & Chamberlain, K. (2011). The power of things. *Qualitative Research in Psychology, 8*(4), 315–332. https://doi.org/10.1080/14780880903490821

Tamboukou, M. (2008). Re-imagining the narratable subject. *Qualitative Research, 8*(3), 283–292. https://doi.org/10.1177/1468794106093623

Taylor, C. A. (2013). Objects, bodies and space: gender and embodied practices of mattering in the classroom. *Gender and Education, 25*(6), 688–703. https://doi.org/10.1080/09540253.2013.834864

Thomson, R., & Østergaard, J. (2021). Open-ended transitions to adulthood: Metaphorical thinking for times of stasis. *Sociological Review, 69*(2), 434–450. https://doi.org/10.1177/0038026120970346

Willig, C. (2017). Reflections on the use of object elicitation. *Qualitative Psychology, 4*(3), 211–222. https://dx.doi.org/10.1037/qup0000054

Woodward, S. (2016). Object interviews, material imaginings and "unsettling" methods: Interdisciplinary approaches to understanding materials and material culture. *Qualitative Research, 16*(4), 359–374. https://doi.org/10.1177/ 1468794115589647

Woodward, S. (2020). *Material methods: Researching and thinking with things.* SAGE.

NINE

 Experience in the Abstract: Exploring the Potential of Graphic Elicitation

Alison Bravington

"GRAPHIC" IS A WORD WITH more than one meaning. As an adjective, it refers to the detailed, explicit rendering of an image in a way that produces emotional impact. As a noun, it denotes a working image that condenses information, representing values, connections, and associations. Graphic elicitation—the use of drawing and diagramming as a basis for exploring human experience—draws on both meanings, using simple visuals to represent experiential depth and complexity. The method is not an invention of qualitative research, but emerged from elicitation practices in education, health services, and social care as a way of exploring a client's personal perspectives and relational processes (Bravington & King, 2019).

Graphic elicitation occupies a methodological niche that is still in development within the "big tent" (Denzin, 2010) of qualitative methodology. It is often broadly categorized under the umbrella of arts-based methods—a label that fails to adequately describe how the properties of drawing and diagramming relate to social inquiry. This chapter explores these issues with reference to previous graphic elicitation studies conducted within the framework of conventional humanist methodologies (Brinkmann, 2017). It is structured around the traditional division between data collection and analysis, with the aim of providing a practical guide. Those of us who are constrained by the approaches to applied research preferred by the institutions where we work or study might already be troubled by the problematization of our situated selves and our audio-recorders as we talk to our research participants. Michael (2004) has already pointed out the potential of furniture and animals to disrupt the tidiness of the research interview—the introduction of paper and pens might seem a step too far. The sections below will unashamedly introduce further responsibilities for the management of materialities in the interview.

As researchers, if we are invested in the concept of methodology, we often take ownership of the interpretive process and situate it within our analytic method. A broader view would encompass the on-the-hop interpretation we undertake as fieldwork progresses, formulating new questions and probes and following up hunches and unexpected turns as we interview. We are forever elaborating our own agenda as we research, and (if we are responsible researchers) forever chasing ways of handing the agenda over to our participants. Graphic elicitation opens up the flow, the hunches, and the unexpectedness to interviewees, engaging them in telling, interpreting, and retelling their experiences.

The aim of this chapter is to give you an understanding of whether graphic elicitation might enhance the reach of your research inquiry, and how the method works. Inevitably, the "how to" draws on mechanistic explanations—we will explore the potential benefits of the method, examine how the dimensions of diagramming and drawing relate to social processes and subjective experience, and touch on systematic approaches to analysis. But the chapter will also push beyond these boundaries to explore some of the less tangible dynamics of graphic representation. In doing so, it will draw on theories of cognition—these are referenced as metaphors for thinking about thinking, rather than cited as scientific fact. In offering ideas around the association between graphic elements and the dynamics of "being in the world," the hope is to unlock your thinking around how assemblages of graphic elements might be customized to help you to conduct inquiry in a way that resonates with the paradigm in which you work.

Why Choose Graphic Elicitation?

While graphics and photographs can both be used to elicit dialogue, what distinguishes graphic elicitation from photo-elicitation is its emphasis on the active, performative process of image construction. Graphic elicitation lends itself to the step-by-step revelation of social, temporal, and/or emotional dynamics. Its abstract nature encourages the spontaneous creation of metaphors to explain our behavior as social actors in a complex world. Elicitation can be researcher- or participant-led—in this chapter we focus on the production of images by the participants as part of the interview process. The use of participant-led drawing and diagramming in qualitative research has steadily increased since the year 2000 (Bravington & King, 2019). The reasons most often cited by researchers to justify their choice of the technique is that it facilitates rapport, stimulates recall, and increases the richness of interview data. How graphic elicitation achieves this is often implicit or poorly described. In this section, we will explore some of the evidence supporting these claims.

Rapport

Good communication relies on feelings of comfort and competence during an interaction. A key claim of participant-led graphic elicitation is that the technique addresses the power imbalance by handing the agenda to the participant (Goldenberg et al., 2016). Rather than a researcher generating a list of questions, the participant creates a visual schematic of their experience to anchor and guide interview dialogue, placing them in a "position of competence" (Ramanan et al., 2021). Participants can make their own judgments about what to represent and how to tell the story around the image; the researcher's role is to find hooks within the visual to prompt the accompanying narrative, rather than to lead the dialogue.

Asking participants to create a drawing or diagram also has implications for the embodied practice of interviewing. It can put the participant at ease by providing opportunities to break the direct eye-gaze that often dominates a close exchange, and can facilitate natural breaks, giving time and space to the participant as they draw, arrange, or rearrange the graphic (Hardy et al., 2012). The creation of a visual can help to dissipate the anxiety experienced by some participants as they try to predict what kind of responses the researcher may be looking for, and the visual anchors the dialogue, reducing the interrogative feel that can sometimes infuse a linear schedule of questions.

Recall

The qualitative research interview, where it chases experiential knowing, depends heavily on participants' power of recall. Asking participants to describe events and connected feelings taps into what cognitive psychologists construe as autobiographical memory, episodic memory, and (more recently) event memory (Rubin & Umanath, 2015). Cognitive scientists distinguish the recall of experience from the perspective of the self from the recall of knowledge. Knowledge, as a phenomenon, is decontextualized, whereas our memory of events relies on additional contextual cues such as spatial awareness and relational stimuli. The ubiquitous use of visuals in learning environments stems from their utility in enhancing this type of recall (Fernandes et al., 2018; Tran et al., 2022). These ideas can be useful in conceptualizing why graphic elicitation might help us to remember experiences and social interactions, and how they felt.

Richness

A graphic representation can convey complexity with simple shapes, often referencing symbols or metaphors that are shared between people or groups of people, across communities or nations, or universally. These shared meanings, or "natural correspondences" (Tversky, 2011), arise from the human experience of embodiment, our spatial awareness, and our ability to draw comparisons. Lines map to journeys, dots to locations. Boxes, circles, or arrows map to events or connections, networks to causes and actions. We can use these shapes to find our way, to record changes or transitions, and to simplify complex experiences. Diagrams in particular can reduce the effort involved in communicating this complexity (Cheng et al., 2001; Tversky, 2011); their abstract nature can introduce ambiguities that are generative (Hurley & Novick, 2006), encouraging new interpretations on the part of the participant or misinterpretations on the part of the researcher that invite further exploration and clarification.

Dialogue focused on a drawing or diagram moves between the meta-view and the detail in an iterative process, mirroring traditional methods of qualitative analysis. As a participant stands back to look at their completed visual, new meanings can arise from the gestalt of the image (Bravington & King, 2019), or from a reconstrual or "re-seeing" of the significance of an experience (Bresler, 2006). Drawing can summon up the intangible—for example, representing happiness (Lu & Da, 2019), pain (Kirkham, 2015), or existential suffering (Cheung et al., 2019).

Choosing and Customizing Graphic Images

The focus of your research inquiry will determine your choice of drawing or diagramming and its graphic scaffolding. Scaffolding refers to the visual

Experience in the Abstract

configurations you choose—whether you wish to capture relational or chronological associations, and/or impose structure using a predetermined metaphor. The choice of scaffolding affects possibilities for representation and interpretation. To explore these issues we will focus on two foundational graphic arrangements used in qualitative research: *egocentric images*, which represent other people or social systems in relation to the self, and *allocentric images*, which represent other people or concepts (such as events or places) in relation to one another. Using examples from research, we will examine how these arrangements might relate to the social and material world, and how they can be further simplified (made more abstract) to encourage flexibility of interpretation. We will then consider other features that free-drawing might bring to the process of elicitation.

Egocentric Images

Egocentric images locate the self (the individual participant) at the hub or center, with spokes or circles expanding outward to link them to surrounding networks. Simpler, related approaches include circle diagrams, in which the participant is placed at the center and connections or associations at varying distances in circles around them, and the use of arrows to represent interaction between the self and others.

Social convoy diagrams. Social convoy diagrams are constructed from concentric circles with the self at the center (Figure 9.1) and are used to explore social networks (Bagnoli, 2009; Emmel & Clark, 2009). Proximity is the dynamic used to suggest the quality of connections—close associations usually appear in the nearest concentric circle and more distant ties in the outer circle. A more abstract application is the arrangement of material phenomena in the circles, with proximity indicating level of preference or significance—examples include studies of information horizons by Savolainen and Kari (2004) and Copeland and Agosto (2012) that explore the materialities of information storage and the values attributed to different media. Copeland and Agosto's participants included unexpected objects on their diagrams, such as clothing and furniture, demonstrating the conceptual flexibility enabled by diagramming where the researcher's brief has a light touch.

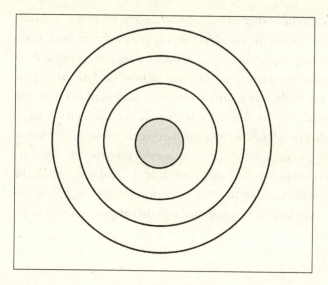

Figure 9.1. Concentric Circles.

Ecomaps. Ecomaps are based on the hub-and-spoke design (Figure 9.2), representing qualities of relationships by the weight, number, or composition of the lines joining the outer circles to the self or hub. They are less abstract and more prescriptive than the concentric circle approach, making them more suitable as a descriptive tool to map the composition of social networks, but have been used in qualitative research to explore experiential issues such as emotional loss and social isolation (Ray & Street, 2007; Washington, 2009).

Releasing the circles from their connecting spokes creates a simpler, more abstract diagram using proximity, size, and overlap to represent connections (Figure 9.3). This doesn't require the participant to fix the quality of the associations, allowing flexibility of interpretation (overlapping symbols can be ambiguous—for example, signifying supportive or oppressive qualities). The elicitative properties of this simplified approach are best illustrated by case studies using the Pictorial Representation of Illness and Self Measure (PRISM) developed by Büchi and Sensky (1999), a therapeutic method used to explore illness burden.

Pictor. Pictor involves the use of arrows to map relationships and interactions (Figure 9.4). The technique was developed from a therapeutic approach exploring family dynamics (Hargreaves, 1979; King et al., 2013), and has been

Experience in the Abstract

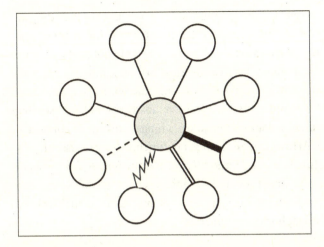

Figure 9.2. Hub-and-Spoke.

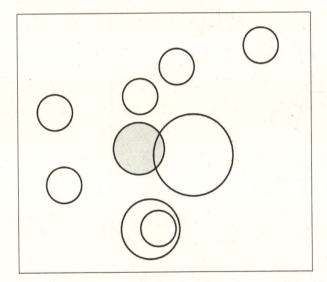

Figure 9.3. Free circles.

used to explore social interaction around specified tasks such as collaborative working (Hardy et al., 2012; Mergenthal & Güthlin, 2018), supportive care (Bulk et al., 2020; Gillespie et al., 2018) and workplace learning (Berkhout et al., 2017; Van den Berg et al., 2017; Olmos-Vega et al., 2019). The interviewee is asked to recall the people involved in a significant event or series of events, write their roles onto semi-adhesive (removable) paper arrows, including an arrow for the self, and use the arrows to "tell the story" of the event or episode (King et al., 2013). Arrows are a uniform size and are not anchored with lines (unless the participant wishes to draw these in). Proximity, directionality, and overlap enable a high degree of flexibility, allowing the representation of the detail of a complex interaction or an abstract view representing qualities of interaction or collaboration across a longer episode of connected events (Figure 9.4a). Arrows can be arranged in timelines or processes if participants prefer (Figure 9.4b) and annotated with drawings. Arrows are not restricted to people who were present during the event or episode—they can be used to represent absent people, pets, and systemic factors, such as legal guidelines or other metaphorical boundaries.

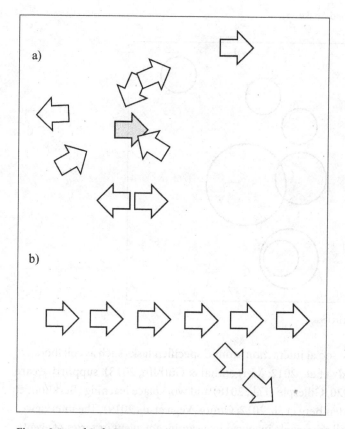

Figure 9.4a and 9.4b. Pictor.

Experience in the Abstract

Allocentric Images

Allocentric images take an external perspective. Participants are asked to map events, objects, or locations in reference to other events, objects, or locations, rather than positioning them in relation to the self. This does not preclude the use of supplementary symbols, annotations, or drawings to add an egocentric perspective, once the external perspective has been established.

Mapping networks. Networks can be diagrammed in the form of processes (Figure 9.5), hierarchies (Figure 9.6), and trees (Figure 9.7), or freeform in relation to concrete geographical features. In participatory approaches such as Participatory Rural Appraisal and Community-Based Participatory Research, both of which have a long history and well-developed epistemological foundations, participants are asked to construct abstract conceptual maps of resources, often combining this with other methods such as participant photography (Benninger et al., 2021) or walk-along interviews (Emmel & Clark, 2009). These approaches move beyond elicitation to capture the act of negotiation between groups or communities, and share and augment some of the dynamics of the focus group method. There is further work to be done to situate group graphic elicitation alongside the methods used in one-on-one interviews.

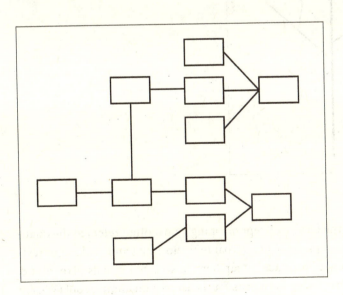

Figure 9.5. Process.

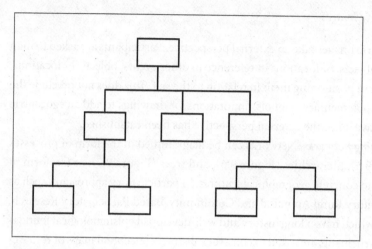

Figure 9.6. Hierarchy.

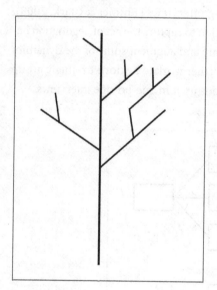

Figure 9.7. Tree.

In research, the term "concept mapping" most often refers to the quantitative analysis of participants' verbal brainstorming and ranking of text-based statements to produce researcher-constructed visuals (Trochim & Kane, 2005). There have been calls for its use as a qualitative tool (Wilson et al., 2016). However, where concepts are linked with lines, these concrete

Experience in the Abstract

associations lose some of the flexibility provided by more abstract approaches. In individual interviews exploring human experience, visuals requiring fixed lines of association between concepts or the reflection of concrete spatial arrangements can lack the explanatory power and dynamism of the abstract image. The fixed nature of mapping is more suited to exploring participants' perceptions of systems and infrastructure (Taysom & Crilly, 2017).

Timelines. Timelining emerged from therapeutic methods in health and social care focused on the recording of life events (McKeown et al., 2006). The majority of qualitative studies using timelines are grounded in the concept of linear time. Participants are presented with a line (most often horizontal) and asked to plot life events relevant to the research question in order of occurrence along the line (Figure 9.8a). Further visual dynamics can then be introduced, to move away from the linear recall and descriptive thinking often encouraged by sequential questioning around life story narratives. When the timeline is complete, participants can stand back and compare events along the line to evaluate similarities and differences. An egocentric perspective can be introduced by asking participants to chart key aspects of personal change or development in parallel with the events timeline. Parallel lines can be introduced (Figure 9.8b) to explore patterns of concurrent events within or across interviews (for an example, see Wilson et al., 2007).

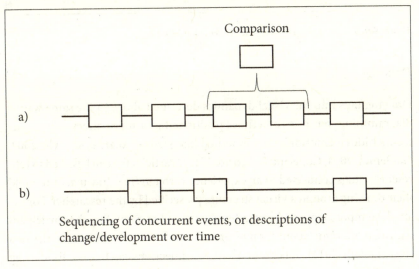

Figure 9.8a and 9.8b. The Dynamics of the Timeline.

A simpler and more intuitive approach to change over time can be introduced by the juxtaposition of axes and a free-drawn line that fluctuates as events progress along the line, denoting movement between two states (Figure 9.9)—for example, showing positive and negative emotions in association with events or change across time (Leung, 2010; Thygesen et al., 2011), or quantifiable change such as weight (Sheridan et al., 2011) or energy levels (Chen, 2016). The fluctuation—what Sheridan and collaborators refer to as the "wiggle in the line"—can elicit meta-narratives around change that are difficult to conceptualize without visualization.

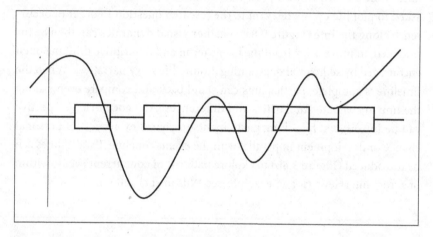

Figure 9.9. The "Wiggle in the Line" (Sheridan et al., 2011).

Drawing

Drawing taps into the visual dynamics described above in the same way as diagramming, but it is sometimes positioned as a more direct way of surfacing hidden emotions and embodied knowledge (Kearney & Hyle, 2004; Guillemin, 2004; Copeland & Agosto, 2012). Participants can be asked to represent feelings connected to an experience through free-drawing, or to mold their drawing around a visual structure prescribed by the researcher. For example, temporal approaches can be encouraged by providing the participant with an *a priori* metaphor for movement through time, such as a journey or a river (Iantaffi, 2011). Talk around family connections can be visualized using trees (Tasker & Granville, 2011; Saarelainen, 2015).

The metaphors we make shape our actions (Lakoff & Johnson, 2003), and it is worth considering how the implicit prescription of a metaphor might shape participants' data and place boundaries around their responses. For example, rivers suggest calm or turbulent waters and obstructive rocks, trees suggest roots or beginnings, growth, direction, connections and/or binary choices or pathways. Lines representing a journey through processes such as medical treatment, if they are unboundaried, may raise ethical issues if metaphors representing the end of the line can be extrapolated from the visual (Saarelainen, 2015).

The boundaries between graphics and free-drawing are sometimes blurred. A simple free-drawn line can wiggle or zigzag to express emotions or change over time (Orland, 2000; Chen, 2016). Diagrams can spontaneously arise during the drawing task (for examples in research with children, see Bagnoli, 2009). The flexibility of drawing enables projective thinking and imagination or anticipation of the future with a few strokes of the pencil or pen.

The Graphic Elicitation Interview

Having consolidated our understanding of how graphic representations might align with subjective experience, we will now consider the practicalities—how you might weave a visual task into your research study and your interview.

Planning and Piloting

When you have chosen a visual that is likely to align with your area of research inquiry, it is essential to pilot the technique to see how this plays out in practice. This will allow you to spot potential points of misunderstanding or discomfort around the task and clarify your approach before briefing your participants. It is wise to draft a conventional topic guide in case a participant decides that they are uncomfortable with the task, and as a prompt for follow-up questions to gather up loose threads where the elicitation task has unraveled experiences in ways that you didn't expect.

Briefing Participants

Participants need to be aware of what they are signing up for at the recruitment stage, so that the visual task is not an unexpected surprise during the interview. Descriptions in recruitment material should be concise and written in plain language. Reassure your participants that they do not require artistic skill, and that no preparation is needed prior to the interview (if this is the case). The details of the task can be communicated during the interview itself. If your research requires governance approvals, your ethics panel will need to understand in detail what you are asking participants to do, and how it might reduce the burden of interviewing for your participants.

The Interview

The act of elicitation is best placed at the beginning of the interview—trusting the technique to carry the dialogue is fundamental to realizing the benefits it can bring. Interviews of less than an hour are unlikely to allow enough time to introduce, construct, and discuss a visual. Opening questions are still necessary to establish rapport, taking an overview of the research area and participants' reasons for participating, and introducing and clarifying the mechanics of the visual.

Leaving the room while the participant creates the visual minimizes the possibilities of co-construction of the image, but this will depend upon the interviewing environment. Your participant may request that you stay. An approach that works in practice is to communicate that you would like to leave the room (but remain nearby in case of questions). If you stay in the room, sit back with your gaze focused elsewhere to allow space and silence for the task. Be clear about a specified time for construction of an initial visual (5–10 minutes is ideal) and that there is no right or wrong way to respond to the brief (to allow flexibility and customization). Keep a record of any assistance you give that is directive (including showing a completed visual as an example or prompt—if this is necessary, perhaps your visual is too complex), with a consideration of its effects on the visual and the dialogue that flows from it. As the interview progresses, questions can be focused around the features of the image. Examples of phrasing for image-focused questions are given in Box 9.1.

Box 9.1. Image-Focused Questions.

IMAGE-FOCUSED QUESTIONS

Opening question:
Could you tell me the story behind the diagram/drawing?

Exploring the details:
Why have you arranged [this visual feature] in this way?
(giving the participant the opportunity to explain the dynamics of their image)
What does this [feature] represent?
Is my understanding of this [feature] correct?
(explaining how you interpret a feature, as an observer, and asking for clarification)
How is/was this [event/experience] different from this [event/experience]?
(comparative questioning to elicit novel thinking)
Is there anything/anyone missing from this scenario?
Did this person [where symbols represent people] see things the same way?
Have you learned anything about the experience from the drawing/diagramming process?
(to consider the bird's-eye view)
In an ideal world, how could this have happened differently?
(to prompt reconfiguration of the diagram)

Reconfiguring the Visual

Participants can be asked to imagine a phenomenon differently in order to clarify essential aspects of an experience—a technique known in phenomenology as imaginative variation (King & Horrocks, 2010). Graphic elicitation lends itself to this approach—visuals can be modified or reconfigured during the course of the interview in response to questions, and this works particularly well with diagramming (Nickerson et al., 2013; Hardy et al., 2012). The participant's initial visual will represent an experience as they remember it, but they can be asked to reconfigure the image to show how things could have happened differently—for example, how a difficult event might have happened in an "ideal" world, or how change might be facilitated.

The Debrief: Audiencing and Confidentiality

As you bring your interview to a close, it is important to address the issue of how and where the constructed image will be viewed, and to communicate this to your participant. Your interview consent form should include a clause that addresses subsequent uses of the image, including who the likely audience will be and allowing participants to give or withhold permission for its reproduction. You will need to be selective in the images you disseminate, and choices should be made in line with participants' permission.

Most research governance panels will insist that data are anonymized. If your chosen drawing or diagramming technique requires symbols representing people, ask participants to label them with roles rather than names (e.g. neighbor, doctor, son, daughter), but be aware that this may be forgotten in the course of the interview, and correcting it can interrupt the flow of an interview. Before the interview closes, check the participant's graphic for identifying labels (this becomes second nature very quickly). You may need to ask some basic questions to clarify roles so that you can anonymize written labels before photographing the image for digital storage.

Remote Interviewing

Using graphic elicitation in online interviews is in its infancy, and its planning and execution present numerous challenges (Pell et al., 2020). Participants will have to work harder to meet the research brief, and any potential vulnerabilities in the population you are studying will need to be considered. Extra time and effort will be needed to create a visual ahead of the interview, and time delays in sharing images may create a significant loss of momentum. Participants will also need access to technology if you wish to interview using videoconferencing tools. Showing visuals on-screen brings its own challenges—drawings and diagrams are inherently more complex than photographs and can be difficult to see on a small screen. The loss of eye-gaze on video as participant and researcher look at the visual may have implications in terms of rapport. The pre-scripting of probes by the researcher, and the inability to reconfigure the diagram in plain sight, also reduces the spontaneity associated with novel thinking, which characterizes the technique when practiced in person.

Understanding the Limitations

Research participants can be subject to some very specific discomforts when they are asked to undertake graphic elicitation. Some participants may not instinctively grasp the abstract nature of a diagram and will configure patterns that do not reflect the relational or sequential arrangement you are anticipating. It is important to hand the agenda to your participants, and flexibility is key. The simpler and more abstract your diagram is, the more adaptable it will be—prescriptive and complex diagrams are more likely to meet with resistance or misunderstanding. If you are wedded to a particular process of visual analysis that relies on all images having common elements, this can lead you to place undue pressure on participants to stick to the rules.

Some participants may perceive a visual task as requiring artistic skill (particularly if it involves drawing). An emphasis on interpretation rather than representation can be helpful, reassuring participants that it will capture a snapshot of experience and help you to focus on their individual situation and context. Consider also whether your participants may have trouble with recall, and what difficulties may arise from this. The social and cultural milieu of your participants will also shape their perspective on fundamental concepts—some participants may not respond to a request to represent events chronologically, dependent on cognitive or cultural differences (Bagnoli, 2009; Ancona et al., 2001; Hinterhuber, 2002), or may read images right-to-left rather than left-to-right (Nickerson et al., 2013). An understanding of egocentric images depends on cultural norms around the self (Schwartz, 2006), and prescribed social norms in particular contexts may affect representations of the dynamics of interaction (Tasker & Granville, 2011).

Images as Data

Whether images constitute data that can be analyzed will depend on how you situate your research practice. The productive tensions created by debates around postqualitative practices melt tasks such as analysis into fluid states freed from conventional frameworks, enabling fragmentation and re-assemblage, and encouraging us as researchers to sit with discomforts and differences and make them matter (St. Pierre & Jackson, 2014). How the particular dynamics of graphic elicitation can merge into these fluidities is still open to exploration. This section will not outline a prescriptive approach to analysis, but will instead signpost sensitizing concepts. If you are working with conventional qualitative approaches, this may prompt you to explore how to integrate visuals into your research findings in a way that works for your inquiry.

Image Production: Analytic Dimensions in Interview Talk

Graphic elicitation draws on a limited range of simple dimensions to provoke reflection in study participants—the simplest graphics make use of proximity, sequence, and metaphor, and (if material resources allow) direction and color. Proximity can indicate emotional allegiance and/or close collaboration, people, or elements that are most significant to the experience described (often appearing central to the image, or grouped in the largest cluster), and the opposite—distance, lack of involvement, and/or group divisions. Direction and overlap can signify similar ambiguities (for example, support or pressure, closeness or conflict). Color or tone can augment or add nuance to the qualities of these relations. Linear sequencing can indicate the passage of time, change, or development, or how a series of processes fit together, and highlight divergent pathways.

The research participant chooses how to operationalize these dimensions as they construct a visual. Dialogue around the dynamics of an image augment and clarify the meanings attributed to it, and participants often flag the sensation of insight as they talk—for example, calling the elicitation process "eye-opening" (Niebauer et al., 2021). Identifying verbal cues around participants' use of color, proximity, grouping, direction, and metaphor from interview transcripts, and the epiphanies they experience as they consider the bird's-eye view, will help you to understand the range of expression enabled by the visual, and how its dynamics might light up the corners and crevices where insights are hidden.

The Image Itself: Possibilities for Systematic Coding

Systematic coding of images has positivist connotations, and its utility and credibility in relation to the visual you have chosen should be carefully considered. Elicitation images are working visuals that drive dialogue and encourage us to reconfigure our thinking. There are dangers in reifying individual images out of the context of the interview, as this invites a different type of audiencing—a third-party interpretation, stripped of the interpretative hooks that grounded the act of construction. The interview dialogue is tied to the visual as an intrinsic part of the elicitation process, contextualizing the image and bringing its invisible dynamics back to life.

Efforts to pin down approaches to image analysis have focused on photographs, film and digital media (for example, Prosser, 1998; Pink, 2001; Rose, 2004), and the resulting frameworks customized for use with other mediums such as drawing (Guillemin & Drew, 2010). The analysis of participant-produced diagrams is less well considered and rarely reported. Systematic approaches are best used to provide grist for the reinterrogation of your interview dialogue. This iterative process is described by King and fellow researchers (2013) in relation to the Pictor technique, by Goldenberg et al. (2016, 2018) in relation to timelines, and by Kirkham (2015) and Wainwright (2018) in relation to drawing.

If you are working within conventional qualitative frameworks, elicited visuals can be usefully contextualized as part of the body of images aggregated across the course of a research inquiry. Using the same visual approach across a series of interviews can create a sense of coherence if you are conducting conventional thematic analysis, as each participant structures their experiences using the same abstract and/or metaphorical anchoring points. Patterns of representation may appear across multiple visuals, which can suggest other avenues in your data. For the purposes of rigor (see Box 9.2), it is vital to recognize where insights developed through thematic analysis are, in fact, an artifact of the visual method. For example, timelines often chart change and development—this is not an insight, it is an *a priori* construction that will evidence itself through interview dialogue.

The analysis of aggregated visuals without their corresponding dialogue requires an attention to their compositional features. Hook and Glaveanu (2013) describe four different compositional elements relevant to image analysis: sensory, structural, dynamic and emerging. These heuristics need a little reinterpretation to make them work for two-dimensional drawings and diagrams. Sensory elements include color, tone, and texture used in ways that represent or induce feelings or emotions. Structural elements include chronological arrangement, the use of axes, and the frequency of use of particular symbols. Dynamic elements include the construction of multiple social perspectives and points of tension, comparison, or ambiguity, and are the fundamental driving force behind diagramming. Emerging elements include focal points and metaphors, and the bird's-eye view. These concepts can provide a pragmatic guide for image-based thinking, and inform your reflections on the discoveries that you make.

Box 9.2. Assessing Rigor in Graphic Elicitation.

WHAT CONSTITUTES RIGOR IN GRAPHIC ELICITATION?

The evaluation of rigor in conventional qualitative research is a much-debated topic, and has not been explored in relation to graphic elicitation. There are some key questions that you might ask yourself as you audit and report your use of the method:

Choice of visual: How does the chosen graphic elicitation technique relate to the research question?
Piloting: How did piloting the interview refine the elicitation approach?
Interview guide: Are the instructions for the graphic elicitation task clearly described? Is the effect of the visual on shaping the data made evident?
Consistency of approach: Did all participants respond to the visual task in the same way? Were there any unexpected interpretations of the brief or customisation of the visual by participants? What did this tell you?
Potential limitations: Did anyone refuse to undertake the visual task? How did you accommodate this? How directive were you during the construction of the visual?
Confidentiality: Was visual data anonymised? If so, how? If not, why?
Analysis: How did the structure of your visual shape the interview dialogue? If you analysed your visuals separately, why and how did you do this? If you integrated your visuals and textual data in a systematic analytic process, how did this process work, and what did it tell you?

Conclusion

Abstract drawings created by humans date back more than 70,000 years (Henshilwood et al., 2018). Asking why our research practices have not traditionally integrated the visual seems imperative. While the aim of this chapter has been to present a practical guide to the use of graphic elicitation as an interviewing method—to consider its benefits, the steps that facilitate its practical application, and its implications for research inquiry—the hope has also been to inspire some novel thinking around how drawings and diagrams might better enable us to share the complexities of human experience. We speculated on the reciprocity between words and pictures that wrestles for equity inside the uncomfortable power dynamics of researcher–participant interaction, and we examined how abstract images might encourage flexibility in the way that we conceive and explain our experiences. While photography seduces us into recording our lives by freezing a moment of "reality," drawing and diagramming allow us to access other dimensions of our experience, and to explore how they make us feel.

References

Ancona, D. G., Okhuysen, G. A., & Perlow, L. A. (2001). Taking time to integrate temporal research. *The Academy of Management Review, 26*, 521–529. https://doi.org/10.5465/amr.2001.5393887

Bagnoli, A. (2009). Beyond the standard interview: The use of graphic elicitation and arts-based methods. *Qualitative Research, 9*(5), 547–570. https://doi.org/10.1177/1468794109343625

Benninger, E., Schmidt-Sane, M., & Spilsbury, J. C. (2021). Conceptualizing social determinants of neighbourhood health through a youth lens. *Child Indicators Research, 14*, 2393–2416. http://dx.doi.org/10.1007/s12187-021-09849-6

Berkhout, J. J., Helmich, E., Teunissen, P. W., van der Vleuten, C. P. M., & Jaarsma, A. D. C. (2017). How clinical medical students perceive others to influence their self-regulated learning. *Medical Education, 51*, 269–279. http://dx.doi.org/10.1111/medu.13131

Bravington, A., & King, N. (2019). Putting graphic elicitation into practice: Tools and typologies for the use of participant-led diagrams in qualitative research interviews. *Qualitative Research, 19*(5), 506–523. http://dx.doi.org/10.1177/1468794118781718

Bresler, L. (2006) Towards connectedness: Aesthetically based research. *Studies in Art Education, 48*(1), 52–69. http://dx.doi.org/10.2307/25475805

Brinkman, S. (2017). Humanism after posthumanism: Or qualitative psychology after the "posts." *Qualitative Research in Psychology, 14*(2), 109–130.

Büchi, S., & Sensky, T. (1999). PRISM: Pictorial Representation of Illness and Self Measure: A brief nonverbal measure of illness impact and therapeutic aid in psychosomatic medicine. *Psychosomatics, 40*(4), 314–320.

Bulk, L. Y., Kimel, G., King, N., & Nimmon, L. (2020). Understanding experiences in hospice: Exploring temporal, occupational and relational dimensions using the Pictor technique. *Qualitative Health Research, 30*(12), 1965–1977. http://dx.doi.org/10.1177/1049732320926134

Chen, A. (2016). The relationship between health management and information behavior over time: A study of the illness journeys of people living with fibromyalgia. *Journal of Medical Internet Research, 18*(10), e269. http://dx.doi.org/10.2196/jmir.5309

Cheng, P. C.-H., Lowe, R. K., & Scaife, M. (2001). Cognitive science approaches to understanding diagrammatic representations. *Artificial Intelligence Review, 15,* 79–94.

Cheung, M. M. Y., Bandana, S., & Smith, L. (2019). "It's a powerful message": A qualitative study of Australian healthcare professionals' perceptions of asthma through the medium of drawings. *BMJ Open, 9,* e027699. http://dx.doi.org/10.1136/bmjopen-2018-027699

Copeland, A. J., & Agosto, D. E. (2012). Diagrams and relational maps: The use of graphic elicitation techniques with interviewing for data collection, analysis, and display. *International Journal of Qualitative Methods, 11*(3), 513–533. https://doi.org/10.1177/160940691201100501

Denzin, N. K. (2010). *The qualitative manifesto: A call to arms.* Left Coast Press.

Emmel, N., & Clark, A. (2009). *The methods used in connected lives: Investigating networks, neighbourhoods and communities.* ESRC National Centre for Research Methods, NCRM Working Paper Series, 06/09. https://eprints.ncrm.ac.uk/id/eprint/800/1/2009_connected_lives_methods_emmel_clark.pdf

Fernandes, M. A., Wammes, J. D., & Meade, M. E. (2018). The surprisingly powerful influence of drawing on memory. *Current Directions in Psychological Science, 27*(5), 302–308. http://dx.doi.org/10.1177/0963721418755385

Gillespie, H., Kelly, M., Gormley, G., King, N., Gilliland, D., & Dornan, T. (2018). How can tomorrow's doctors be more caring? A phenomenological investigation. *Medical Education, 52,* 1052–1063. http://dx.doi.org/10.1111/medu.13684

Goldenberg, T., Darbes, L. A., & Stephenson, R. (2018). Inter-partner and temporal variations in the perception of sexual risk for HIV. *AIDS Behaviour, 22,* 1870–1884. http://dx.doi.org/10.1007/s10461-017-1876-5

Goldenberg, T., Finneran, C., Andes, K. L., & Stephenson, R. (2016). Using participant-empowered visual relationship timelines in a qualitative study of sexual behaviour. *Global Public Health, 11*(5–6), 699–718. http://dx.doi.org/10.1080/17441692.2016.1170869

Guillemin, M. (2004). Embodying heart disease through drawings. *Health: An Interdisciplinary Journal for the Social Study of Health, Illness and Medicine, 8*(2), 223–239. http://dx.doi.org/10.1177/1363459304041071

Guilleman, M., & Drew, S. (2010). Questions of process in participant-generated visual methodologies. *Visual Studies, 25*(2), 175–188. https://doi.org/10.1080/1472586X.2010.502676

Hardy, B., King, N., & Firth, J. (2012) Applying the Pictor technique to research interviews with people affected by advanced disease. *Nurse Researcher, 20*(1), 6–10. https://doi.org/10.7748/nr2012.09.20.1.6.c9302

Hargreaves, C. P. (1979). Social networks and interpersonal constructs. In P. Stringer & D. Bannister (Eds.), *Constructs of sociality and individuality* (pp. 153–175). Academic Press.

Henshilwood, C. S., d'Errico, F., van Niekerk, K. L., Dayet, L., Queffelec, A., & Pollarolo, L. (2018). An abstract drawing from the 73,000-year-old levels at Blombos Cave, South Africa. (Letter.) *Nature, 562,* 115–128. http://dx.doi.org/10.1038/s41586-018-0514-3

Hinterhuber, H. H. (2002). "Taking time to integrate temporal research": Some comments. *The Academy of Management Review, 27*, 170.

Hook, D., & Glaveanu, V. P. (2013). Image analysis: An interactive approach to compositional elements. *Qualitative Research in Psychology, 10*(4), 355–368. http://dx.doi.org/10.1080/14780887.2012.674175

Hurley, S. M., & Novick, L. R. (2006). Context and structure: The nature of students' knowledge about three spatial diagram representations. *Thinking & Reasoning, 12*(3), 281–308. https://doi.org/10.1080/13546780500363974

Iantaffi, A. (2011). Travelling along "rivers of experience": Personal construct psychology and visual metaphors in research. In P. Reavey (Ed.), *Visual methods in psychology: Using and interpreting images in qualitative research* (pp. 271–283). Psychology Press.

Kearney, K. S., & Hyle, A. E. (2004). Drawing out emotions: The use of participant-produced drawings in qualitative inquiry. *Qualitative Research, 4*, 361–382. https://doi.org/10.1177/1468794104047234

King, N., Bravington, A., Brooks, J., Hardy, B., Melvin, J., & Wilde, D. (2013). The Pictor technique: A method for exploring the experience of collaborative working. *Qualitative Health Research, 23*(8), 1138–1152. https://doi.org/10.1177/1049732313495326

King, N., & Horrocks C. (2010). *Interviews in qualitative research*. SAGE.

Kirkham, J. A. (2015). Painting pain: An interpretative phenomenological analysis of representations of living with chronic pain. *Health Psychology, 34*(4), 398–406. http://dx.doi.org/10.1037/hea0000139

Lakoff, G., & Johnson, M. (2003). *Metaphors we live by*. University of Chicago Press.

Leung, P. P. Y. (2010). Autobiographical timeline: A narrative and life story approach in understanding meaning-making in cancer patients. *Illness, Crisis, & Loss, 18*(2), 111–127. https://doi.org/10.2190/IL.18.2.c

Lu, H., & Da, S. (2019) The relationships between leisure and happiness—A graphic elicitation method. *Leisure Studies, 39*(1), 111–130. http://dx.doi.org/10.1080/02614367.2019.1575459

McKeown, J., Clarke, A., & Repper, J. (2006). Life story work in health and social care: Systematic literature review. *Journal of Advanced Learning, 55*(2), 237–247. https://doi.org/10.1111/j.1365-2648.2006.03897.x

Mergenthal, K., & Güthlin, C. (2018). Kooperationen sichtbar machen durch Anwendung der Pictor Technique (Visualizing Cooperation Using the Pictor Technique). *Zeitschrift für Allgemeinmedizin, 94*(10), 401–404. http://dx.doi.org/10 10.3238/zfa.2018.00401–0404

Michael, M. (2004). On making data social: Heterogeneity in sociological practice. *Qualitative Health Research, 41*(1), 5–23.

Nickerson, J. V., Corter, J. E., Tversky, B., Roh, Y.-J., Zahner, D., & Yu, L. (2013). Cognitive tools shape thought: Diagrams in design. *Cognitive Processing, 14*(3), 255–272. http://dx.doi.org/10.1007/s10339-013-0547-3

Niebauer, E., Fry, N., Auster-Gussman, L. A., & Wahbeh, H. (2021) Patient perspectives on the causes of breast cancer: A qualitative study on the relationship between stress, trauma, and breast cancer development. *International Journal of Qualitative Studies on Health and Well-being, 16*(1), 1983949. http://dx.doi.org/10.1080/17482631.2021.1983949

Olmos-Vega, F. M., Dolmans, D. H. J. M., Guzmán-Quintero, C., Echevveri-Rodriguez, C., Tennissen, P. W., & Stalmaijer, R. E. (2019). Disentangling residents' engagement with communities of clinical practice in the workplace. *Advances in Health Sciences Education, 24*, 459–475. http://dx.doi.org/10.1007/s10459-019-09874-9

Orland, L. (2000). What's in a line? Exploration of a research and reflection tool. *Teachers and Teaching: Theory and Practice, 6*(2), 197–213. http://dx.doi.org/10.1080/713698715

Pell, B., Williams, D., Phillips, R., Sanders, J., Edwards, A., Choy, E., & Grant, A. (2020). Using visual timelines in telephone interviews: Reflection and lessons learned from the Star Family Study. *International Journal of Qualitative Methods, 19*, 1–11. http://dx.doi.org/10.1177/1609406920913675

Pink, S. (2001). *Doing visual ethnography: Images, media and representation in research*. SAGE.

Prosser, J. (Ed.). (1998). *Image-based research: A sourcebook for qualitative researchers*. Routledge.

Ramanan, N., Adriaenssens, P., Derlyn, I., & De Haene, L. (2021). "The mother I was born to or the one I worked for?": An exploratory study on family separation in live-in child domestic workers in Karnataka, India. *Child Abuse & Neglect, 117*, 105081. http://dx.doi.org/10.1016/j.chiabu.2021.105081

Ray, R. A., & Street, A. (2007). Non-finite loss and emotional labour: family caregivers' experiences of living with motor neurone disease. *Journal of Clinical Nursing, 16*(3a), 35–43. http://dx.doi.org/10.1111/j.1365-2702.2006.01722.x

Rose, G. (2004) *Visual methodologies: An introduction to researching with visual materials* (4th ed.). SAGE.

Rubin, D. C., & Umanath, S. (2015). Event memory: A theory of memory for laboratory, autobiographical, and fictional events. *Psychological Review, 122*(1), 1–23. http://dx.doi.org/10.1037/a0037907

Saarelainen, S. (2015). Life tree drawings as a methodological approach in young adults' life stories during cancer remission. *Narrative Works: Issues, Investigations, & Interventions, 5*(1), 68–91.

Savolainen, R., & Kari, J. (2004). Placing the Internet in information source horizons. A study of information seeking by Internet users in the context of self-development. *Library & Information Science Research, 26*, 415–433. http://dx.doi.org/10.1016/j.lisr.2004.04.004

Schwartz, S. H. (2006). A theory of cultural value orientations: Explication and applications. *Comparative Sociology, 5*(2–3): 137–182.

Sheridan, J., Chamberlain, K., & Dupuis, A. (2011). Timelining: Visualizing experience. *Qualitative Research, 11*(5), 552–569. http://dx.doi.org/10.1177/1468794111413235

St. Pierre, E. A., & Jackson, A. Y. (2014). Data analysis after coding. *Qualitative Inquiry, 20*(6), 715–719. http://dx.doi.org/10.1177/1077800414532435

Tasker, F., & Granville, J. (2011). Children's views of family relationships in lesbian-led families. *Journal of GLBT Family Studies, 7*(1/2), 182–199. https://doi.org/10.1080/1550428X.2011.540201

Taysom, E. & Crilly, N. (2017). Resilience in sociotechnical systems: The perspectives of multiple stakeholders. *she ji: The Journal of Design, Economics, and Innovation, 3*(3), 165–182.

Thygesen, M. K., Pedersen, B. D., Kragstrup, J., Wagner, L., & Mogensen, O. (2011). Utilizing a new graphic elicitation technique to collect emotional narratives describing disease trajectories. *The Qualitative Report, 16*(2), 596–608.

Tran, S. H. N., Isaac Beech, I., & Fernandes, M. A. (2022). Drawing compared to writing in a diary enhances recall of autobiographical memories. *Aging, Neuropsychology, and Cognition.* Advance online publication. http://dx.doi.org/10.1080/13825585.2022.2047594

Trochim, W., & Kane, M. (2005). Concept mapping: An introduction to structured conceptualization in health care. *International Journal for Quality in Health Care, 17*(3), 187–191. http://dx.doi.org/10.1093/intqhc/mzi038

Tversky, B. (2011) Visualizing thought. *Topics in Cognitive Science, 3,* 499–535. http://dx.doi.org/10.1111/j.1756-8765.2010.01113.x

Van den Berg, J. W., Verberg, C. P. M., Scherpbier, A. J. J. A., Jaarsma, A. D. C., & Lombarts, K. M. J. M. H. (2017). Is being a medical educator a lonely business? The essence of social support. *Medical Education, 51,* 302–315. http://dx.doi.org/10.1111/medu.13162

Wainwright, M. (2018). Imaging and imagining chronic obstructive pulmonary disease (COPD): Uruguayans draw their lungs. *Disability and Rehabilitation, 40*(26), 3094–3103. http://dx.doi.org/10.1080/09638288.2017.1376357

Washington, L. (2009). A contextual analysis of caregivers of children with disabilities. *Journal of Human Behavior in the Social Environment, 19*(5), 554–571. http://dx.doi.org/10.1080/09638288.2017.1376357

Wilson, J., Mandich, A., & Magalhães, L. (2016). Concept mapping: A dynamic, individualized and qualitative method for eliciting meaning. *Qualitative Health Research, 26*(8), 1151–1161. http://dx.doi.org/10.1177/1049732315616623

Wilson, S., Cunningham-Burley, S., Bancroft, A., Backett-Milburn, K., & Masters, H. (2007). Young people, biographical narratives and the life grid: Young people's accounts of parental substance use. *Qualitative Research, 7*(1), 135–151. https://doi.org/10.1177/1468794107071427

TEN

 Mobile Methods, Go-Alongs, and Walking Interviews

Kathryn Roulston and Maureen A. Flint

W E ARE FAMILIAR WITH JOURNALISTS walking alongside interviewees in order to gain in-depth accounts of people's lives, loves, and legacies for news stories and television documentaries. We read accounts in news outlets that describe how authors accompanied their interviewees on outings. Similarly, ethnographers have long accompanied their participants during their daily activities as they documented the cultures of peoples all over the world. Anthropologist Bronislaw Malinowski (2014 [1922]), for example, described the hazards of going on a sailing expedition with a key informant. When the winds changed in an unfavorable direction, they returned to shore. Subsequently, Malinowski's guide no longer trusted him as a passenger. Malinowski (2014) wrote: "Unfortunately, To'uluwa got it into his head that I had brought him bad luck, and so when he planned his next trip, I was not taken into his confidence or allowed to form one of the party" (p. 494). Malinowski's thwarted sailing expedition was a "go-along" long before the term had been used. Go-alongs are used to generate knowledge about the world that involves becoming mobile in some way, whether walking, sailing, riding, or otherwise moving through space.

Buscher and fellow researchers (2011) have described mobile methods as examining "fleeting, distributed, multiple, non-causal, sensory, emotional and kinaesthetic" phenomena (p. 1). The turn to examining mobilities in the social sciences aligns with work that decenters the human and attends to the more-than-human in the environment (Roulston, 2022). Through pursuit of research agendas in mobility studies, Buscher et al. (2011) proposed a range of phenomena that highlight the importance of space, place, temporality, social interaction, movement, embodiment, and sensorial experience within the mobilities turn. Geographer Peter Merriman (2014) cautioned researchers using mobile methods to not overstate the benefits of these approaches in the conduct of research, but rather to remain open to the possibilities of what mobile methods are, can, and should be (p. 183).

In this chapter we discuss some historical antecedents for walking, prior to defining go-alongs and walking interviews and reviewing how scholars across disciplines have used them. The second author presents her use of walking interviews in research, and we provide questions for other researchers using go-alongs and walking interviews to consider when designing studies. We conclude the chapter by discussing innovations in mobile methods and questions related to the evaluation of quality.

On Walking

As well as being a primary means of locomotion for people all over the world and central to the act of pilgrimage, walking is frequently linked with artistic practice (O'Neill & Roberts, 2020). Artists, musicians, and writers have talked about walking as both a source of inspiration and part of the creative process. Philosophers from Immanuel Kant (1724–1804) to Henry David Thoreau (1817–1862), poets from John Keats (1795–1821) to Arthur Rimbaud (1854–1891), to Mary Oliver (1935–2019), and writers such as Bruce Chatwin (1940–1989), Alice Walker (b. 1944), and Rebecca Solnit (b. 1961) have all written about walking. Whether walking was part of a daily routine (Kant), a reflective or spiritual practice (Solnit and Walker), related to a specific life event (Keats), a crucial part of attending to the natural world (Thoreau and Oliver), or a central mode of traversing the world (Rimbaud and Chatwin), walking has long been inextricably tied to thinking and creative practice. Some artists identify walking as a central part of their practice (e.g., the Walking Artists Network https://www.walkingartistsnetwork.org/). Walking as a way of moving about the world predates all other forms of mobility, and is indelibly part of Indigenous cultures, pointing to how human life is intertwined with the land (Phillips, 2022).

In their research, ethnographers have long used walking to examine what people do throughout the day, how they move and interact with one another, and how events and activities occur within specific settings. Recent work has explored the role of place through sensory (Pink, 2015) and sounded ethnography (Wozolek, 2018). Anthropologists Lee and Ingold (2006) wrote about the resonances between walking and anthropological fieldwork—those of attunement to the environment, understanding of place, and the social aspect of walking with others (pp. 68–69). They advocate that the "record of the walk, and of the experience that it affords, is just as important—and just as valid a source of field materials—as the 'discourse' that might have accompanied it" (p. 83). More recently, interest in "go-alongs" and "walking interviews" has surged among scholars examining how humans perceive and interact with space and place, and people's sensory experiences, embodiment, and interactions with the environment and the non-human.

Go-Alongs and Walking Interviews

As noted, going-along with participants to observe their everyday activities and ask questions is not a new research approach. However, we locate the formalizing of the term "go-along" as a research method with Margarethe Kusenbach (2003, 2018), who described "go-alongs" as combining participant observation with interviews, bringing phenomenological sensibility to ethnographic research. In Kusenbach's framing, go-alongs encompass walk-alongs and ride-alongs (i.e., in automobiles or public transit). More recently, other researchers have extended and nuanced the combination of movement, interview, and observation to conduct "swim-alongs" (Denton et al., 2021) and ride-alongs (Scott, 2020; Spinney, 2009). Scholars have used go-alongs while jogging and traveling on ferries and airplanes (Riley et al., 2021), and proposed being-alongs, including "harvesting-alongs, nature-sleepovers, and horseback ride-alongs" (Duedahl & Stilling Blichfeldt, 2020, p. 454).

Since walking interviews involve researchers walking alongside interviewees and talking about research topics, they appear deceptively simple. What could be easier than carrying an audio-recording device to record a conversation while walking with a participant or jotting down notes during or after a walk? Readers should note that the kinds of "mobility" involved in different forms of "go-along" vary considerably from "sedentary" (e.g., while accompanying a participant on a bus or in an automobile), to the relaxed stroll of a walk in the countryside, to high levels of physical activity involved in swimming, cycling, or running. The talk that is facilitated during go-alongs is necessarily different, depending on the activity and the physical capacity of participants involved (e.g., people with mobility issues might have difficulty walking up a hill; people swimming or cycling might minimize talk). For this reason, researchers using mobile methods should think carefully before inviting participants to "go along," both because of the physical nature of the method and the type of data generated. Walking does not necessarily generate "better" or "richer" data. This is discussed by May and Lewis (2020), who conducted walk-alongs as well as "in-situ" interviews and noted that the "in-situ" interviews, which were conducted on a bench in a housing development, resulted in data that were richer and more sensory than the walk-alongs.

Attention to walking as an activity can limit involvement among people with physical impairments, or those for whom walking in public is fraught. Researchers working from critical perspectives have troubled the idea of walking interviews as an egalitarian approach to research (Castrodale, 2018; Warren, 2017, 2021). Warren (2021) has critically examined how mobile methods can marginalize certain groups because of the social differences of gender, ethnicity, and health. In disability studies, mobile methods are employed to provide insight into the privileges afforded by able-bodiedness (e.g., Castrodale, 2018). Mobile methods have also been used to make visible hidden barriers, discourses, and challenges in navigating everyday life. For example, Parent (2016) discussed the problems of conducting a form of go-along called "wheeling interviews," where video cameras mounted on wheelchairs became unfastened as the researcher and participants traversed bumpy sidewalks, and the researcher and the participants encountered inaccessible spaces. Other examples include Ware (2022), who "cripped" walking by attending to the ways in which disability disrupts "nature" and hiking trails through a disability justice lens, and Martinez and Gois (2022), who employed walking as interruption to explore the effects of racism, sexism, and colonialism as researchers who "do not belong" to a space (p. 209). Walking, rather than simply extracting or tracing truth, brings up complicated questions about response-ability to and with participants, and the entangled production of place and identity.

How Researchers Use Go-Alongs and Walking Interviews

Thus far, we have provided a broad overview of the purpose and history of walking methods in qualitative research. In what follows, we focus specifically on the relationship between walking and the interview. Researchers who use walking while asking questions use a variety of labels to discuss what they do. For example, Anderson (2004) used the term "bimbling" to describe "aimless walking while talking" (p. 257). Evans and Jones (2011) described undertaking "participatory walking interviews," while Inwood and Martin (2008) used the term "roving focus groups" in their study of African American students' experiences of being on a predominantly White campus. Tong and collaborators (2016) developed an approach to walking interviews with foreign-born older adults that they called "interACTIVE interviews." Interviews involved the researcher and an interpreter walking on a participant-led route through the participants' neighborhoods, where the interpreter acted as a "co-interviewer" (p. 209). When Wiederhold (2015) returned to her hometown to conduct research, she labeled her use of walking interviews "peripatetic interviews" in order to capture the idea that participants were teachers, while the researcher took on the role of student. In a similar vein, Chang (2017) engaged in participant-led walking interviews of sites of interest as part of a three-stage process referred to as the "docent method." This involved an initial interview, a walking interview that was audio-recorded with accompanying photos, and a follow-up interview. O'Neill and Roberts (2020) developed an approach to research that they call the Walking Interview as a Biographical Method (WIBM) as a way to "render the 'meaning' of walking or a particular route for the individual (or group), its 'functions(s)' for them in daily life [so that] other deeper 'philosophical' life meanings can emerge, in the 'story' that is told" (p. 36).

Yet other researchers have focused on the researcher's experience in order to capture and attend to what is going on in the environment. For example, Hall and fellow researchers (2008) described "soundwalking," in which they focused on listening to and recording the everyday sounds in the environments they traversed, and "touring interviews," in which they took fieldnotes and photographs and sketched maps. Powell (2020, 2022) used the term "StoryWalk" for her approach to walking with residents of San Jose, California. Powell drew on Donna Haraway's notion of SF (an abbreviation indicating the ambiguity between science fact and speculative fiction), and the work of Derek McCormack and Erin Manning to envision walking as experimental, speculative, and propositional (Powell, 2020, p. 36).

As in other approaches to interviews for research purposes, how go-alongs and walking interviews are practiced varies considerably across disciplines and the purposes for which these methods are used. For example, walking interviews have been employed by scholars in India to examine people's perspectives of air and noise pollution in their daily commute (Marquart et al., 2022). These researchers used geographic information system (GIS) devices to trace the routes that participants took. At various points during the walking interviews, participants responded to questions using a Likert scale. Findings were analyzed statistically. In contrast, qualitative researchers have used a range of approaches that involve participants' involvement as "tour guides" within local communities (e.g., Bergeron et al., 2014; Kullberg & Odzakovic, 2018), on farms (e.g., Mackay et al., 2018; Thomas et al., 2019) and in domestic spaces (e.g., Ratzenböck, 2016).

Researchers ask specific questions of participants or encourage unstructured conversations based on the surroundings. Those who facilitate less structured talk propose that this provides opportunities for conversations that orient to the environment and whatever occurs, thereby generating rich data related to environments such as smells, sights, sounds, movements, and haptic sensations (Ross et al., 2009). In a study of community members' sense of the local community, Sáenz de Tejada Granados and Van der Horst (2020) described an approach to "natural go-alongs" in which the researcher approached people on the street and asked them about the local area. Since these pedestrians were averse to having conversations recorded, the researcher jotted down key words and sketched the route, taking photos at key points during the go-along. Teff-Seker et al. (2022) designed an open-ended protocol in which participants were asked to first walk in silence before being asked a series of prompts concerning their sensory experiences. Advocates assert that go-alongs and walking interviews can be participant-led, creating more equitable relationships between researcher and researched and lessening power differences (Shareck et al., 2021).

As further variations, researchers have used images (Madsen, 2017), video (O'Neill et al., 2017; Pink, 2007), and mapping (Flint, 2019b), sometimes created with the aid of Geographic Positioning Systems (GPS) (Hand et al., 2017; Jones & Evans, 2012; Martini, 2020; Motala & Bozalek, 2022; Wilmott, 2016, 2017) as ways to represent walking interviews and go-alongs. Another variation involves researchers and participants working collaboratively to create soundscape compositions using recordings of sonic environments encountered in participant-led walks (Stevenson & Holloway, 2017). Scholars have also used artistic representations such as creative non-fiction and poetry (Bell & Bush, 2020; Palmgren, 2018) to present findings from research using walking interviews. As can be seen from these examples, walking interviews and go-alongs are well suited to examine questions to do with space, place, and how people navigate particular routines and routes.

Justifying the Use of Go-Alongs and Walking Interviews

While O'Neill and Roberts's (2020) proposal for an integration of biographical methods with walking in the WIBM discussed earlier is situated in the field of sociology, the use of walking interviews has been discussed by researchers across diverse disciplines, including dementia studies (Adekoya & Guse, 2020; Kullberg & Odzakovic, 2018; Odzakovic et al., 2018), disability studies (Castrodale, 2018; Parent, 2016), geography (Evans & Jones, 2011; Finlay & Bowman, 2017; Isakjee, 2016; Jones & Evans, 2012; Lager et al., 2015), gerontology (Lőrinc et al., 2022), health (Garcia et al., 2012; Lauwers et al., 2021; Saint-Onge et al., 2021), higher education (Flint, 2019a, 2019b; Harris, 2016), landscape design (Colley et al., 2016), leisure sciences (Burns et al., 2020), marketing (Johnstone et al., 2019), museum studies (Madsen, 2017), outdoor education (Lynch & Mannion, 2016), social work (Ferguson, 2016), tourism (Mackay et al., 2018), and urban planning (Sun & Lau, 2021). This list is by no means exhaustive, since researchers all over the world in multiple disciplines use walking interviews and go-alongs, justifying their use for a range of reasons.

Mobile methods have been used to explore indoor and outdoor spaces in rural and urban environments. Reed and Ellis (2019) used go-alongs to examine indoor spaces in their study of postmortem imagery. They argued that this allowed them to explore the sensory experiences of navigating secret places. Thomas and fellow researchers (2019) used walk-along interviews with farmers, arguing that this allowed insights into spaces and practices not discussed in sedentary interviews (p. 7). These mobile methods have been found helpful in encouraging people to discuss their local situated knowledge (e.g., Brannelly & Bartlett, 2020) and enabling an embodied approach to the study of human-nature experience. Spinney (2009) asserted that videoing cycling in combination with interviews enables scholars in mobility studies to explore the sensory, affective, and technological aspects of phenomena (p. 828). Stevenson and Holloway (2017) argued for the use of participant-led walking interviews as a way to facilitate the creation of soundscape compositions that reflected participants' voices. In this approach, the focus was on participants attuning to sonic environments they encountered and creating soundscapes. Let's look in more detail at how the second author, Maureen, used walking interviews in her research on a college campus.

College Student Navigations of Place

"Take me on a tour of campus," I invited students. This study spanned three years and ultimately included 20 participants. My interest in walking had originated from a broader study that explored first-year college students' sense of belonging across race and gender (Garvey et al., 2018). In higher education research, belonging is understood as a motivating factor in student outcomes such as matriculation, success, persistence, and graduation (Gopalan & Brady, 2020; Strayhorn, 2012). I had become interested in mobile and participant-led methods after reading work by feminist geographer Massey (2005) and Indigenous scholars (Tuck & McKenzie, 2015) and had begun wondering how walking and talking along with other participant-generated materials might unfold different questions or possibilities for understanding belonging. In what follows, I describe three examples of moments that occurred during walking interviews that provide greater detail to themes discussed in the literature, including (1) encountering (in)visible histories; (2) interview logics; and (3) walking as intervention.

Walking, (In)visibility, and History

One of my first walking interviews had been with Jon (all student names are pseudonyms), a White man who was a senior in the engineering program. We met at the center of campus, and he immediately walked me toward a large boulder located at the center of the campus green that bore a plaque commemorating the soldiers of the American Confederacy. As we stood in front of the boulder, a campus tour of prospective students walked by us. The tour leader did not mention the boulder but did tout the achievements and opportunities of the honors college, housed in a building visible from the boulder. At the time, the honors college was named after an individual who had published extensively on eugenics based on racial characteristics and racist assumptions. The talk of the tour tugged at the conversation Jon and I had been having about the history of the boulder and its context, and we ended up discussing Jon's activism to change the name of the building. (It would be four more years before the building's name would be changed to "Honors Hall.") Following the resurgence of media attention on the movement for Black life in the summer of 2020, the boulder was also moved to an undisclosed location. This moment with Jon, the campus tour, the boulder, and the honors building made visceral the paradoxical histories of Alabama and the American South, and it also began to complicate the ways in which I was thinking about belongingness. I wondered how belongingness and place were co-implicated, how place mattered in student belongingness. More specifically, I wondered how students encountered and navigated histories of race and racism that were both visible and invisible in the landscape. Through walking, Jon and I *felt* the histories of place and their contradictions. The recording of the walking interview makes audible how the talk of the tour guide caused us to stop talking, to turn toward them, and how it shaped our conversation in response. This is not to say that Jon had not noted these contradictions before—indeed, he had described them as "quintessentially Alabamian" in the focus group he had participated in earlier. However, the act of walking, of encountering the place, brought together these discourses in a visceral and felt way that would not have been possible in a "neutral" research site. This moment is explored in more depth in Flint (2019b).

Disentangling Interview Logics

As described in this chapter, some researchers look to walking as a form of interruptive and disruptive data generation, a way to think beyond the logics of extraction that mark the traditional interview (Kuntz, 2015). Many of these researchers offer walking as being open to the unexpected, such as the bimble (Anderson, 2004). However, what I found in conducting walking interviews was the ways in which the traditional methods of "doing research" still pulled at me. For example, while on a walking interview with Kathleen, a White woman in her sophomore year, we encountered a hawk feeding on a squirrel on the central grounds of campus. Before coming across the hawk, I had been asking her basic questions about her experience on campus. As we came across the hawk, our conversation was pulled off course as we exclaimed in surprise. However, despite the violence of this moment, its unexpectedness, and its absurdity, I quickly brought us back to our original conversation, picking up as if the event had never happened. The pull of traditional methodologies is so powerful, as St. Pierre (2013) suggested, that "we can slip back into it with a single, telltale word" (p. 655). Even as Kathleen and I embarked on this walk to think *with* place and remain open to its encounters, the pull of the idea that particular types of talk are "right" or "correct" asserted its power.

Interestingly, several months later, the hawk reappeared while I was on a walking interview. This time, however, the hawk was there only in memory. On this occasion, the act of walking by a particular place on campus caused another participant, Owen, to remember seeing a feeding hawk on campus. This time, rather than move on, we entertained the story, and it led her to share her experience as a Black student at a predominately White campus, about the exclusive culture of fraternities and sororities on campus. Specifically, Owen shared a story about visiting a White, all-female sorority on campus for the first time, and the feelings of discomfort she experienced there. This example demonstrates the danger of using mobile methods unreflectively as "keys" to unlock the unexpected, as well as what might become possible by entertaining the unexpected and surprising. I examine the hawk and two other "objects" encountered on campus in Flint (2019a).

Intervening in Place, Walking as Activism

A final example returns us again to the boulder, a year after Jon and I first encountered the rock. On this occasion, I was walking with Leo, a Black student in his final year of college. As we approached the monument, again talking about its history and Leo's first memory of encountering it, we were joined by a faculty member and two visiting historians. "*I wanted to make sure they saw this, it doesn't get much attention I think [even] with all the controversy about Confederate monuments, but here it is, right?*" the faculty member had said. As we stood around the boulder, discussing its history and the complicated legacy of the boulder, the university, Alabama, and the country, another tour walked by us. This time, a group lingered behind, watching us, and as we talked, one of them clicked a picture of the boulder. As Leo and I walked away, Leo wondered about the image that was now on that phone. Would they zoom in to read the text on the placard? Would they look up the boulder later? How would it fit into or against their understanding of campus? As we wondered, two campus tour guides began walking up the path toward us. Leo paused, then greeted one of the tour guides and asked, "*Do you ever take people to the rock? Is that part of the tour?*" The tour guide responded no, then asked, "*Do you have any advice on the story we should tell?*" After Leo summarized what we had talked about with the historians moments before, we each continued on our way.

After a few moments, Leo turned around, and quietly stated, noting that they had diverted from the path (which skirted the rock) to stop in front of the boulder, both leaning toward the inscription. *"Wow!"* Leo had said, *"Even just merely talking about it, in that interaction, can get someone interested enough to stop and read and see what's around."*

From a critical perspective, scholars have written about the interview as an emancipatory practice, an interaction with transformative potential (Wolgemuth & Donohue, 2006). What this moment with Leo demonstrates is the potential of the walking interview to be an intervention into understandings of—or the production of—place. In this example, both the act of pausing by the boulder and stopping to talk with the tour guides brings others into the inquiry. Even as Leo and I continued on our walk, the implications of us standing by the boulder, talking to the historians, and questioning the tour guides continue to ripple as a moment of visual and mobile activism. This moment, along with an engagement with another monument on campus commemorating the work of civil rights activists, is explored in Flint (2021).

How to Design Research Using Go-Alongs and Walking Interviews

Figure 10.1 reviews questions that researchers ask when designing studies that use go-alongs or walking interviews. When using mobile methods that involve traveling in a car, bus, plane, or boat, activities such as cycling or swimming, or the use of mobility devices such as wheelchairs, additional questions must be asked. For example, when public transportation is involved, what are the ethical issues involved in conducting interviews near overhearing audiences? When automobiles are involved, what are the safety issues involved in talking while driving? Who will drive? When interviewers and interviewees are running or swimming (Denton et al., 2021), how will interviews be recorded? What physical issues related to moving while talking are relevant? If speakers use wheelchairs or mobility aids, what accessibility issues must be considered? And for any go-along approach taken, there is always the possibility of unexpected disruptions that cannot be anticipated. Thompson and Reynolds (2019) provide recommendations for how researchers might prepare for disruptions.

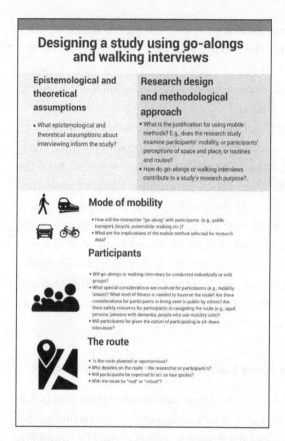

Figure 10.1a. Designing a Study Using Go-Alongs and Walking Interviews (p. 1).

Moving Along With Mobile Methods

Researchers continue apace to innovate in their use of mobile methods such as go-alongs and walking interviews. One set of innovations encompasses the integration of technologies with mobile methods. Spinney (2015), for example, has suggested combining go-alongs with technologies of "bio-sensing" (e.g., electroencephalography [EEG] technologies that measure brain waves and technologies that measure galvanic skin response). Such technologies, Spinney argued, provide "more detailed and pre-personal intensities of feeling" (p. 235) in mobile video ethnographies. For a review of other bio-sensory methods that scholars have used, see Versey (2021). "Virtual go-alongs" have been trialed by researchers who have created immersive virtual reality

Mobile Methods, Go-Alongs, and Walking Interviews

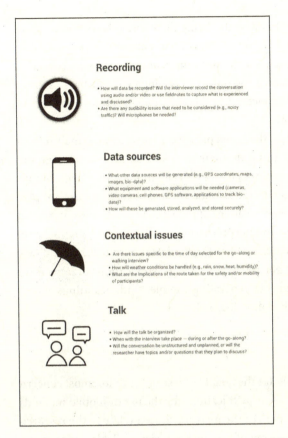

Figure 10.1b. Designing a Study Using Go-Alongs and Walking Interviews (p. 2).

environments (Vindenes & Wasson, 2021). In these go-alongs, participants moved through a virtual reality environment that showed images of real spaces while the interviewer asked questions.

In the midst of the COVID-19 pandemic, Shareck et al. (2021) offered a range of approaches to conducting walk-along interviews in a post-pandemic world. These included conducting walking-interviews "at a distance" via telephone, having participants record their walks using photos, voice-memos, or video—after which the researcher conducts an interview (p. 3)—conducting a live "virtual" walk involving synchronous communication with a participant wearing a camera or using a hand-held device, and asking questions of participants using a smartphone app at different points in time in combination with tracking the route using GPS technology (pp. 2–3). These technological solutions for possible ways to integrate "being there" provide ways to conduct research in a world in which in-person research might not always be possible. Nevertheless, these approaches also raise significant ethical issues related to the security of data generated using digital technologies, cloud-based storage of data, as well as privacy concerns to do with tracing the whereabouts of participants in the real world.

How researchers theorize the concepts used in a study and analyze data generated from go-alongs and walking interviews continues to change and develop in new ways. Researchers using walking interviews and go-alongs have theorized the data generated using a wide variety of theoretical perspectives to research that span positivist approaches to research (Marquart et al., 2022; Sun & Lau, 2021), to interpretivist (Kusenbach, 2003; Teff-Seker et al., 2022), critical (Castrodale, 2018), postcolonial (Wilmott, 2016), and new materialist (Powell, 2022) perspectives. Scholars' applications of innovative theoretical perspectives assist in generating complex understandings of data generated (e.g., Motala & Bozalek, 2022).

Conclusion

When considering how to judge the quality of research, our foremost concern is that researchers provide clear justifications for the use of mobile methods that show how the affordances of the method chosen relate to the research questions posed. Given the array of new technologies available, we advocate that researchers think carefully about how much data they will generate, for what purposes, how these data will be stored securely and analyzed, how findings will be represented, and what relevant ethical issues might be. We recommend that researchers carefully consider the ethical implications for their decisions, account for steps taken, and provide detailed accounts of the researcher's decisions and research process throughout the life of a study.

In this chapter we have introduced readers to the wide array of ways in which mobile interviewing can take place. We are excited by the innovations occurring in how go-alongs and walking interviews have been used to conduct qualitative research. With careful preparation and planning, these methods have the potential to add depth and nuance to how qualitative researchers make use of interview accounts to inform research topics about the social world.

References

Adekoya, A. A., & Guse, L. (2020). Walking interviews and wandering behavior: Ethical insights and methodological outcomes while exploring the perspectives of older adults living with dementia. *International Journal of Qualitative Methods, 19*. https://doi.org/10.1177/1609406920920135

Anderson, J. (2004). Talking whilst walking: A geographical archaeology of knowledge. *Area, 36*(3), 254–261.

Bell, S. L., & Bush, T. N. (2020). "Never mind the bullocks": Animating the go-along interview through creative nonfiction. *Mobilities, 16*(3), 1–16. https://doi.org/10.1080/17450101.2020.1817685

Bergeron, J., Paquette, S., & Poullaouec-Gonidec, P. (2014). Uncovering landscape values and micro-geographies of meanings with the go-along method. *Landscape and Urban Planning, 122*, 108–121. https://doi.org/https://doi.org/10.1016/j.landurbplan.2013.11.009

Brannelly, T., & Bartlett, R. (2020). Using walking interviews to enhance research relations with people with dementia: Methodological insights from an empirical study conducted in England. *Ethics and Social Welfare, 14*(4), 432–442. https://doi.org/10.1080/17496535.2020.1839115

Burns, R., Gallant, K. A., Litwiller, F., White, C., & Hamilton-Hinch, B. (2020). The go-along interview: A valuable tool for leisure research. *Leisure Sciences, 42*(1), 51–68. https://doi.org/10.1080/01490400.2019.1578708

Buscher, M., Urry, J., & Witchger, K. (2011). Introduction: Mobile methods. In M. Buscher, J. Urry, & K. Witchger (Eds.), *Mobile methods* (pp. 1–19). Routledge.

Castrodale, M. A. (2018). Mobilizing dis/ability research: A critical discussion of qualitative go-along interviews in practice. *Qualitative Inquiry, 24*(1), 45–55. https://doi.org/10.1177/1077800417727765

Chang, J. S. (2017). The docent method: A grounded theory approach for researching health and place. *Qualitative Health Research, 27*(4), 609–619. https://doi.org/10.1177/1049732316667055

Colley, K., Brown, C., & Montarzino, A. (2016). Restorative wildscapes at work: An investigation of the wellbeing benefits of greenspace at urban fringe business sites using "go-along" interviews. *Landscape Research, 41*(6), 598–615. https://doi.org/10.1080/01426397.2016.1197191

Denton, H., Dannreuther, C., & Aranda, K. (2021). Researching at sea: Exploring the "swim-along" interview method. *Health & Place, 67*. https://doi.org/10.1016/j.healthplace.2020.102466

Duedahl, E., & Stilling Blichfeldt, B. (2020). To walk the talk of go-along methods: Navigating the unknown terrains of being-along. *Scandinavian Journal of Hospitality and Tourism, 20*(5), 438–458. https://doi.org/10.1080/15022250.2020.1766560

Evans, J., & Jones, P. (2011). The walking interview: Methodology, mobility and place. *Applied Geography, 31*(2), 849–858. https://doi.org/https://doi.org/10.1016/j.apgeog.2010.09.005

Ferguson, H. (2016). Researching social work practice close up: Using ethnographic and mobile methods to understand encounters between social workers, children and families. *British Journal of Social Work, 46*(1), 153–168. https://doi.org/10.1093/bjsw/bcu120

Finlay, J. M., & Bowman, J. A. (2017). Geographies on the move: A practical and theoretical approach to the mobile interview. *The Professional Geographer, 69*(2), 263–274. https://doi.org/10.1080/00330124.2016.1229623

Flint, M. A. (2019a). Hawks, robots, and chalkings: Unexpected object encounters during walking interviews on a college campus. *Educational Research for Social Change, 8*(1), 120–137. https://doi.org/https://doi.org/10.17159/2221-4070/2018/v8i1a8

Flint, M. A. (2019b). Ruptures and reproductions: A walking encounter with a campus tour and a Confederate monument. *Cultural Studies ↔ Critical Methodologies, 19*(2), 91–104. https://doi.org/10.1177/1532708618809136

Flint, M. A. (2021). Racialized retellings: (Un)ma(r)king space and place on college campuses. *Critical Studies in Education, 62*(5), 559–574. https://doi.org/10.1080/17508487.2021.1877756

Garcia, C. M., Eisenberg, M. E., Frerich, E. A., Lechner, K. E., & Lust, K. (2012). Conducting go-along interviews to understand context and promote health. *Qualitative Health Research, 22*(10), 1395–1403. https://doi.org/10.1177/1049732312452936

Garvey, J. C., Guyotte, K. W., Latopolski, K. S., Sanders, L. A., & Flint, M. A. (2018). Belongingness in residence halls: Examining spaces and contexts for first-year students across race and gender. *Journal of the First-Year Experience & Students in Transition, 30*(2), 9–25.

Gopalan, M., & Brady, S. T. (2020). College students' sense of belonging: A national perspective. *Educational Researcher, 49*(2), 134–137. https://doi.org/10.3102/0013189x19897622

Hall, T., Lashua, B., & Coffey, A. (2008). Sound and the everyday in qualitative research. *Qualitative Inquiry, 14*(6), 1019–1040. https://doi.org/10.1177/1077800407312054

Hand, C., Huot, S., Laliberte Rudman, D., & Wijekoon, S. (2017). Qualitative–geospatial methods of exploring person-place transactions in aging adults: A scoping review. *The Gerontologist, 57*(3), e47–e61. https://doi.org/10.1093/geront/gnw130

Harris, J. (2016). Utilizing the walking interview to explore campus climate for students of color. *Journal of Student Affairs Research and Practice, 53*(4), 365–377. https://doi.org/10.1080/19496591.2016.1194284

Inwood, J. F. J., & Martin, D. G. (2008). Whitewash: White privilege and racialized landscapes at the University of Georgia. *Social & Cultural Geography, 9*(4), 373–395.

Isakjee, A. (2016). Dissonant belongings: The evolving spatial identities of young Muslim men in the UK. *Environment and Planning A: Economy and Space, 48*(7), 1337–1353. https://doi.org/10.1177/0308518x16641110

Johnstone, J. H., Bryce, D., & Alexander, M. J. (2019). Using mobile methods to understand multifaceted heritage organisations. *International Journal of Contemporary Hospitality Management, 32*(2), 1675–1691. https://doi.org/10.1108/ijchm-04-2019-0400

Jones, P., & Evans, J. (2012). The spatial transcript: Analysing mobilities through qualitative GIS. *Area, 44*(1), 92–99. https://doi.org/10.1111/j.1475-4762.2011.01058.x

Kullberg, A., & Odzakovic, E. (2018). Walking interviews as a research method with people living with dementia in their local community In J. Keady, L.-C. Hyden, A. Johnson, & C. Swarbrick (Eds.), *Social research in dementia studies: Inclusion and innovation* (pp. 23–37). Routledge.

Kuntz, A. M. (2015). *The responsible methodologist: Inquiry, truth-telling, and social justice*. Routledge.

Kusenbach, M. (2003). Street phenomenology: The go-along as ethnographic research tool. *Ethnography, 4*(3), 455–485. https://doi.org/10.1177/146613810343007

Kusenbach, M. (2018). Go-Alongs. In U. Flick (Ed.), *The SAGE handbook of qualitative data collection* (pp. 344–361). SAGE.

Lager, D., Van Hoven, B., & Huigen, P. P. P. (2015). Understanding older adults' social capital in place: Obstacles to and opportunities for social contacts in the neighbourhood. *Geoforum, 59*, 87–97. https://doi.org/10.1016/j.geoforum.2014.12.009

Lauwers, L., Leone, M., Guyot, M., Pelgrims, I., Remmen, R., Van den Broeck, K., Keune, H., & Bastiaens, H. (2021). Exploring how the urban neighborhood environment influences mental well-being using walking interviews. *Health & Place, 67*. Article 102506. https://doi.org/10.1016/j.healthplace.2020.102497

Lee, J., & Ingold, T. (2006). Fieldwork on foot: Perceiving, routing, socializing. In S. Coleman & P. Collins (Eds.), *Locating the field: Space, place and context in anthropology* (pp. 67–85). Berg.

Lőrinc, M., Kilkey, M., Ryan, L., & Tawodzera, O. (2022). "You still want to go lots of places": Exploring walking interviews in research with older migrants. *The Gerontologist, 62*(6), 832–841. https://doi.org/10.1093/geront/gnab152

Lynch, J., & Mannion, G. (2016). Enacting a place-responsive research methodology: Walking interviews with educators. *Journal of Adventure Education and Outdoor Learning, 16*(4), 330–345. https://doi.org/10.1080/14729679.2016.1163271

Mackay, M. H., Nelson, T., & Perkins, H. C. (2018). Interpretive walks: Advancing the use of mobile methods in the study of entrepreneurial farm tourism settings. *Geographical Research, 56*, 167–175.

Madsen, T. A. (2017). Walking and sensing at Faaborg Museum. Atmosphere and walk-along interviews at the museum. *Nordisk Museologi, 2*, 124–141. https://doi.org/10.5617/nm.6351

Malinowski, B. (2014 [1922]). *Argonauts of the western Pacific: An account of native enterprise and adventure in the archipelagoes of Melanesian New Guinea*. Routledge.

Marquart, H., Schlink, U., & Nagendra, S. M. S. (2022). Complementing mobile measurements with Walking Interviews: A case study on personal exposure of commuters in Chennai, India. *International Journal of Urban Sciences, 26*(1), 148–161. https://doi.org/10.1080/12265934.2020.1871060

Martinez, C. A. F., & Gois, G. R. (2022). Walking as political utterance: The walking subjects and the production of space. *Qualitative Inquiry, 28*(2), 209–218. https://doi.org/10.1177/10778004211042351

Martini, N. (2020). Using GPS and GIS to enrich the walk-along method. *Field Methods, 32*(2), 180–192. https://doi.org/10.1177/1525822x20905257

Massey, D. (2005). *For space*. SAGE.

May, V., & Lewis, C. (2020). Researching embodied relationships with place: Rehabilitating the sit-down interview. *Qualitative Research, 20*(2), 127–142. https://doi.org/10.1177/1468794119834186

Merriman, P. (2014). Rethinking mobile methods. *Mobilities, 9*(2), 167–187. https://doi.org/10.1080/17450101.2013.784540

Motala, S., & Bozalek, V. (2022). Haunted walks of District Six: Propositions for counter-surveying. *Qualitative Inquiry, 28*(2), 244–256. https://doi.org/10.1177/10778004211042349

Odzakovic, E., Hellström, I., Ward, R., & Kullberg, A. (2018). "Overjoyed that I can go outside": Using walking interviews to learn about the lived experience and meaning of neighbourhood for people living with dementia. *Dementia, 19*(7), 2199–2219. https://doi.org/10.1177/1471301218817453

O'Neill, M., Mansaray, S., & Haaken, J. (2017). Women's lives, well-being and community: Arts-based biographical methods. *International Review of Qualitative Research, 10*(2), 211–233. https://doi.org/10.2307/26372257

O'Neill, M., & Roberts, B. (2020). *Walking methods: Research on the move*. Routledge.

Palmgren, A. (2018). Standing still: Walking interviews and poetic spatial inquiry. *Area, 50*(3), 372–383. https://doi.org/https://doi.org/10.1111/area.12410

Parent, L. (2016). The wheeling interview: Mobile methods and disability. *Mobilities, 11*(4), 521–532.

Phillips, S. (2022). Walking while Aboriginal. *Qualitative Inquiry, 28*(2), 198–199. https://doi.org/10.1177/10778004211043496

Pink, S. (2007). Walking with video. *Visual Studies, 22*(3), 240–252. https://doi.org/10.1080/14725860701657142

Pink, S. (2015). *Doing sensory ethnography* (2nd ed.). SAGE.

Powell, K. (2020). Walking refrains for storied movement. *Cultural Studies ↔ Critical Methodologies, 20*(1), 35–42. https://doi.org/10.1177/1532708619884975

Powell, K. (2022). Moving encounters with spatial racism: Walking in San Jose Japantown. *Qualitative Inquiry, 28*(2), 257–266. https://doi.org/10.1177/10778004211042345

Ratzenböck, B. (2016). "Let's take a look together": Walking interviews in domestic spaces as a means to examine ICT experiences of women 60+. *Romanian Journal of Communication and Public Relations, 18*(1), 49. https://doi.org/10.21018/rjcpr.2016.1.201

Reed, K., & Ellis, J. (2019). Movement, materiality, and the mortuary: Adopting go-along ethnography in research on fetal and neonatal postmortem. *Journal of Contemporary Ethnography, 48*(2), 209–235. https://doi.org/10.1177/0891241618769997

Riley, M., Turner, J., Hayes, S. J., & Peters, K. (2021). Mobile interviews by land, air and sea. In N. von Benzon, M. Holton, C. Wilkinson, & S. Wilkinson (Eds.), *Creative methods for human geographers* (pp. 141–152). SAGE.

Ross, N. J., Renold, E., Holland, S., & Hillman, A. (2009). Moving stories: Using mobile methods to explore the everyday lives of young people in public care. *Qualitative Research, 9*(5), 605–623. https://doi.org/10.1177/1468794109343629

Roulston, K. (2022). Bursting forth: Attending to the more-than-human in qualitative research. In N. K. Denzin & M. D. Giardina (Eds.), *Transformative visions for qualitative inquiry* (pp. 65–84). Routledge.

Sáenz de Tejada Granados, C., & Van der Horst, D. (2020). Tabula non-rasa: Go-along interviews and memory mapping in a post-mining landscape designated for urban expansion. *Landscape Research, 45*(1), 6–25. https://doi.org/10.1080/01426397.2019.1569220

Saint-Onge, K., Bernard, P., Kingsbury, C., & Houle, J. (2021). Older public housing tenants' capabilities for physical activity described using walk-along interviews in Montreal, Canada. *International Journal of Environmental Research and Public Health, 18*(21), 11647. https://doi.org/10.3390/ijerph182111647

St. Pierre, E. A. (2013). The posts continue: Becoming. *International Journal of Qualitative Studies in Education, 26*(6), 646–657. https://doi.org/10.1080/09518398.2013.788754

Scott, N. A. (2020). Calibrating the go-along for the Anthropocene. *International Journal of Social Research Methodology, 23*(3), 317–328. https://doi.org/10.1080/13645579.2019.1696089

Shareck, M., Alexander, S., & Glenn, N. M. (2021). In-situ at a distance? Challenges and opportunities for health and place research methods in a post-COVID-19 world. *Health & Place, 69*. Article 102545. https://doi.org/10.1016/j.healthplace.2021.102572

Spinney, J. (2009). Cycling the city: Movement, meaning and method. *Geography Compass, 3*(2), 817–835. https://doi.org/10.1111/j.1749-8198.2008.00211.x

Spinney, J. (2015). Close encounters? Mobile methods, (post)phenomenology and affect. *cultural geographies, 22*(2), 231–246. https://doi.org/https://www.jstor.org/stable/26168640

Stevenson, A., & Holloway, J. (2017). Getting participants' voices heard: Using mobile, participant led, sound-based methods to explore place-making. *Area, 49*(1), 85–93. https://doi.org/10.1111/area.12296

Strayhorn, T. L. (2012). *College students' sense of belonging: A key to educational success for all students*. Routledge.

Sun, G., & Lau, C. Y. (2021). Go-along with older people to public transport in high-density cities: Understanding the concerns and walking barriers through their lens. *Journal of Transport & Health, 21*, Article 101072. https://doi.org/10.1016/j.jth.2021.101072

Teff-Seker, Y., Rasilo, T., Dick, J., Goldsborough, D., & Orenstein, D. E. (2022). What does nature feel like? Using embodied walking interviews to discover cultural ecosystem services. *Ecosystem Services, 55*. Article 101425. https://doi.org/10.1016/j.ecoser.2022.101425

Thomas, E., Riley, M., & Smith, H. (2019). A flowing conversation? Methodological issues in interviewing farmers about rivers and riparian environments. *Area, 51*(2), 371–379. https://doi.org/10.1111/area.12507

Thompson, C., & Reynolds, J. (2019). Reflections on the go-along: How "disruptions" can illuminate the relationships of health, place and practice. *Geographical Journal, 185*(2), 156–167. https://doi.org/10.1111/geoj.12285

Tong, C., Sims-Gould, J., & McKay, H. (2016). InterACTIVE Interpreted Interviews (I3): A multi-lingual, mobile method to examine the neighbourhood environment with older adults. *Social Science & Medicine, 168*, 207–213. https://doi.org/10.1016/j.socscimed.2016.08.010

Tuck, E., & McKenzie, M. (2015). *Place in research: Theory, methodology, and methods*. Routledge.

Versey, H. S. (2021). Can mobile methods bridge psychology and place-based research? *Qualitative Psychology, 9*(2), 156–170. https://psycnet.apa.org/doi/10.1037/qup0000187

Vindenes, J., & Wasson, B. (2021). Show, don't tell: Using go-along interviews in immersive virtual reality. *Designing Interactive Systems Conference*, 190–204. https://doi.org/10.1145/3461778.3462014

Ware, S. M. (2022). Foraging the future: Forest baths, engaged pedagogy, and planting ourselves into the future. *Qualitative Inquiry, 28*(2), 236–243. https://doi.org/10.1177/10778004211046601

Warren, S. (2017). Pluralising the walking interview: Researching (im)mobilities with Muslim women. *Social & Cultural Geography, 18*(6), 786–807. https://doi.org/10.1080/14649365.2016.1228113

Warren, S. (2021). Pluralising (im)mobilities: Anti-Muslim acts and the epistemic politics of mobile methods. *Mobilities, 16*(6), 905–920. https://doi.org/10.1080/17450101.2021.1922068

Wiederhold, A. (2015). Conducting fieldwork at and away from home: shifting researcher positionality with mobile interviewing methods. *Qualitative Research, 15*(5), 600–615. https://doi.org/10.1177/1468794114550440

Wilmott, C. (2016). Small moments in Spatial Big Data: Calculability, authority and interoperability in everyday mobile mapping. *Big Data & Society, 3*(2). https://doi.org/10.1177/2053951716661364

Wilmott, C. (2017). In-between mobile maps and media: Movement. *Television & New Media, 18*(4), 320–335. https://doi.org/10.1177/1527476416663637

Wolgemuth, J. R., & Donohue, R. (2006). Toward an inquiry of discomfort: Guiding transformation in "emancipatory" narrative research. *Qualitative Inquiry, 12*(5), 1022–1039.

Wozolek, B. (2018). In 8100 again: The sounds of students breaking. *Educational Studies, 54*(4), 367–381. https://doi.org/10.1080/00131946.2018.1473869

ELEVEN

 # Photo Elicitation With Native STEM Students and Professionals

Nuria Jaumot-Pascual, Tiffany Smith, Maria Ong, and Kathy DeerInWater

OUR TEAM HAS CONDUCTED PHOTO elicitation (PE) in two projects with Native[1] participants. The first was a small study with eight participants called *Native Women and Two-Spirit Individuals in Computing* (NAWC2) and was funded by the Women of Color in Computing Collaborative. TERC and the American Indian Science and Engineering Society (AISES) partnered to study: (a) the hurdles and supports experienced by Native students in undergraduate computing education, and (b) how participants experienced the intersections of their identities as Native individuals and computing students. The second project is an ongoing, national study with forty PE participants called *Native STEM Portraits: A Longitudinal, Mixed-Methods Study of the Intersectional Experiences of Native Learners and Professionals in STEM* (NSP) and is funded by the National Science Foundation. Researchers at TERC, AISES, and the University of Georgia partnered to conduct this study, with TERC and AISES researchers conducting the PE section of the study, and researchers at the University of Georgia focusing on the surveys. Similar to NAWC2, NSP addressed research questions regarding the hurdles and supports that Native STEM students and professionals experience and their intersecting identities. We consider NAWC2 to be the pilot that allowed us to develop the larger NSP study and secure funding for it. We use images and participants' quotes from both projects to illustrate the questions of process that we share in this chapter.

Defining Photo Elicitation

PE interviewing is a data collection method where photographs are used in interviews to elicit conversation. Harper (2002) described it as follows:

The difference between interviews using images and text, and interviews using words alone lies in the ways we respond to these two forms of symbolic representation. This has a physical basis: the parts of the brain that process visual information are evolutionarily older than the parts that process verbal information. Thus, images evoke deeper elements of human consciousness that [sic] do words; exchanges based on words alone utilize less of the brain's capacity than do exchanges in which the brain is processing images as well as words. These may be some of the reasons the photo elicitation interview seems like not simply an interview process that elicits more information, but rather one that evokes a different kind of information. (p. 13)

Note Harper's emphasis on the differences between how different types of information are processed in the brain and how it results in different kinds of responses. Collier (1957) noted that using PE generated more emotional statements and "elicited longer and more comprehensive interviews but at the same time helped subjects overcome the fatigue and repetition of conventional interviews" (p. 858). Harris and Guillemin (2012) and Padgett et al. (2013) have found that photographs create intimacy between participants and researcher and help participants to critically reflect on meaningful aspects of their lives due to photographs' potential for the expansion of sensory awareness and increased self-reflexivity. This has also been our experience, with interviews eliciting a degree of intimacy and trust between interviewee and interviewer that was often startling for members of our team who were accustomed to traditional interview formats. In our studies, we paired photographs with semi-structured interview protocols that included prompts requesting examples and stories. This format facilitated interactions that felt more like conversations than interviews, further aligning our methods with Indigenous methodologies seeking relationality and the co-construction of knowledge (Archibald, 2008).

Among scholars of PE methods, there has been some disagreement about the analysis of resulting data (Guillemin & Drew, 2010). Bessette and Paris (2020) pointed out that validity of images as data is often a concern among researchers due to the potential of having multiple, subjective interpretations. There are researchers who consider that the researchers themselves should analyze the images as well (e.g., Carlson et al., 2006) and others who consider that the weight of the analysis needs to be conducted by participants and researchers together during the interview (e.g., Drew & Guillemin, 2014).

In participant-generated PE, where participants take the photos used in the interviews, the analysis of the images is generally done during the interview, centering the participant's interpretation and meaning-making while the researcher gently guides the conversation. As we describe below, to align with our theoretical framework, we used participant-generated PE, considering participants as experts in their photos' meaning.

History of the Method

PE originated in anthropology in the 1950s with John Collier's experimentation on how photographs could aid interviews in the context of a study of the relation of environment to mental health (Collier, 1957). This method was only cited a handful of times until 1967, when John Collier and his son, Malcolm Collier, published a book on the method, which they later expanded in 1986. Since then, the citations have steadily climbed and diversified across multiple social science disciplines. Visual methodologies that use photography have also diversified to include approaches that vary in how photos are generated and how participatory they are.

Photovoice (Wang & Burris, 1997) is one such participatory method that grew in popularity over the past two decades. Wang and Burris defined photovoice as "a process by which people can identify, represent, and enhance their community through a specific photographic technique. It entrusts cameras to the hands of people to enable them to act as recorders, and potential catalysts for change, in their own communities" (p. 369). Photovoice differs from PE as we describe it here in that photovoice involves community engagement processes to catalyze local change using the photographs generated in the study.

Photo methods, like PE and photovoice, with increased involvement from participants rather than researcher-controlled methods, have been identified by Indigenous and non-Indigenous researchers as culturally relevant methods to conduct research with Indigenous participants. They are considered culturally relevant due to their empowering, trust-building, and conversational nature. The earliest examples of the use of photo methods, in this case photovoice, with Indigenous participants are studies in the allied health sciences by Moffitt and Vollman (2004) and Castleden and Garvin (2008). In both studies, authors underscored how empowering the method was for participants. Castleden and Garvin, for example, identified the method as being supportive of building a sense of ownership and of trust. PE and photovoice have more recently been taken up in the study of Native students in higher education, focusing on topics such as participants' sense of belonging in institutions of higher education, their supports and barriers, and their use of on-campus resources (e.g., Beatty et al., 2020; Chelberg, 2019; Coble, 2019; McMillan, 2020; Minthorn & Marsh, 2016). In research with Native participants, PE is characterized as "radical, ethical, and revolutionary" due to its potential for addressing issues of social inequity and promoting policy change (Minthorn & Marsh, 2016, p. 5).

Our Team's Implementation of Photo Elicitation

Our team used theoretical frameworks that stem from Critical Race Theory as applied to higher education (Solórzano, 1998; Solórzano et al., 2000), such as Tribal Critical Race Theory (TribalCrit) (Brayboy, 2005), Intersectionality (Collins, 2019; Collins & Bilge, 2016), and Community Cultural Wealth (Yosso, 2005). In alignment with our theoretical framework, we also follow Indigenous social scientists' and educational researchers' (e.g., Brayboy & Deyhle, 2000; Smith, 1999) recommendations to conduct studies with Native communities in ways that respect the cultural background of participants, promote community participation and empowerment, consider the community's interests, and create rapport with and avoid the exploitation of the community.

Our team used participant-generated PE where participants took photographs in response to a series of prompts that addressed our research questions. In both of our studies, we used three prompts, and participants submitted up to five photographs and captions per prompt: supports that helped them persist in STEM; hurdles they experienced; and how they identified as both Native individuals and scientists in their STEM discipline. Before the interview, participants submitted the photographs and captions (brief explanations for each photograph) so that the researcher could prepare for the interview. Having a caption for each photo helped in providing a context for any photographs that were not addressed during the interview due to time constraints.

We worked from the assumption that "increased participant control of data generation through production of visual images [would] help to illuminate important aspects of lived experience that might otherwise have been overlooked or ignored by researchers—perhaps even been invisible" (Guillemin & Drew, 2010, p. 176). We also worked from the perspective that participant-generated PE provides an "opportunity for both sides to engage in talk rather than only one party doing most of the talking" (Archibald, 2008, p. 47). This conversational style stems from our commitment to conducting our research in a relational manner from start to finish, being intentional in using the language of "conversations" for a more informal understanding of the projects' data collection than the westernized method of researcher-controlled interviews (Archibald, 2008; Smith, 2019). It is a means to co-construct knowledge collectively and for communal gain and intentionally incorporates Indigenous notions of relationality, reciprocity, and respect in sharing with one another (Wilson, 2008).

After participants submitted the images and captions, we used their photos in individual interviews where the images were at the center of the conversation, decentering the role of the researcher. Each participant became the expert on the topic through their ownership and their interpretations of their photographs. The use of photographs also pushed us to try to listen with all our senses (Archibald, 2008), or, at a minimum, with more senses than traditional interviews. After data collection, we analyzed the interview recordings and transcripts from all participants. We will further discuss how our team has conducted analysis below.

Methodological Affordances of PE

PE "takes seriously participants as knowers" and "provide[s] participants with the opportunity to produce an image that allows them to portray what is often difficult to express in words" (Guillemin & Drew, 2010, pp. 177–178). These can also have the effect of being therapeutic opportunities for self-reflection for participants, who find that they can express thoughts and experiences that had previously been inaccessible to themselves (e.g., Jaumot-Pascual, 2018). In addition, PE has affordances related to expressivity and introspection, representation of Native cultures and values, and creativity, to name a few.

Portraying Native Cultures and Values

In our studies, PE provided the opportunity to portray Native cultural artifacts as part of participants' representation. This was particularly poignant in our prompt that asked about how they identified as Native STEM students and professionals. Many participants found this question to be difficult to answer, as it asked about something intangible and, as some acknowledged, something that they had never considered before. Many participants depicted their ideas by juxtaposing cultural artifacts (such as turquoise and beaded jewelry, pottery, dolls, baskets, and moccasins) with STEM-related artifacts (such as measuring tools, calculators, and computers). By showing cultural objects and STEM tools together, participants asserted that both identities fit together, even if the fit might not be obvious to the viewer. An example of this is one of Diana's photos portraying Indigenous pottery and her computer (Figure 11.1).

Figure 11.1. A Collection of Art.
Author: Diana*, undergraduate computing student (NAWC2)
"I see what I'm doing as, code and programming as, it's an art. It's an art, because you can express yourself in so many different ways with what you do, and what you use it for, what you use your code for.... I want to bring the two worlds together. They're pretty separate. Or they would be, they would have no connection if you were an outsider. But... I want to bring my two identities together.
* All names in this chapter are pseudonyms.

Participants also used their photos as an opportunity to portray the Native values that they were trying to embody through their STEM work. Some of these values include respect for their elders and community, the cultural and spiritual significance of place, nature, and the Earth, and the responsibility to give back. Participants portrayed respect for their elders and community through images of their elders or objects that represented them. To portray community, some participants would show places where their community gathers and things that were important to their communities. Participants also portrayed the significance of place and nature through landscapes that were culturally and spiritually significant for them.

Introspection

Participants in both studies highlighted that the process of PE provided an opportunity for introspection to assess their own values and to reflect on the path taken so far. Participants shared that the PE process was both difficult and rewarding. On the one hand, creating images that expressed ideas was not always easy. Confirming Guillemin and Drew's (2010) claims, our participants worried about whether they were doing it "right" or if they were showing the types of things we wanted to see. At the same time, they appreciated the opportunity for creativity and reflection, both as they prepared their photographs to respond to the prompts and during the interview when talking about the photos with the researchers. For example, Charlie (pharmacy professional, NSP) expressed how his participation in the project made him reflect and pulled him in two directions, from "this is a lot of work" to "this is a lot of fun," commenting:

> It took me a while to kind of get my head around how I wanted to approach it. But like I said, it was kind of rewarding. It was rewarding, and it was an interesting process. Looking back, I appreciate the chance—At first, I was like, oh my god, this is a lot of work. . . . But then when I got into it, I'm like, oh, this is a lot of fun.

Similarly, Libby, an undergraduate student in computing (NAWC2) shared: "I just want to say that this was a really wonderful experience, and it was really fun to take all the photos. It was just great to get so introspective, so I want to say thank you for letting me participate."

For other participants, the self-reflection and introspection facilitated by PE provided an avenue to reflect on their identities as Native scientists and connect with the emotions brought up by looking at their past and thinking about their future. Callie's example (computing undergraduate, NAWC2, Figure 11.2) shows how participating in a PE project was an emotionally complex opportunity to reflect on her difficult path and her successes. In Callie's case, these emotions were particularly poignant because we talked with her as she was starting her last semester in her senior year in what was her second bachelor's degree to change careers from teaching to computing. It was a moment of reckoning for her, as the end of her degree and the beginning of her second career approached. North (computing graduate student, NSP) explained that the photo elicitation process helped him reflect on his career path leading up to the current moment, while also helping him reflect on how he planned on giving back to his community going forward.

Figure 11.2. New Formation.
Author: Callie, undergraduate student in computer science (NAWC2)
"[What] I kind of enjoyed about this project is in that I could use pictures or metaphorical ways of looking at my life and what I've gone through. I enjoyed that a lot.... [It was emotional] 'cause it's sad to think about challenges that I've had, and then super happy to think about all that I've overcome. And then, it's exciting and scary to think about the future, 'cause you never really know what's going to happen. So, there was a wide variety of emotions that I've been able to think about as I was doing the project."

Creativity and Representation

Metaphor, Image Manipulation, and Collage

PE also provided flexibility in how participants chose to represent their ideas and responses to the prompts, from metaphor to representational images, from candid to staged photographs, from compositions and photocollages to portraits. Many participants used staging with different levels of complexity. Several participants photographed stacks of books that included works written by Indigenous authors, collections of Indigenous stories, and books from their STEM disciplines. Others used figurines and Native dolls to stage groups of people representing relationships with others and the feelings associated with them. Such was the case with Reed (STEM teacher, NSP) (Figures 11.3 and 11.4), who showed his sense of belonging and isolation through how he positioned a set of kachinas, or small, carved figures of tribal ancestral spirits. In Figure 11.3, Reed showed that he had been able to connect with his culture and tribe. However, in other photos he shared with us, such as Figure 11.4, he portrayed a single kachina standing on its own on the table's corner to show how he often felt isolated.

Callie (Figure 11.2), on the other hand, used a landscape photograph as a metaphor to express her ideas. In this case, the "New Formation" in the image was a metaphor for her future: something new that was still taking shape.

Figure 11.3. Connection.
Author: Reed, professional in STEM secondary education (NSP)
"As I have gained connection with my past, I have also sought that type of connection with the world. Mine has been a journey attempting to understand and later to teach understanding of the world and STEM concepts."

Figure 11.4. Isolation.
Author: Reed, professional in STEM secondary education (NSP)
"As part of being different, there is an isolation that comes with it. One can attempt to be part of the majority group, but you never really will be."

Other participants manipulated their images through changes in the lighting and focus, by juxtaposing images, by using filters, or by creating collages. These images showed participants' creativity and skills and provided them with additional ways to express the complexity of their experiences in STEM. Participants used visual language (e.g., blurring, transparencies, overlapping) to display how their experiences and identities were shaped. Some examples in these studies are the blurring of images to express how experiencing microaggression depletes one's mental energy, and using collage to bring together complex meanings difficult to express in one single image.

Creativity Beyond Photography

The use of photography provided participants with an avenue for the expression of their creativity, and many took advantage of the opportunity by doing more than taking candid photos, with solutions such as manipulating the photos, as described above. Other participants took their creativity in different directions according to their skills and interests. Some of the non-photographic creative expressions included more traditional forms of representation such as pencil, crayon, and marker drawings, hand-lettered posters, and the use of icons and stock images to create compositions. Drawings spanned different skill levels, from simple stencil tracings to life-like renderings. Such was the case with Sage (Figure 11.5), who used her artistic skills to draw a salmon's tail. To many viewers, the fish's tail will look beautifully done. However, Sage herself considered it not to be up to her professors' standards or even her own, given that she had taken many art courses that would allow her to create what she called "beautiful works."

Figure 11.5. Make It Beautiful.
Author: Sage, graduate student in environmental science (NSP)
"[STEM discipline] is scientific, yet my professors want us to also create beautiful work. This etching is rather shoddy, a representative salmon from my parents' homeland. The director of the program probably would not like it. I took so many art classes, so I should know how to create beautiful works."

Other participants used our request for photographs as a jumping-off point to unleash their creativity that required artistic processes beyond photography, drawing, and the use of preexisting icons. These unexpected forms of expression included creative streak plates (Figure 11.6), a music playlist, and a recording of a participant playing the violin. Except for the violin recording, we received all these forms of expression as photographs. The streak plates were a way for Meadow (postdoctoral fellow in microbiology, NSP) to speak to her persistence in STEM through the representation of her tribal affiliation by using skills from her discipline.

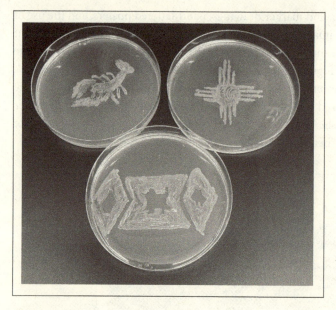

Figure 11.6. Saktce and Tribal Plates.
Author: Meadow, graduate student in microbiology (NSP)
"These are images of streak plates that I have done of bacterial strains to show how I try to introduce my culture into my science. . . . Science gives me the ability to be creative, which I enjoy as an Indigenous crafter. I also would like to use my work to give back to my community and other Indigenous communities by researching infectious disease."

Challenges of Using Photo Elicitation

Although we have found photography to be an accessible medium for most participants, we have also encountered some challenges that we would like to highlight and that have to do with the technology itself, participants' responses, and ownership of the images. We asked participants to share images with us that were at least 300 dpi. However, even though most participants were relatively tech-savvy, sometimes they were not aware of what 300 dpi meant or were not aware of how to change their camera's settings. We received images that were photographs of printed photographs, collages, PowerPoint presentations, and other formats. These often meant low-resolution images that were not adequate for use in certain formats, such as large print. This often limited how the images could be used for later dissemination and reciprocity with Native communities.

Another technical issue that we encountered was participants taking images from the Internet without checking whether they were open access. Unfortunately, we could not use these images because they were usually copyrighted, unless they came from websites where content was explicitly open source. Other technical or logistical issues included difficulties with sharing the images due to the technology used (e.g., uploading files to a shared drive), connectivity issues, and lack of access to the locations where participants wanted to take pictures (e.g., university campuses during the pandemic). With a bit of creativity, these issues were often possible to address or to find alternatives to, such as by extending uploading deadlines to after campus in-person classes resumed, or participants choosing images they had taken before their participation in the project.

As described above, though photography is a familiar format, some participants felt intimidated by the idea of responding to a prompt through images. In NAWC2, for example, Johanna narrowly interpreted the prompts relative to other participants. She limited her images mostly to pieces of technology to literally depict her interest and training in computing. During her interview, the researcher decided to ask beyond the technology portrayed in the pictures to include people and organizations. When Johanna realized that she could have included photos of supports such as her parents and her volunteering efforts, she was dismayed that she hadn't thought to submit them. Nevertheless, she was pleased to share her thoughts on them, even if they were not accompanied by images. The takeaway lesson for us in this interaction with Johanna is that there are topics (e.g., volunteering) that participants may not think to include in their photos about which researchers may want to probe. Researchers should be as prepared as possible by reviewing photos and captions ahead of time and being aware of what is depicted and what is potentially missing.

We found that another way that participants were intimidated by the PE format was not quite knowing how to begin. Dawn, a geology undergraduate student participating in NSP, could not think of ways to respond to the project's prompts with photos. As a result, she kept delaying the interview to the point that we thought she was not going to participate. Finally, a team researcher met with her to show her how other participants had used photos to respond to the prompts, being careful to show a broad diversity of responses so as to avoid directing her in a particular direction. As this meeting unfolded, it was apparent that Dawn expressed a sense of relief at seeing other participants' pictures, particularly the different levels of craft and creativity, and was starting to have ideas about how she wanted to shape her responses. She shared that she thought that her photos needed to be particularly beautiful or technical, and that it was refreshing to see a wide range among other participants' images.

Although the goal for PE interviews is to discuss all the images that participants share with us, sometimes that is not possible. In some cases, it is a matter of time and not wanting to overstep the amount of time participants have agreed to spend with us. In other cases, it is a matter of having lively storytellers or participants with complex stories that do not fit into the average interview times. Krista, a NAWC2 undergraduate computing student, was an extraordinary storyteller, so one interview was not sufficient to share all the ideas and stories that she had collected in her images. She was so disappointed in the fact that we did not talk about all the images that she volunteered to do an additional interview to ensure that all images were properly covered.

Some participants contributed images without captions. When this was paired with the need to prioritize photos during the interview due to time constraints, we ended up with images for which we did not have any context, so we did not have a way to interpret them. Unfortunately, we do not have many options for including these caption-less images in publications and dissemination efforts, which can be frustrating, particularly when the image is striking.

We attempted to pre-empt or address these issues by providing detailed instructions to participants using different formats. We typically offered instructions by at least two of the following three means: a meeting, in writing, and via videorecorded presentation. The different formats helped because repetition of the information aided with recollection, particularly on topics that might have been unfamiliar, such as image resolution.

Interpreting Visual Data

As described above, Bessette and Paris (2020) noted that validity of images alone is often a concern among researchers, due to their being open to multiple, subjective interpretations. Indeed, in our two projects, the ways in which participants' images responded to our prompts were often not evident without the captions and our conversations during interviews. Guided by our theoretical framework and Tribal Crit Theory and Indigenous scholars' calls to respect participants' cultural backgrounds and knowledge (e.g., Brayboy, 2005;

Brayboy & Deyhle, 2000), our team takes a participant-centered approach to the PE method. We work from the perspective that participants, as the generators of the images, are the experts in their meaning. Thus, participants interpret the images, and we contribute to the analysis with the participants through the facilitation of the participants' process during the interview. Interview transcripts and captions are further analyzed like other textual data using methods from the qualitative research tradition. In the transcripts, photos are inserted at appropriate places to provide context for the words.

In the case of NAWC2, our analysis process started with deductive coding (Patton, 2002) using codes that we developed from our theoretical frame and our knowledge of the literature on minoritized and marginalized groups in STEM. An example of a deductive code that we used was "navigation strategies," which we based on Tara Yosso's (2005) "navigational capital" from her community cultural wealth framework. As we conducted deductive coding, we developed inductive codes (Strauss & Corbin, 1998) for any relevant data that did not fit the deductive codes. An example of an inductive code we used was "Convergence/divergence of Native science/culture & Western science/culture," which we used when participants told us about their experiences of trying to bring together their Native knowledges with what they were learning in school. We then brought together both types of codes into a hybrid codebook (Fereday & Muir-Cochrane, 2006). After coding, we conducted thematic analysis (Braun & Clarke, 2006) to identify patterns across the data, to group codes, and to develop themes.

In centering Indigenous ways of conducting research in NSP, the team records, transcribes, and analyzes the data from PE to gain an understanding of the interconnectedness of the participants in relation to their experiences and to each other (Archibald, 2008). We follow Smith's (2019) recommendation to sit with the stories to critically reflect on their meanings as an important practice to drawing out significant themes. The team reads and re-reads transcripts to pull out overarching themes from the participant stories organically. Additionally, the team comes together for critical discussion and reflection after each layer of thematic analysis, as the themes become stronger and more stories align with each area. We pay special attention to sharing participant stories along with their photos with the team during our meetings, which is a testament to the true loving and caring nature we model in maintaining these relationships and elevating these important stories.

Ethical Considerations

With the new Institutional Review Board rules approved and implemented across the United States in 2018, both NAWC2 and NSP became exempt studies because all participants were adults voluntarily participating in studies that involved minimal risk. However, in both studies, we considered that we needed to be sensitive to the history of extractive research with Native populations and to the fact that this is a relatively small population, so we internally implemented protections beyond what was required from our overseeing IRB.

Indigenous people are often not included in studies on STEM education due to their low numbers. The reason usually offered is that conventional research tools would not have rigorous results and that participants' characteristics would make them easily identifiable (Pawley, 2019). Given that PE encompasses different types of data, including words and images, along with the small numbers, this heightens the likelihood of participants being identified, making the research team particularly sensitive to the need to carefully protect participants' identities. Our first step always consisted of removing language that might inadvertently identify a participant, such as the name of their tribe or the state where they resided. As an effort to ensure participants' anonymity, we asked them to avoid including faces in their photographs. Most participants understood the reasons for our request and complied by using images that did not include faces. Other participants who wanted to portray people used creative solutions, such as showing people from the back, showing only parts of the body such as hands or feet, portraying people wearing lab masks, goggles, or other equipment covering parts of the face, or even showing people from the neck down.

Although we asked participants to avoid faces as much as possible, particularly of other people, to avoid issues of identification, lack of consent, and potential breaches of confidentiality, a few submitted self-portraits as part of the project. This injected an added level of complexity into the project. Although we have participants' signed consent to use the photographs they shared with us, we avoided using self-portraits that clearly showed participants' features due to the risk of identification already mentioned. We only used those from participants with whom we had double-checked that they were aware of our inclusion of the images in presentations and publications and insisted that they are the best representation of their answers to our prompts. In all other cases, we either blurred faces or shared only their captions. The self-portraits that participants submitted were empowering images in a variety of formats, from business-like portraits to creative self-portraits with valued objects, where they showed how their STEM and Native identities converged. Bell, an undergraduate student in computing (NAWC2), submitted a self-portrait that showed her from the waist up wearing a grey business suit and a white shirt, a simple necklace, beaded earrings, and her long, straight hair parted in the middle and pushed back. Bell shared: "I chose this headshot because as a college student it is important to portray myself as professional as possible. Another element to this picture is my beaded earrings. It shows both sides of me—being a dedicated young professional and my cultural background." For Bell, it was important to show through her self-portrait that her professionalism and her identity as a Native woman did not conflict with each other. Arcadia, on the other hand, chose to share a series of self-portraits where he stained different parts of his body with red paint (a color signifying empowerment) to emphasize the symbolism of each: his throat for voice and clarity, his head as the strongest element in the body and symbol of loneliness, his eyes as the gateway to the head and in observance of being the only one, and his hands as a symbol for his work. Though his use of red paint on his face was striking, we decided against fully showing his face to avoid identification.

Reciprocity

In our work with Native individuals in STEM, one of our main priorities has been and continues to be to engage in reciprocity, meaning we bring back what we learn from our research to the Indigenous communities that have welcomed us, so that our work does not continue building on the legacy of extraction and colonization that is so common in research done with Native participants (Archibald, 2008; Smith, 1999; Wilson, 2008). For example, the first dissemination efforts for the NAWC2 pilot included the publication of a piece published in *Winds of Change* (Silva et al., 2021a), the bimonthly magazine published by AISES for its membership. We have also presented NAWC2 and NSP findings at primarily Native conferences (e.g., AISES, STEMS² Symposium at the University of Hawaii at Manoa). One of these presentations has included an NSP participant as a co-presenter with a focus on his PE experiences.

The possibilities afforded by PE images allow for more flexible, dynamic, visually attractive, and creative possibilities of how to present findings encompassing both images and words in different formats. So far, we have found that the use of images and words together is a powerful combination to convey ideas and that viewers have strong responses to presentations and publications using these materials. It seems that PE's power to elicit emotions does not end with the participants who take the photos and caption them; those who view the photos along with their captions are similarly compelled and moved by them.

Our team has utilized visually rich formats, including video and photo exhibitions. First, we developed a 3-minute video presenting some of NSP's initial findings around the concept of "giving back" to retain Native students and professions in STEM (Jaumot-Pascual et al., 2022). This video was part of the 2022 STEM for All Video Showcase, a yearly event where studies that have received funding from federal sources can present their work through short videos. The video received a Presenters' Choice Award and was warmly received by Native and non-Native researchers alike. According to comments on the public discussion wall, the video resonated with others both at the content and visual levels. The second is a traveling photos and text exhibition from NSP that the team has developed with a professional designer. Its inaugural exhibition was at the 2022 AISES conference, where attendees had the opportunity to respond to the images and captions with written comments. As one of the attendees shared: "Thank you for this beautiful opportunity to have people reflect the challenges that come with academic pursuits away from our communities + people.... Nothing like art to bring us to connect with our emotional experience." The exhibition will travel to other institutions in the country with high Indigenous representation, such as Tribal Colleges and Universities and Native cultural centers.

Additional avenues for dissemination that benefit from the visual power of photographs include: (a) blog posts (e.g., D'Souza, 2022); (b) academic manuscripts (e.g., Jaumot-Pascual et al., forthcoming); (3) short articles in trade publications (e.g., Silva et al., 2021b); and (d) highly visual presentations (e.g., Ong et al., 2022; Torres-Gerald et al., 2022). We plan on continuing to prioritize dissemination efforts that aim to engage in reciprocity with Native audiences and those who work with them.

As we have emphasized, participant-generated PE is a data collection method where a participant's voice is centered. We used it in NAWC2 and NSP, seeking to follow the recommendations of Indigenous researchers regarding conducting research with Indigenous participants, such as respecting their cultural background and promoting community participation. PE's versatility in portraying Native cultures and values, its potential to encourage introspection, as well as its flexibility around representation and creativity, make PE a culturally relevant method for projects with Indigenous participants. Our study participants were able to represent their culture and values by depicting cultural artifacts and objects that symbolized their elders, community, and concepts such as the cultural and spiritual significance of place and the responsibility to give back. Though we experienced some issues in the implementation of PE with Indigenous participants, we found that its affordances provided for creative opportunities to disseminate project findings and to reciprocate with Indigenous communities. The development of a short video highlighting initial findings and of an exhibition of photos and text are two examples of these creative dissemination and reciprocation efforts. We continue to explore avenues to reciprocate with the Native communities that have generously shared their stories with us.

Acknowledgments

Our Funders: for NAWC2, Women of Color in Computing Researcher/Practitioner Collaborative/Pivotal Ventures; for NSP, National Science Foundation, HRD-2000619

Our NAWC2 and NSP Teams: Matthew Madison (UGA), Selay Zor (UGA), Lisette Torres-Gerald (TERC), Christina B. Silva (TERC), Maria Jimenez (Community Consulting), Janet Smith (Edscape Consulting), Anya Carbonell (TERC), Angela D'Souza (TERC), Katie Yao (TERC)

Our Partnering Institutions: Montana State University (Brittany Fasy); New Mexico State University (Jonathan Cook); Oklahoma State University (Jovette Dew and Christopher Bingham); University of Oklahoma (Lisa Morales); Salish Kootenai College (Judy Hudgins); Arizona State University (Kimberly Scott) and Kapor Center (Allison Scott, Frieda McAlear)

Our Advisors and Consultants: Frieda McAlear, Stephanie Masta, Marigold Linton, and Sarah Berkeley

Note

1. We use the terms Native and Indigenous interchangeably throughout this paper. Shotton et al. (2013) define these terms (along with American Indian and Native American) as "Indigenous populations of North America, particularly those located in what we now know as the United States and those who identify as Native American or Alaska Native" (p. 4). We also include Native Hawaiians in our definition of the terms Native and Indigenous.

References

Archibald, J. A. (2008). *Indigenous storywork: Educating the heart, mind, body, and spirit*. UBC Press.

Beatty, S., Hayden, K. A., & Jeffs, C. (2020). Indigenizing library spaces using photovoice methodology [Paper presentation]. In S. Baughman, J. Belanger, E. Durnan, E. Edwards, M. Kyrillidou, K. Maidenberg, A. Pappalardo, & M. Strub (Eds.). Proceedings of the 2020–2021 Library Assessment Conference: Building effective, sustainable, practical assessment, October 29, 2020–March 2021, virtual conference. Washington, DC: Association of Research Libraries, 2021. https://www.libraryassessment.org/wp-content/uploads/2021/08/186-Beatty-Indigenizing-Library-Spaces.pdf

Bessette, H. J., & Paris, N. A. (2020). Using visual and textual metaphors to explore teachers' professional roles and identities. *International Journal of Research & Method in Education*, 43(2), 173–188.

Braun, V., & Clarke, V. (2006). Using thematic analysis in psychology. *Qualitative Research in Psychology*, 3(2), 77–101. https://doi.org/10.1191/1478088706qp063oa

Brayboy, B. M. J. (2005). Toward a tribal critical race theory in education. *The Urban Review*, 37(5), 425–446. https://doi.org/10.1007/s11256-005-0018-y

Brayboy, B. M., & Deyhle, D. (2000). Insider-outsider: Researchers in American Indian communities. *Theory into Practice*, 39(3), 163–169.

Carlson, E. D., Engebretson, J., & Chamberlain, R. M. (2006). Photovoice as a social process of critical consciousness. *Qualitative Health Research*, 16(6), 836–852.

Castleden, H., & Garvin, T. (2008). Modifying photovoice for community-based participatory Indigenous research. *Social Science & Medicine*, 66(6), 1393–1405.

Chelberg, K. (2019). *Using photovoice and photo-elicitation to understand successes and barriers related to Tribal College students' education* [Unpublished doctoral dissertation]. Edgewood College.

Coble, J. (2019). *Exploring Aboriginal student experiences with post-secondary education through photography and story* [Unpublished doctoral dissertation]. University of Calgary.

Collier, J. (1957). Photography in anthropology: A report on two experiments. *American Anthropologist*, 59(5), 843–859.

Collier, J., & Collier, M. (1986). *Visual anthropology: Photography as a research method*. University of New Mexico Press.

Collins, P. H. (2019). *Intersectionality as critical social theory*. Duke University Press.

Collins, P. H., & Bilge, S. (2016). *Intersectionality*. John Wiley & Sons.

Drew, S., & Guillemin, M. (2014). From photographs to findings: Visual meaning-making and interpretive engagement in the analysis of participant-generated images. *Visual Studies, 29*(1), 54–67.

D'Souza, A. (2022). From teacher to social science researcher on Native students' experiences and community cultural wealth. TERC Blog. https://blog.terc.edu/from-teacher-to-social-science-researcher-on-native-students-experiences-and-community-cultural-wealth

Fereday, J., & Muir-Cochrane, E. (2006). Demonstrating rigor using thematic analysis: A hybrid approach of inductive and deductive coding and theme development. *International Journal of Qualitative Methods, 5*(1), 80–92. https://doi.org/10.1177/160940690600500107

Guillemin, M., & Drew, S. (2010). Questions of process in participant-generated visual methodologies. *Visual Studies, 25*(2), 175–188.

Harper, D. (2002). Talking about pictures: A case for photo elicitation. *Visual Studies, 17*(1), 13–26.

Harris, A., & Guillemin, M. (2012). Developing sensory awareness in qualitative interviewing: A portal into the otherwise unexplored. *Qualitative Health Research, 22*(5), 689–699.

Jaumot-Pascual, N. (2018). *Conducting a culturally responsive evaluation: Values engagement, self-reflexivity, and photo elicitation* [Unpublished doctoral dissertation]. University of Georgia.

Jaumot-Pascual, N., DeerInWater, K., Ong, M., & Silva, C. B. (forthcoming). "I can do data for my people": Experiences of giving back for Native undergraduates in computing. *Cultural Studies of Science Education*.

Jaumot-Pascual, N., Smith, T., Madison, M., Ong, M., Torres-Gerald, L., Silva, C. B., & Zor, S. (2022). *Portraits of giving back by Native individuals in STEM*. 2022 STEM for All Video Showcase. https://stemforall2022.videohall.com/presentations/2449

McMillan, A. (2020). *"It's more than an organization": Exploring the role of a Native student organization in creating a culturally relevant and culturally responsive campus environment for Native American college students* [Unpublished doctoral dissertation]. North Carolina State University.

Minthorn, R. S., & Marsh, T. E. (2016). Centering indigenous college student voices and perspectives through photovoice and photo-elicitation. *Contemporary Educational Psychology, 47*, 4–10.

Moffitt, P. M., & Vollman, A. L. (2004). Photovoice: Picturing the health of Aboriginal women in a remote northern community. *Canadian Journal of Nursing Research = Revue Canadienne de Recherche en Sciences Infirmières, 36*(4), 189–201.

Ong, M., Madison, M., Smith, T., Jaumot-Pascual, N., Torres-Gerald, L., Zor, S., & Silva, C. (2022, April 21–April 26). *Native STEM portraits: A mixed-methods study of persistence of Native undergraduate students in STEM* [Paper presentation]. American Educational Research Association Annual Meeting, San Diego, CA.

Padgett, D. K., Smith, B. T., Derejko, K. S., Henwood, B. F., & Tiderington, E. (2013). A picture is worth…? Photo elicitation interviewing with formerly homeless adults. *Qualitative Health Research, 23*(11), 1435–1444.

Patton, M. Q. (2002). *Qualitative research and evaluation methods*. SAGE.

Pawley, A. L. (2019). Learning from small numbers: Studying ruling relations that gender and race the structure of U.S. engineering education. *Journal of Engineering Education, 108*(1), 13-31.

Shotton, H. J., Lowe, S. C., & Waterman, S. J. (Eds.). (2013). *Beyond the asterisk: Understanding Native students in higher education*. Stylus.

Silva, C. B., Jaumot-Pascual, N., Ong, M., & DeerInWater, K. (2021a, Spring). What motivates Native computer science students? A new study looks at how giving back helps undergraduates stick with a challenging major. *Winds of Change*. https://read.nxtbook.com/aises/winds_of_change/spring_2021/what_motivates_native_compute.html

Silva, C. B., Jaumot-Pascual, N., Ong, M., & DeerInWater, K. (2021b, Spring). "I think around the box." Experiences of a Native two-spirit undergraduate student in computing. *Hands On!* https://www.terc.edu/wp-content/uploads/2021/04/TERC_HandsOn_Spring-2021_final.pdf

Smith, L. T. (1999). *Decolonizing methodologies: Research and indigenous peoples*. Zed Books.

Smith, T. D. (2019). *Indigenizing the academy: A story-telling journey to determine pathways for Native student success in engineering* [Unpublished doctoral dissertation]. University of Oklahoma.

Solórzano, D. G. (1998). Critical race theory, race and gender microaggressions, and the experience of Chicana and Chicano scholars. *International Journal of Qualitative Studies in Education, 11*(1), 121-136.

Solórzano, D., Ceja, M., & Yosso, T. (2000). Critical race theory, racial microaggressions, and campus racial climate: The experiences of African American college students. *Journal of Negro Education, 69*(1/2), 60-73.

Strauss, A. L., & Corbin, J. M. (1998). *Basics of qualitative research techniques: Techniques and procedures for developing grounded theory* (2nd ed.). SAGE.

Torres-Gerald, L., Madison, M., & Silva, C. (2022, June 28-June 30). [Paper presentation]. *"It's this dichotomy of ways of doing things": Lived experiences of Native faculty in STEM*. STEMS² Symposium at the University of Hawaii at Manoa.

Wang, C., & Burris, M. A. (1997). Photovoice: Concept, methodology, and use for participatory needs assessment. *Health Education & Behavior, 24*(3), 369-387.

Wilson, S. (2008). *Research is ceremony: Indigenous research methods*. Fernwood Publishing.

Yosso, T. J. (2005). Whose culture has capital?: A critical race theory discussion of community cultural wealth. *Race Ethnicity and Education, 8*(1), 69-91.

About the Authors

Darci Bell is a registered dietitian and Ph.D. candidate in the Department of Nutritional Sciences at the University of Georgia. Her research interests include developing and evaluating nutrition education for limited-resource audiences, implementation science, qualitative methods, and the reduction of weight stigma among health professionals providing nutrition education. Her current research focuses on the feasibility of implementing eLearning nutrition education programs for low-income audiences in community- and clinic-based settings.

Alison Bravington is an applied health researcher working with diverse qualitative methodologies and implementation science frameworks to explore and improve patient, caregiver, and practitioner experiences in cancer and palliative care, interdisciplinary collaboration in health and social care, and students' experiential learning on practice placements or internships. Alison combines skills from a previous career as an editor and writer with an educational background in English literature, psychology, and social research methods.

Janie Copple is an assistant professor in the Department of Educational Policy Studies at Georgia State University. Her research explores qualitative research methodologies, specifically feminist critical materialist approaches to narrative, autoethnographic and arts-based research, and topics on motherhood and puberty education. Janie has published works in *The Qualitative Report* and *Qualitative Inquiry* and is co-editor and contributing author of *Conservative Philanthropies and Organizations Shaping U.S. Educational Policy and Practice*.

Kathy DeerInWater, Ph.D. (Cherokee Nation of Oklahoma) is the Chief Program Officer at AISES. She oversees program development, implementation, evaluation, and reporting for all AISES special projects. She serves as the PI or program director on all research projects, including the National Science Foundation-funded Lighting the Pathway to Faculty Careers for Natives in STEM project. Dr. DeerInWater completed her Ph.D. in Ecology at the University of California, Davis.

Emma Elliott, Ph.D., M.S.W. is an assistant professor in the Department of Learning Sciences and Human Development in the College of Education at the University of Washington. Her research centers ethical frameworks generated by Indigenous and place-based knowledges and practices to create process-centered approaches that illuminate Indigenous pathways toward collective livelihood. The interdisciplinary intersections of her research include contemporary Indigenous issues; culture, learning, and human development; and trauma, prevention, and recovery.

Maureen A. Flint is an assistant professor in Qualitative Research at the University of Georgia where she teaches courses on qualitative research design and theory. Her scholarship explores the theory, practice, and pedagogy of qualitative methodologies, artful inquiries, and questions of social (in)justice, ethics, and equity in higher education. Representations of her artful inquiries can be found on her website at maureenflint.com.

Jori N. Hall, Ph.D., professor in the Qualitative Research and Evaluation Methodologies program at the University of Georgia, is an award-winning author and multidisciplinary researcher. Dr. Hall's research is concerned with social inequalities and the overall rigor of social science research. Her work addresses issues of research methodology, cultural responsiveness, and the role of values and privilege within the fields of evaluation, education, and health. Dr. Hall has published numerous peer-reviewed works in scholarly venues; authored the book *Focus Groups: Culturally Responsive Approaches for Qualitative Inquiry and Program Evaluation*; and was selected as a Leaders of Equitable Evaluation and Diversity (LEEAD) fellow by The Annie E. Casey Foundation. Dr. Hall currently serves as the Co-Editor-in-Chief for the *American Journal of Evaluation*.

Brigette A. Herron, Ph.D., is a Development Associate at the Empowerment Collaborative of Long Island-Victims Information Bureau of Suffolk (ECLI-VIBES). Her research interests include teaching qualitative research methods and interviewing, feminist pedagogy in adult and higher education, and trauma-informed approaches to research, evaluation, and education for limited-resource audiences. She has co-authored several books and book chapters and has published articles about qualitative interviewing in the journals *LEARNing Landscapes*, *Qualitative Inquiry*, and *Cultural Studies ↔ Critical Methodologies*.

About the Authors

Nuria Jaumot-Pascual, Ph.D., is a Research Scientist at TERC. She researches the experiences of people of color in STEM higher education and careers. She specializes in qualitative, literature synthesis, and visual inquiry methods. Dr. Jaumot-Pascual is currently Co-PI for Native STEM Portraits (NSP, NSF-funded) and is currently a fellow of the Georgia Education Policy Fellowship Program. She holds a doctorate in Qualitative Research and Evaluation Methodologies from the University of Georgia.

Lorien S. Jordan, Ph.D., is an assistant professor of Educational Statistics and Research Methods at the University of Arkansas's College of Education and Health Professions. She is a critical qualitative methodologist who studies the cultural reproduction of (non)belonging. Lorien's current work includes critical theoretical analyses of institutional discourses, policies, and practices that maintain injustice, including assessing the cultural-political mechanisms of knowledge production. She has conducted this work in the United States, New Zealand, and Cambodia.

Joseph-Emery Lyvan Kouaho is a proud descendant of the Cote d'Ivoire, and a Ph.D. Candidate in the Educational Administration Policy program at the University of Georgia. Joseph's research interests center on how federal education policies impact the lived and educational outcomes of Black persons. Joseph earned his Master of Public Policy from Duke University's Sanford School of Public Policy, and a Bachelor of Arts in Political Science from the University of North Carolina at Chapel Hill. He is currently in the process of developing his dissertation project, which focuses on the parental involvement of college-educated Black men.

Jung Sun Lee, Ph.D., R.D.N., is a professor in the Department of Nutritional Sciences and faculty of Gerontology at the University of Georgia. Her research focuses on food insecurity, food and nutrition assistance programs, community-based nutrition interventions, and policies addressing nutrition-related health disparities in low-income populations. She conducts interdisciplinary research-outreach projects to better understand the extent and nature of food insecurity and to improve the capacity of food and nutrition assistance programs using mixed methods.

Travis M. Marn is an assistant professor of educational psychology and research methods at Southern Connecticut State University's College of Education. Their research agenda focuses on the use and development of qualitative and post-qualitative methodologies and exploring questions of justice, identity, and subjectivity through new materialist, posthumanist, and poststructural frameworks.

Susan Naomi Nordstrom is an associate professor of Educational Research in the Department of Counseling, Educational Psychology, and Research at The University of Memphis. She studies poststructural and post-humanist theories, Deleuze, new materialism, human–nonhuman relationships, onto-epistemology, and qualitative research methodology. She has published on post-qualitative methodologies as well as human and nonhuman relationships in post-qualitative methodologies in leading qualitative research journals.

Maria (Mia) Ong, Ph.D., is a Senior Research Scientist and Evaluator at TERC. For over 20 years she has conducted empirical research focusing on women of color in higher education and careers in STEM and has led evaluation of several STEM equity and inclusion programs. Dr. Ong serves as PI for the Native STEM Portraits study. She holds a Ph.D. in Social and Cultural Studies in Education from the University of California, Berkeley.

Kathryn Roulston is Professor of Qualitative Research in the Mary Frances Early College of Education at the University of Georgia. Her research interests include qualitative research methods, qualitative interviewing, and analyses of talk-in-interaction. She is the author of *Interviewing: A Guide to Theory and Practice* (2022), *Exploring the archives: A beginner's guide for qualitative researchers* (with K. deMarrais, 2021), and editor of *Interactional Studies of Qualitative Research Interviews* (2019). She has contributed chapters to handbooks of qualitative research as well as articles to *Qualitative Research, Qualitative Inquiry*, the *International Journal of Research and Method in Education*, and the *International Journal of Qualitative Methods*, among other journals. In her spare time, she enjoys textile arts, including hand-dyeing, spinning, and weaving.

Timothy San Pedro is an associate professor of Critical Studies in Race, Justice, and Equity at Ohio State University. He is Filipino-American and grew up on the Flathead Indian Reservation in Western Montana. His latest work focuses on the ways in which Indigenous families teach tribal knowledges, sovereignty rights, and everyday resurgence efforts. He is an inaugural Gates Millennium Scholar, Cultivating New Voices Among Scholars of Color Fellow, Ford Fellow, CAE Presidential Fellow, and Spencer Fellow.

Tiffany Smith, Ph.D. (Cherokee Nation and descendant of Muscogee [Creek] Nations, both of Oklahoma) is the Director of Research and Career Support at AISES and serves as Co-PI for the NSF-funded Native STEM Portraits project. Her scholarship focuses on applying Indigenous methodologies and her own Tsalagi (Cherokee) epistemology to decolonizing academic spaces, particularly in STEM fields. Dr. Smith holds a Ph.D. in adult and higher education/student affairs from the University of Oklahoma.

Morgan P. Tate is a doctoral candidate in the Department of Educational Theory and Practice at the University of Georgia. Tate utilizes artful method(ologies) in/with research on teacher preparation and social studies education.

Jennifer R. Wolgemuth is an associate professor in educational research at the University of South Florida, where she directs the Graduate Certificate in Qualitative Research. Her research agenda focuses on ethics and validity of social science research. Drawing on critical, poststructural, and new materialist theories, she explores inquiry as an agential process that simultaneously investigates and creates lives and communities to and for which the researcher is responsible.

Acknowledgments

This volume began with a panel I organized for the International Congress of Qualitative Inquiry (ICQI) in 2020. To panelists' collective dismay, the 2020 meeting was cancelled as people the world over grappled with living through the shutdowns that occurred as a result of the COVID-19 pandemic. Nevertheless, several of the authors in this volume reconvened with me to present a panel at the virtual ICQI conference in 2021. We each talked about creative approaches to interviewing, which led me to thinking about the numerous ways that qualitative researchers use interviews in ways that do not conform to the semi-structured qualitative interviewing practices that most of us are familiar with and have been trained in. Although I've written a little about some of the approaches included in the volume elsewhere, I've found that space constraints always prevented me from attending to the details. Further, I needed to learn more about these approaches. Later in 2021 I invited other authors to share their ideas about innovations in interview practice. This volume is the result. As always, there are many people to thank.

First, I extend my deepest gratitude to all of the authors for accepting my invitations to write about interviewing, contributing to this volume, and addressing requested revisions. Your work has sharpened my thinking about interview practices, and the examples and ideas you discuss are inspiration for others.

Second, I thank my co-editors of the book series, *Qualitative research methodologies: Traditions, designs, and pedagogies*—Kathleen deMarrais, Melissa Freeman, and Jori Hall—for early conversations that helped me think about how to shape this collaborative endeavor to speak to qualitative researchers and teachers of qualitative research.

Third, I thank members of my reading group with whom I had the pleasure of sharing a writing retreat in 2022 that enabled me to work on this project: Susan Cannon, Maureen Flint, and Amy Stich. What could be better than laughter and good times while writing?

Fourth, I thank my husband Mike Healy for his unfailing support.

Finally, thanks to the team at Myers Education Press—Stephanie Gabaree, Chris Myers, Carl Young and Tom Bechtle—for their timely support and guidance to bring this book to completion. Thanks also to Caprial Farrington for assistance with indexing.

Index

A
Aagaard, Jesper, 116
Abildgaard, Mette Simonsen, 150
accountability, xiii, 13, 70
    cultural accountability, 14–16
    relational accountability, 14–16
Adamov Ferguson, Katya, 25
Adams, Catherine A., 151, 153
Adekoya, Adebusola A., 201
Affirmative ethics, 87, 89–91, 138
agential realism, xiv, 109, 147
    agential cuts, 110, 114, 117–118
Agosto, Denise E., 173, 180
Allen, Louisa, 151
Altheide, David L., 130
Alshenqeeti, Hamza, 49
analytical realism, 130–131
Ancona, Deborah G., 185
Anderson, Jon, 198, 203
Anzaldúa, Gloria E., 8
Archibald, Jo-ann, xiii, 24–27, 32–33, 35, 40, 219, 229, 231
Arellano, Sonia C., 100
art, 16, 35
    collage, 91–95
    quilting art, 100–101
    use in representation, 16, 55
artifacts. *See* objects
assemblage, xi, xiv, Chapter 7
    definition, 128
    of data, 99, 127, 134–135
audiencing, 184, 187
Ayrton, Rachel, 58–59

B
Bagnoli, Anna, 173, 181, 185
Bailey, Michelle J., 53
Bang, Megan, 23, 25, 28, 40
Banks, Marcus, 149
Barad, Karen, xi, xiv, 109–112, 114, 117, 119–120, 123–124, 147, 152–153
Barlott, Tim, 111, 153
Bartlett, Ruth, 201
Bayeck, Rebecca Yvonne, 13,
Beatty, Susan, 218
Bebe Silva, Christina, 231–232

Bell, Sarah L., 200
Bennett, Jane, 147
Benninger, Elizabeth, 177
Bergeron, Julie, 200
Berkhout, Joris J., 175
Berryman, Mere, 3, 6, 9
Bessette, Harriet J., 216, 228
Bilge, Sirma, 218
bimbling, 198
biographical methods, 199, 201
biometrics, 206
Bird, Tess, 150
Birt, Linda, 51
Bishop, Russell, 13, 36, 129
Bissell, Susan, 149
Bonilla-Silva, Eduardo, 53
Bowman, Jay A., 201
Bozalek, Vivienne, 200, 208
Brady, Shannon T., 202
Braidotti, Rosi, xi, 87–91, 93, 95–98, 102, 104–105, 109, 138
Brannelly, Tula, 201
Braun, Virginia, 229
Bravington, Alison, xiv, Chapter 9
Brayboy, Bryan McKinley Jones, 25, 218, 228–229
Bresler, Liora, 172
Bridges-Rhoads, Sarah, 111, 121, 123
Briggs, Charles L., 6
briefing participants, 181–182
Brien, Julie, 100–101
Brinkmann, Svend, xv, 169
Brown, Lesley, xi
Büchi, Stefan, 174
Bulk, Laura Yvonne, 175
Burns, Robyn, 201
Burris, Mary Ann, 217
Büscher, Monika, 195,
Butler, Judith, 114, 118–119

C
Campbell, Patricia B., 50
Canagarajah, A. Suresh, 12
Care Collective, The, 113
Carlson, David Lee, 121
Carlson, Elizabeth D., 216

Caronia, Letizia, 151, 153
cartography, xi, xiv, Chapter 5
    critical cartography, 88
    quality, 104
    thinking cartographically, 87, 89, 104
Casey, Mary A., 66–67
Castleden, Heather, 217–218
Castrodale, Mark Anthony, 198, 201, 208
Catungal, John Paul, 70
Chamberlain, Kerry, 150
Chang, Jamie Suki, 199
Charmaz, Kathy, 51
Chelberg, Kelli, 218
Chen, Annie T., 180–181
Cheng, Peter C.-H., 172
Cheung, Melissa M. Y., 172
Chilisa, Bagele, 3, 5–6, 9, 16
Chouinard, Jill Anne, 3–5, 16–17, 44
Chow, Rey, 118
Clandinin, D. Jean, 25
Clark, Andrew, 173, 177
Clarke, Victoria, 229
cognition, 170
Cohen, Jeffrey H., 132–133, 149
Cohen, Nancy L., 67
Colebrook, Claire, 128, 138
Colley, Kathryn, 201
Collier, John, 132–133, 216–217
Collier, Malcolm, 133, 149
Collins, Patricia Hill, 4, 218
confidentiality, 57–58, 69, 184, 188, 230
Connelly, F. Michael, 25
conventional qualitative research, 14, 131, 133, 150, 169, 186–188, 216
conversation bombing, 13
conversational method, 12–13, 38, 127, 131, 133, 219
Copeland, Andrea J., 173, 180
Copple, Janie, Chapter 8
Corbin, Juliet, 229
Cousins, J. Bradley, 44
Cowan, Sue, 51
Cram, Fiona, 3–5, 16–17
Creswell, John W., 50
Critical Race Theory, 17, 50, 218
critical reflexivity, xiii, 9–10, 70
cultural competence, 5
culturally relevant pedagogy, 43–44
culturally responsive research, xii–xiii, 4–5, 7, 217
    characteristics, 44
    conceptualization and implementation, 45–51
    culturally responsive focus groups, Chapter 3. *See* focus groups
    culturally responsive interviews, 5–7, 18–19
    defined, 44
    quality, 50

D
Da, Shuyang, 172
damage discourses, 14, 29
Daniels, Nicola, 67
data analysis, 51–52
    creative analytic practices, 54
    images, 186–187, 228–229
    qualitative data analysis software (QDAS), 52
data collection, 25, 38, 65, 67, 70, 78–81, 110, 115, 169, 215–216, 219, 233
    notetakers, 46, 52
De', Rahul, 67–69
DeerInWater, Kathy, Chapter 11
de Freitas, Elizabeth, 89
De Leon, Jason Patrick, 132–133, 149
Deleuze, Gilles, xi, xiv, 87, 89, 131, 133, 136–137, 139, 141
Deloria, Vine, 25
Denham, Magdalena A., 52
Denton, Hannah, 197, 205
Denzin, Norman K., 43, 52, 169
DePaoli, Jennifer, 23
Derrida, Jacques, 129
Deyhle, Donna, 218, 229
dialogic process, 6, 8–9, 18, 39
    dialogic interaction, 29–30, 35
    dialogic spiral, 35, 37
disability studies, xii, 198, 201
dissemination, 56, 226, 228, 231–233. *See* publishing
Donohue, Richard, 205
Dos Santos Marques, Isabel C., 67–68
drawings and diagrams. *See* graphic elicitation, images
Drew, Sarah, 187, 216, 219
Duedahl, Eva, 197
Duff, Wendy, 129
Duffy, Michelle, 97–98
Durie, Mason, 12

Index

E
ecomaps, 174
Edwards, Rosalind, 54
Eldh, Ann Catrine, 55
Ellis, Julie, 201
Elliott, Emma, xiii, Chapter 2
Emmel, Nick, 173, 177
Engward, Hilary, 67–69, 82
entanglement. *See* Barad, Karen
Esposito, Noreen, 55
ethics, 15–16, 69, 119, 133, 230–233
Evans, James, 198, 200–201
Ezzy, Douglas, 153

F
Falter, Michelle, 58
feminist approaches, 50, 54, 65–66, 69–71, 80
    feminist new materialism, 87
Fereday, Jennifer, 229
Ferguson, Harry, 201
Fernandes, Myra A., 172
Fine, Michelle, 19
Finlay, Jessica M., 201
Finlay, Linda, 9
Flint, Maureen A., xiii–xiv, Chapters 5 & 10
Flynn, Rachel, 46
focus groups, Chapters 3 & 4
    challenges, 56–59, 68–69, 76–77
    culturally responsive focus groups, chapter 3
    moderation, 45–46
    online focus groups, 66–67
    recruitment, 56–57, 73–74, 76–77, 79, 182
fold, xi, xiv, 131, 133, 137, 150
Fosi Palaamo, Alesana, 7
Foucault, Michel, 118
Fowler, Chris, 151
Fricker, Miranda, 4, 16
Fuller, Danielle, 150

G
Garcia, Carolyn M., 201
Garvey, Jason C., 202
Garvin, Theresa, 217–218
genealogy, 10, 18, 129–131, 137–138
Gershon, Walter S., 88–89
Gillespie, Hannah, 175
Gilligan, Carol, 54
Glaser, Barney, 51
Glaveanu, Vlad P., 187

go-alongs, Chapter 10. *See also* mobile methods
    definition, 197
Gois, Gabriela R., 198
Goldenberg, Tamar, 171, 187
Gondwe, Mzamose, 150
Gopalan, Maithreyi, 202
Granville, Julia, 180, 185
graphic elicitation interviews, xiv, Chapter 9
    definition, 169
    limitations, 185
    planning, 181–184
    purpose, 170
    quality, 188
Guattari, Félix, xi, 87, 89, 139, 141
Guest, Greg, 46
Guillemin, Marilys, 180, 187, 216, 219, 221
Gullion, Jessica, 55–56
Guse, Lorna, 201
Güthlin, Corina, 175
Guyotte, Kelly W., 119, 151–152

H
Hackstaff, Karla B., 129–131
Halcomb, Elizabeth J., 57–58
Hall, Jori N., xii–xiii, 6, Chapter 3
Hall, Tom, 199
Hanawalt, Christina, 93
Hand, Carri, 200
Hannan, Leonie, 151
Haraway, Donna J., 119–120, 159
Hardy, Beth, 171, 175, 183
Harevan, Tamara, 130
Harper, Douglas, 149, 215
Harris, Anna, 48, 216
Harris, Jessica, 201
Harris, Oliver J. T., 151
Harris, Robie, 157
Hartley, Laura, 12, 16
Harvey, David, 88
Hays, Charles A., 56
Helfenbein, Robert J., 88
Henare, Amiria, 148
Henshilwood, Christopher S., 188
hermeneutic humility, 11–12, 17
Herron, Brigette A., Chapter 4
Hicks, Dan, 148
Hinterhuber, Hans H., 185
Hodder, Ian, 151
Holloway, Julian, 200–201

Holmes, Andrew G. D., 45
Holmes, Helen, 150
Hood, Stafford, 44
Hook, Derek, 187
hooks, bell, 37–38
Horrocks, Christine, 183
Hoskins, Janet, 148
Hudson, Maui, 16
Hultin, Lotta, 151
humanism, 96, 113, 169
   posthumanism, 96
Hurdley, Rachel, 148
Hurley, Sean M., 172
Hyle, Adrienne E., 180

I
Iantaffi, Alex, 180
identity, 6, 115, 118, 152, 198
   identity performance, 115, 118
images, Chapters 9 & 11
   allocentric images, 177–181
   egocentric images, 173–176
   image as metaphor, 222–223
   image manipulation, 222–224
imaginative variation, 183
Indigenous knowledge systems, 25, 28
   Indigenous Storywork, xiii, 24–25, 27, 33, 35
   Indigenous paradigms, 38
Indigenous peoples, 28, 38, Chapters 1, 2 & 11
   Indigenous values
informed consent, 48, 69
Ingold, Tim, 148, 196
institutional review boards, 230
Interpretation, 15–18, 228–229
interviewing
   bodily proximity of interviewing, 114–115
   interview logics, 203–204
   interview spaces, 116, chapter 10
   materiality of interviewing, 114, 116
   romance of interviewing, 111–113
intra-action, xi, xiv, 152, 157–158, Chapter 6
Inwood, Joshua F. J., 198,
Isakjee, Arshad, 201

J
Jackson, Alecia Y., 123, 185
Jaumot-Pascual, Nuria, xv, Chapter 11
Jensen, Tenna, 150
Jiang, Qianzhi, 67
Johnson, Catherine A., 130

Johnson, Corey W., 43, 50–51, 54
Johnson, Jeremiah, 55–56
Johnson, Johnny M., 130
Johnson, Mark, 181
Johnstone, Jane H., 201
Jones, April M., 47
Jones, Phil, 198, 200–201
Jordan, Lorien S., xiii, Chapter 1
journaling, 53

K
Kane, Mary, 178
Kari, Jarkko, 173
Kearney, Kerri S., 180
Keating, AnaLouise, 8
Kerr, Jeannie, 25
Killam, Rachel K., 113
Kim, Annette M., 92
Kim, Jeong-Hee, 159
King, Nigel, 169–170, 172, 174, 176, 183, 187
Kinloch, Valerie, 28–29, 36
Kirkham, Jamie A., 172, 187
Kommers, Heleen, 150
Koro, Mirka, 12, 113. See also Koro-Ljungberg, Mirka
Koro-Ljungberg, Mirka, 89, 119, 121
Kovach, Margaret E., xii, 4, 15–16, 33, 38, 40
Krueger, Richard A., 66–67
Kuberska, Karolina, 150
Kullberg, Agneta, 200–201
Kuntz, Aaron M., 25, 88, 110, 138, 203
Kusenbach, Margarethe, xii, 197, 208
Kwan, Mei-Po, 92

L
Ladson-Billings, Gloria, 23, 43
Laestadius, Linnea, 68–69
Lager, Debbie, 201
Lahman, Maria K. E., 43
Lakoff, George, 181
Lambert, Ronald D., 130
land, 7–8, 13, 24, 31, 97, 130, 137, 196
language, 11, 149, 182, 219
   inclusive language, 55
   language translation, 17–18, 55
   linguistic mapping, 101–102
Lathen, Lorraine, 68–69
Latour, Bruno, 117
Latz, Amanda O., 149
Lau, Cheuk Yin, 201, 208
Lauwers, Laura, 201

Index

Lavrakas, Paul J., 48
Law, John, 148
Lee, Jo, 196
Lee, Jung Sun, Chapter 4
Lee-Morgan, Jenny B. J., 26
Leung, Pamela P. Y, 180
Lewis, Camilla, 198
Li, Jingxian, 103
Linnentown Quilting Project, 100–101
Lobe, Bojana, 67–68
Longnecker, Nancy, 150
Lörinc, Magdolna, 201
Lynch, Jonathan, 201

M

Mackay, Michael, 200–201
MacLure, Maggie, 157
Madison, D. Soyini, 55
Madsen, Tina Anette, 200–201
Madriz, Esther, 43
Malinowski, Bronisław, 195
Mannion, Greg, 201
mapping. *See* cartography
mapping networks, 177–179
Marn, Travis M., xiv, Chapter 6
Marquart, Heike, 199, 208
Marsh, Tyson E. J., 218
Martin, Deborah G., 198
Martin, Georgina, 26
Martinez, César A. F., 198
Martini, Natalia, 200
Masny, Diana, 89
Massey, Doreen, 88, 202
Massey, Oliver T., 52
Matthiesen, Noomi, 116
May, Vanessa, 198
Mazzei, Lisa A., 96, 120, 123, 154
McClary, Ben H., 99
McCoy, Meredith L., 23
McCracken, Grant, 132–133
McCulliss, Debbie, 54–56
McDaid-Morgan, Nikki
McKenzie, Marcia, 202
McKeown, Jane, 179
McKittrick, Katherine, 88
McLeod, John, 51
McMillan, Ashley, 218
Mello, Michelle M., 29
member checking, 51
memos, 53, 69, 74, 78, 154, 207
Mergenthal, Karola, 175

Merriman, Peter, 195
methodological pluriversalism, 12–14
Michael, Mike, 169
Mignolo, Walter D., 12
Mila-Schaaf, Karlo, 16
Miller, Daniel, 148
Minthorn, Robin Z., 218
Mitchell, Jennifer, 51
mobile methods, Chapter 10. *See also* go-alongs, walking interviews
  designing research, 205–208
  disability communities, 198, 201
  justifying use of, 201
  quality, 208
Moffitt, Pertice, 217
Mol, Annemarie, 115
more-than-human, xi, 96–97, 109, 157
Morgan, David L., 67–68
Morrison, Dirk, 67
Motala, Siddique, 200, 208
Muir-Cochrane, Eimear, 229
Mulvihill, Thalia M., 149
Mutua, Kagendo, 13

N

narrative, 6–7, 12, 14, 171, 179, Chapter 8
  materializing narratives, 152, 159–163
  use in representation, 55, 79–80, 94
Nash, Catherine, 129
native peoples. *See* Indigenous peoples
new materialism. *See* agential realism
Newman, Peter A., 69, 82
Nickerson, Jeffrey V., 183, 185
Niebauer, Erica, 186
Nobrega, Suzanne, 67,
nomadic ethics, 90
nonhuman animals, 138–139
nonhuman objects, 109, 128, 130–131, 133–134, 138, 141
Nordstrom, Susan N., xiv, 116, Chapter 7, 150, 153, 159
Notermans, Catrien, 150
Novick, Laura R., 172

O

objects, see Chapters 7, 8
  definition, 148
  object elicitation, 149–150
  object encounters, 147, 151–152, 157, 160–162

object-interviews, xiv, Chapters 7, 8
    definition, 150
    justifying use of, 161
    planning, 162–163
Odzakovic, Elzana, 200–201
Olmos-Vega, Francisco N., 175
O'Neill, Maggie, 196, 199–201
Ong, Maria, xv, Chapter 11
ontoethicoepistemology, 119
Onwuegbuzie, Anthony John, 52
oral traditions, 6
Orland, Lily, 181
Osei-Kofi, Nana, 93
Østergaard, Jeanette, 150

P

Padgett, Deborah K., 216
Pahl, Kate, 150
Pain, Helen, 149
Palmgren, Ann-Charlotte, 200
Parent, Laurence, 198, 201
Parham, Angel A., 130
Paris, Django, 23, 25
Paris, Nita A., 216, 228
Parnet, Claire, 136
Parry, Diana C., 43, 50–51, 54
Pasque, Penny A., 43
Patton, Michael Q., 44, 229
Paulus, Trena M., 67
Pawley, Alice L., 230
Pell, Bethan, 184
Pe-Pua, Rogelia, 7
Perdue, Theda, 99
Perry, Mia, 89
Phillips, Sandra, 196
photo elicitation, xv, 149, Chapter 11
    affordances, 219–225
    challenges, 226–228
    conduct of, 218–219
    data analysis, 216–217
    definition, 216
    participant-generated, 217
    photovoice, xii, 14–15, 217–218
pictor, 174–177
Pink, Sarah, 148–149, 187, 196, 200
poetry, 200
    use in data analysis and representation, 16, 54–55, 155–157
Poth, Cheryl N., 50
Pottinger, Laura, 150

positionality, 50. *See* researcher positionality
positivism, 186, 208
post-positivism, 136
Powell, Kimberly, 199, 208
power dynamics, 58–59
Projects in Humanization, 28–29, 32–33, 36
Prosser, Jon, 187
publishing, 18, 56

Q

Qin, Dongxiao, 50
questions, 163, 170–171, 181, 183, 200
    derivation, xi
    open-ended questions, 47, 162–163, 200
quotation, 17

R

Rahman, Syahirah A., 67–70, 82
Rajchman, John, 137
Ramachandran, Vignesh, 68
Ramanan, Namratha, 171
rapport, 49, 68, 70, 156–157, 171, 182, 184, 218
Ratzenböck, Barbara, 200
Ray, Robin A., 174
reciprocity, 26, 30, 231
recording device, 135–136
Reed, Kate, 201
reflexivity, 51, 53
Reilly, Rosemary C., 54
relational research, 7, 24, 28, 34, 134
representation, 15–18, 54–56, 78–79, 80, 121, 159
research questions, xv, 161–162, 208
researcher positionality, 7–9, 23–24
response-ability, 120, 198
responsivity, 4–5, 53, 133
Reynolds, Joanna, 205
Riley, Mark, 197
Roberts, Brian, 196, 199
Roberts, J. Kessa, 65, 68–69, 78
Roberts, Rosanne E., 47
Robinson, Dylan, 38
Rodriguez, Katrina L., 45, 50–51
Rodriguez Medina, Leandro, 11, 17
Rolón-Dow, Rosalie, 53
Romano, Donna, 150, 152
Rose, Gillian, 98, 187
Rosenthal, Meagen, 47–48
Rosenzweig, Roy, 130
Ross, Nicola J., 200

Index

Roulston, Kathryn, Introduction, 3–4, 47, 96, 111, 117, 119, 149, Chapter 10
Rubin, David C., 171
Ryan, Katherine E., 46

S

Saarelainen, Suvi-Maria K., 180–181
Sáenz de Tejada Granados, Carlota, 200
Saint-Onge, Kadia, 201
Salmons, Janet, 69
San Pedro, Timothy, xiii, Chapter 2
Savolainen, Reijo, 173
Schadler, Cornelia, 121
Scheurich, James J., 132
Schroedl, Gerald F., 97
Schwandt, Thomas A., 11, 152
Schwartz, Shalom H., 185
Scott, Nicholas A., 197
Sczesny, Sabine, 55
Semetsky, Inna, 89
sensemaking, 153, 159, 161
Sensky, Tom, 174
Seponski, Desiree M., 5
Shareck, Martine, 200
Shelton, Stephanie A., 47
Sheridan, Joanna, 150, 180
Sim, Julius, 49, 57
Smith, Linda Tuhiwai, 6, 7, 18, 25, 218
Smith, Tiffany D., xv, Chapter 11
social convoy diagram, 173–174
social justice, 36, 43–44, 46, 50, 54, 56, 59
Soja, Edward W., 88
Solórzano, Daniel, 218
Somerville, Margaret, 12, 16,
sonic methods, 88, 200
sonic mapping, 96–100
  Soundwalking, 199
space and place, xiv, 91, 96, 99, 197
Spinney, Justin, 197, 201, 206
Stake, Robert E., 4
Stanton, Christine R., 52
Stearns, Peter N., 130
Stevenson, Andrew, 200–201
Stilling Blichfeldt, Bodil, 197
storytelling, xiii, 6, 13, 24, 31–32, 36, 38
  story extraction, 10, 25, 37–38, 203, 231
  storying, xiii, 13, 27–29, 35–37, 39
St. Pierre, Elizabeth A., 134, 185, 203
Strauss, Anselm, 51, 229
Strayhorn, Terrell Lamont, 202

Street, Annette F., 174
subjectivity, 10, 90
Sun, Guibo, 201, 208
Swadener, Beth B., 13
Sy, Michael, 67–69
symbolic representation, 216
Symbolic role, 152, 163
symonette, Hazel, 44
synergistic conversation, xiii, 24–27, 30–31, 34, 39–40, Chapter 2
  characteristics of, 31–32
  tenets, 35–38

T

Talking circles, 6
Tamasese, Kiwi, 8
Tamboukou, Maria, 159
Tasker, Fiona, 180, 185
Taylor, Carol A., 121, 151
Taylor, Janette Y., 7, 9
Teff-Seker, Yael, 200, 208
Teti, Michelle, 69
Thelen, David P., 130
theorizing interviews, xiii–xiv, Chapters 5, 6, 7
Thomas, Emma, 200–201
Thomas, Veronica G., 50
Thompson, Claire, 205
Thompson, Terrie Lynn, 151, 153
Thomson, Rachel, 150
Thygesen, Marianne K., 180
timelines, 176, 179, 187
Tong, Catherine, 199
Torres-Gerald, Lisette, 232
Tran, Sophia H. N., 172
transcription, 46
  of objects, 135
  transcript review, 51
trauma-informed research, 70–71, 80–81
Tremblay, Stephanie, 67–68
Trevisan, Filippo, 68
triangulation, 52
Trochim, William, 178
Tuck, Eve, 14–15, 40, 202
Tungohan, Ethel, 70
Tutton, Richard, 129
Tversky, Barbara, 172
Tyler, Katherine, 129

U

Ulmer, Jasmine B., 89, 121, 123

Umanath, Sharda, 171

V
Van Cleave, Jessica, 112, 123
van den Berg, Joost W., 175
van der Horst, Dan, 200
Vázquez-Montilla, Elia, 6
Veale, Kylie H., 130
Venn, Couse, 128
Versey, H. Shellae, 206
vibrant matter, 147
Vindenes, Joakim, 207
virtual research, 69
    go-alongs, 206
    technology, 57–58
    virtual focus groups, 66–69
    virtual interviewing, 68–70, 81, 153, 184
Vizenor, Gerald R., 25
Vollman, Ardene R., 217
Vossoughi, Shirin, 23

W
Wainwright, Megan, 187
walking interviews, 196–300, *See* bimbling
    intervention, 204–205
    walking interview as biographical method, 199
Wang, Caroline, 217
Wang, Yixuan, 102
Ware, Syrus Marcus, 198
Warren, Saskia, 198
Washington, Leon, 174
Waterfield, Jackie, 49, 57
Weller, Susie, 54
westernized methods, xiii, 3–4, 16, 25, 28, 33–34, 39, 110
Whitehead, Hattie T., 101
Wiederhold, Anna, 199
Wilkinson, Sue, 66
Willgerodt, Mayumi Anne, 46
William, Elder Jean, 26
Willig, Carla, 150
Wilmott, Clancy, 200, 208
Wilson, Jessie, 178
Wilson, Sarah, 207
Wilson, Shawn, 7, 40, 219, 231
Winn, Maisha T., 23, 25
Winter, Patricia L., 99
witnessing, 7, 13, 15, 26
Wolf, Leslie E., 29
Wolgemuth, Jennifer R., xiv, Chapter 6, 205

Wozolek, Boni, 88–89, 196
Woodward, Sophie, xii, 148, 150–151, 160, 163
Woodyatt, Cory R., 46
Wooten, Michelle M., 89

Y
Yang, K. Wayne, 14–15
Yarbrough, Donald B., 44
Yip, Tiffany, 23
Yosso, Tara J., 218